GREAT MARQUES OF BRITAIN

ETX 66

GREAT MARQUES OF BRITAIN

Compiled and edited by
JONATHAN WOOD

Foreword by
STIRLING MOSS

VISCOUNT BOOKS

CONTENTS

This edition published 1989 by
Viscount Books
an imprint of the
Octopus Publishing Group
Michelin House, 81 Fulham Road
London SW3 6RB

© Hennerwood Publications Limited 1983

ISBN 1 600 56442 8

The chapters on Jaguar, M.G. and
Rolls-Royce originally appeared in
the Great Marques series published
by Octopus Books Limited. These
sections have been abridged and
updated.

The chapters on Jaguar and M.G.
were written by Chris Harvey and
edited by Jonathan Wood. All the
other sections were written by
Jonathan Wood.

Reproduction of Rolls-Royce and
Bentley Trademarks and copyright
material is made with the kind
permission of its owners.

Produced by
Mandarin Offset
22a Westlands Road, Quarry Bay
Hong Kong

Printed and Bound in Hong Kong

PAGE 1 1939 Triumph Dolomite; *PAGES 2–3* 1937 M.G. VA. Provided by Frances Adam;
PAGES 4–5 1963 lightweight racing E type Jaguar. Provided by Nigel Dawes Collection.

Stirling Moss in action.

FAR LEFT **1958 Tourist Trophy,**
Goodwood, *in a factory-entered*
Aston Martin DBRI, where,
sharing the wheel,with Tony
Brooks, he won the event at
142.15 km/h (88.33 mph).

LEFT **1961 Monaco Grand Prix,** *in*
Rob Walker's Lotus 18, which he
won at 113.78 km/h (70.70 mph).

BELOW **1953 Daily Express**
Production Sports Car Race,
Silverstone *when, following a*
crash in practice, he was placed
seventh in the Jaguar C type. On
the same day he won the
Production Touring Car event in
a Mark VII Jaguar.

FOREWORD

by Stirling Moss

During the late 'seventies and early 'eighties, we all read a lot about the decline of the British car industry, and how difficult it was to remain competitive and profitable in the teeth of opposition from the all-conquering Japanese. So it's good to remember that the British car industry has much to be proud of; for most of the history of the automobile, British names have earned an honoured place in that epic story. Indeed, there have been times when the names of the more famous British cars seem to have dominated the life-story of the motor car, and most worthwhile developments tended to happen in the workshops of the Midlands.

And what names they are. Anyone who grew up in the exciting pre-war and post-war years, when companies like M.G. symbolized all that was best in British sports car design and engineering, can't help but remember the days when the Abingdon plant was the largest sports car factory in the world, and classics like the TC were dreamed of by any young man with a spark of enthusiasm in his veins. When Jaguar raced at Le Mans, and dominated this test of endurance against the best the European opposition could throw at them, it was comforting to reflect you could enjoy the 'Grace, Space and Pace' on which the company prided itself for a fraction of the price of any of their real overseas competitors.

However, there were many other marques which kept British engineering respected overseas: from the large, powerful and opulent luxury cars like the Rolls-Royces and Bentleys to humble but well-loved designs like the Morris Minor and the Austin Seven; from sports cars for the less wealthy enthusiasts such as the Triumph Spitfire and the Austin Healey Sprite to sophisticated thoroughbreds like the Lotus Elite and the Aston Martin DB4. All of them have a vital part to play in a story which is all too easily forgotten today, even by present-day enthusiasts, and a story which needs retelling. Jonathan Wood is just the man for the job. As an author of several books on cars of the past and former features editor of *Thoroughbred and Classic Cars*, he has every reason to know the history of each make and model, both in the workshop and on the track, and the story he tells is entertaining and encouraging.

Stirling Moss.

London

INTRODUCTION

The 90 years or so of the British motor industry's existence have seen an extraordinary variety of makes (or marques) and models offered to the public. Of these some were good, others plain indifferent and a few downright bad. However, some British marques have outstanding qualities and these form the subject of this book.

Britain came rather late to the motor car. It was in 1886 that the German Benz company began manufacturing its products for public sale and the French immediately seized on the invention so that their industry was soon the world's largest. Britain, however, did not really get into its stride until around the turn of the century and the vast majority of pre-First World War car companies were established in the 1901–05 era.

Just two makes that date from this time are Rolls-Royce, established in 1904, and Austin created the following year. Henry Royce's 10 hp car was not a triumph of original design

though it had a precision of line and clear-sighted refinement that was to be found in all Royce's subsequent work. Following the historic meeting with motoring pioneer, the Hon. Charles Rolls, from this small two-cylinder car sprang a range of three-, four- and six-cylinder models which culminated in the superlative 40/50 which was later to be known as the Silver Ghost. It was the Ghost, soon to become Rolls-Royce's one and only model, that raised the marque head and shoulders above its British Daimler and Napier contemporaries and successfully challenged such makes as Mercedes and Delaunay-Bellville on continental Europe. This, coupled with Claude Johnson's undoubted marketing and managerial skills, proclaimed the product of Henry Royce's genius as 'The Best Car in the World'. The coming of the First World War saw Rolls-Royce extend its interests into the aero engine field, which was to expand during the subsequent inter-war years, so that by the mid 1930s Rolls-

Royce was first and foremost an aero engine manufacturer.

Herbert Austin was not a creative designer but tended to rely on other engineers' creations for his inspiration. His first design was an improvement on the French Léon Bollée, while his own models from 1906 onwards were more often than not copied from other sources. For like many of his contemporaries Austin possessed a natural aptitude for mechanics, but this essentially empirical standpoint was backed up with the minimum of theoretical knowledge. It resulted in a cautious approach to design and the cars were rarely innovative. Nevertheless Austins were reliable and well built with carefully conceived and executed bodywork. Austin possessed a good eye for style and proportion, and his coachwork was built at Longbridge rather than being farmed out to a specialist; an unusual state of affairs.

Diametrically opposed to the Austin in concept was William Morris's Bullnose Morris Oxford that appeared in 1913. Austin was far more steeped in British engineering traditions than the young bicycle maker from Cowley; so whereas Austin made as much as possible on the premises and *manufactured* his car at his Longbridge factory, Morris ordered practically all his car's parts from outside suppliers and then *assembled* them at his Cowley works. In 1914 Morris

built 909 cars, 364 more than Austin who made 545, and established a manufacturing advantage that was to be maintained for virtually the next 35 years.

The arrival of Bentley
The coming of the First World War saw practically all the car companies rapidly expand to cope with the insatiable demands for munitions and aircraft which introduced the

1914 Rolls-Royce Silver Ghost. *This chassis was exported to Australia in July 1914 and the body is by Waring Brothers of Melbourne. It is now in America, having been there since 1972. Provided by Dick Philippi*

concept of mass production to many. The ending of the war in 1918 saw the following year's Motor Show play host to no less than 90 firms. One was Bentley Motors, formed only in January of that year, displaying its 3-litre model. Unfortunately parts for its engine were not completed in time, so the crankcase and camshaft cover were made of wood and realistically painted. The model did not reach production until 1921 and there followed 6½-, 4½- and 8-litre cars. Although the firm was largely unprofitable, Bentley's successes at the newly instituted Le Mans 24-hour race, winning on no less than five occasions, were reassuring to a public who needed reminding that British technology could still give the Continental opposition a run for its money. W.O. Bentley's rugged and reliable cars presented a clear, unflickering image of the spirit of Victorian England, mirroring an era of stability, prosperity and self-confidence; thinking that in many ways seemed out of place in Britain of the 1920s. It was, unfortunately, an ideal that flew in the face of reality and Bentley's approach of designing cars strictly from an engineering standpoint (which is a good reason for so venerating them today) was only possible from 1926 onwards by Woolf Barnato raising his financial umbrella and shielding the firm from the harsh realities of the decade. In all only 3037 'W.O.' Bentleys were produced in the ten years between 1921 and 1931 which accounted for only about a week of William Morris's Bullnose production in 1925. But how boring motoring history would be without such extravagances!

The hand-built high-performance Bentley had little in common with the mass-produced Bullnose which was an American at heart, the car's engine and gearbox having been designed in Detroit. After the First World War Morris had been able to build on his well-prepared pre-war ground. In 1919 the modern, reliable 11.9 hp Cowley and more expensive Oxford were just the sort of medium-sized cars that the post-war public was wanting. By 1924 Morris was Britain's top-selling car maker and, apart from 1933–4 when Austin built more cars, was to remain so until the outbreak of the Second World War.

Austin had not been so lucky. He had started off in 1918 by scrapping his pre-war range and producing just one model, a massive 20 hp car in the spirit of a 16 hp Hudson he had run during the war. It was as unsuitable for the 1920s as the Bullnose Morris was ideal, but Austin soon saw the errors of his ways and produced his successful 12 hp model in 1921 by the simple expedient of scaling down the design of his larger car. Even more significant, however, was his famous Seven, introduced in 1922. When it appeared Austin's baby car had the smallest capacity four-cylinder engine on the British market and it was not until the late 1920s that his rivals responded to the wisdom of its conception.

Austin deserves credit for deciding to manufacture a small car but, ironically, he was not responsible for the model's diminutive 696 cc four-cylinder engine which lies at the very core of the model's appeal. For the Seven is basically a large car scaled down and that sector of the market was usually

confined to noisy and crude contrivances powered by rough-running two-cylinder engines. As was his way, Austin was all for doing the same and had in mind to copy the two-cylinder air-cooled Rover Eight. But a young 18-year-old draughtsman, Stanley Edge, because he possessed far more technical knowledge than his 55-year-old employer, coupled with his direct no nonsense approach, managed to convince Austin of the sense of adopting a small four. With Austin's agreement, Edge then proceeded to design the unit which went on to power 290,000 or so Sevens. The car was to prove the Austin Motor Company's salvation and was soon to outstrip the larger 12 in manufacturing output. From 1926 until 1932 it was the firm's best-selling model and remained in production until 1939 after output had peaked in 1935, 13 years after its appearance, when over 27,000 Sevens left Austin's Longbridge factory.

was a visual triumph; the cars were old fashioned by continental standards though greater things were to follow in the post-war years.

The 1930s were, however, the heyday of the small family saloon. British car manufacturing output doubled between 1929 and 1939, and in 1935 Great Britain overtook France as Europe's largest car manufacturer and thus became second only to America in motor vehicle output. It was during the decade that the Big Six car manufacturers established themselves. In 1929 Austin, Morris and Singer had accounted for no less than three-quarters of the country's motor vehicle output. By 1939 Morris was still the market leader but was pursued by Austin, Ford (whose 1932 Model Y gave it a strong grip on the British market it has never relinquished), followed by Standard, Vauxhall and Rootes.

Although the mass production market grew and was

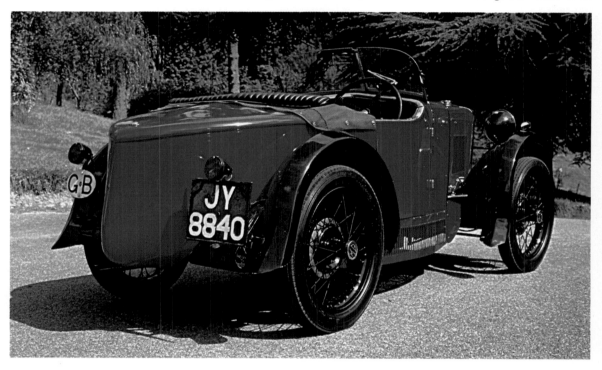

BELOW LEFT **1937 Austin Seven Ruby.** *Austin's famous 'baby' car was introduced in 1922 and continued in production until 1939. This is an example of the Ruby saloon, announced in 1934 and offering such modest refinements as bumpers, trafficators, and opening bonnet vents. Provided by the Patrick Collection.*

RIGHT **1930 M.G. M-type.** *William Morris's answer to the Austin Seven was the Morris Minor which shared its 847 cc overhead camshaft engine with the M-type. The model remained in production until 1932 and its derivatives until 1935. Output and profits fell and were not revived until the late 1930s. Provided by Keith J. Portsmore.*

The M.G. sports car

It was the Austin Seven that prompted William Morris to introduce his Minor model in 1929. Sales were disappointing, however, but the lively 847 cc overhead camshaft four was far more at home in the M Type M.G. introduced simultaneously. This marque had come to the fore in the 1920s when Cecil Kimber, the manager of the Oxford-based Morris Garages, began producing sporting versions of the contemporary Morris products. Before long M.G. (for Morris Garages) emerged as a make in its own right and gained great individuality with a move to Abingdon, 10 km (6 miles) from Oxford, in 1929. Up until 1935 the M.G. two-seaters were competitively active, attracting works support, and upheld British laurels as far afield as the Italian Mille Miglia. It was sad that such activities were not reflected in increased M.G. sales and it was paradoxical that only after the mid 1930s, with its racing programme cancelled and its products cheapened and simplified, that sales, and no doubt profits, rose. By 1939 M.G. was by far and away Britain's largest sports car manufacturer.

M.G.s used Wolseley- and Morris-derived engines but the same could not be said of the Aston Martin which, from 1927, exclusively relied on a well-conceived 1½-litre overhead camshaft four that had, ironically, been conceived as a proprietary engine. The cars were possessed of an inherent honesty, with their good looks reflecting a potent performance which was certainly not always the way with every 'sports' car of the 1930s. Although well made, the Ulster 100

consolidated in the 1930s, the decade also witnessed the birth of one of the post-war world's most famous marques. It had been in 1931, at the very nadir of the world depression, that William Lyons revealed his low, stylish SS1 at that year's Motor Show. Lyons, whose Irish father had established his Music and Pianoforte Warehouse in Blackpool at the turn of the century, had first gone into partnership producing motorcycle sidecars in the town and then progressed to car bodies. A move to Coventry was followed by the creation of the Standard-based SS in which Lyons established his successful formula of astounding good looks coupled with a sensationally low price. The performance would have to wait until 1935 and more powerful overhead-valve engines.

Post-war car production

After the Second World War the British motor industry's circumstances differed greatly from the conditions that had greeted trading in 1919. The country's economic reserves had been exhausted by the beginning of 1941 and a buoyant balance of payments surplus became an economic prerequisite of Clement Attlee's post-war Labour government. Therefore, after a generation of producing cars almost exclusively for the home market, British car makers were directed to export their products to the Commonwealth – Australia and New Zealand in particular – and to the United States of America.

It was Jaguar (as SS was renamed in 1945) and later M.G. that showed the potential of the trans-Atlantic sports car market and it was this buoyant sector that triggered the birth of the Austin Healey marque in 1952. Healey, along with Bristol, had been two of the new British makes to appear at the 1948 Motor Show, the first to be held for ten years. Donald Healey's cars were sporting, fast but expensive and the make looked like becoming Jaguar fodder when BMC's Leonard Lord instantly took up the firm's new 100 model and the Austin Healey marque was born. The really significant event of 1952, however, was the birth of the British Motor Corporation, formed by an alliance of the Austin and Morris companies with Lord at its head. Post-war he had directed Austin to become the country's largest car producer and, with the creation of BMC, its headquarters were firmly established at Longbridge; Morris was very much the junior partner of the merger. The union had been effected to cancel out a duplication of resources and model overlaps but, above all, it was intended to challenge the growing strength and market penetration of the American-owned, Dagenham-based Ford Motor Company which was being skilfully and farsightedly directed by Sir Patrick Hennessy.

Fortunately for most British manufacturers, it was largely a seller's market in the 1950s though Britain ceded its number-one manufacturing place to West Germany in 1956. The decade also witnessed an eruption of small specialist sports cars, often clad in glass-fibre bodies of dubious quality, of which the most illustrious is the Lotus marque. Colin Chapman's technical expertise and sheer guts saw Lotus evolve from an enthusiast's kit car to the visually impressive Elite coupé of 1957, a position fortified by the arrival of the Elan sports car in 1962. The 1960s saw Chapman move decisively into the grand prix field with Britain gaining pre-eminence on the racing circuits of the world which culminated in no less than seven manufacturers' championship wins.

Nineteen fifty-nine was a year of extraordinary significance for the British motor industry when BMC unveiled its revolutionary Mini with transverse engine, front-wheel drive and all-independent rubber suspension. Alec Issigonis's baby has since gone on to change the course of small car design throughout the world and in 1962 he followed with his 1100 on a similar theme. It was destined to be Britain's top-selling car for close on ten years. Ford's reply, however, was the scrupulously costed but conventional Cortina, and as the 1960s evolved the heady trading

conditions that had featured in the previous decade were replaced by a far more realistic buyer's market. Although BMC was doing well with its 1100 it failed to generate sufficient profits for the corporation and this led to its merging with Jaguar in 1966 to form British Motor Holdings.

Sir William Lyons (knighted 1956) had fulfilled all his pre-war promise and in 1948 had shown the world that a twin overhead camshaft engine could be a mass production reality. The famous XK power unit was intended for the big Mark VII Jaguar saloon, mostly for sale in America, and was equally at home in the sensational but low production sports cars. These evolved into the sports racers that triumphed at Le Mans in the 1950s and echoed Bentley's victories of 30 years previously. A Jaguar alliance with BMC, as the country's largest motor manufacturing combine, seemed to make sense.

Yet 18 months later BMH had new masters in the shape of the rapidly expanding Leyland Motors, headed by Sir Donald Stokes. In 1961 the commercial vehicle manufacturers had taken over the Standard Triumph company. Triumph, a bankrupted firm in 1939, had been bought at the end of the war by Standard. Until the arrival of the Herald in 1959 the Triumph saloons had been low production rather awkward products which never quite managed to find their niche. The sports car line, of which the TR2 of 1953 was the

ABOVE **1968 Triumph TR5.** *Basically externally similar to its TR4 and 4A predecessors, the Michelotti-styled TR5 was the first of the sports car range to be six-cylinder powered, in this case a 2½-litre, fuel-injected unit that rendered the bonnet bulge (for the previous engine's carburettors) superfluous.*

LEFT **Jaguar XK120.** *This Ecurie Ecosse team car was raced in the 1950s by Sir James Scott-Douglas. This car, which was re-sprayed in its original Flag Blue livery, was magnificently restored by Tom May, a former owner. Scott-Douglas drove this car at the Nürburgring 1000 km in 1953. Provided by Tony Hildebrand of Straight Six.*

first, was far more successful and soon found a ready market in America. Leyland's resources were to see a new, successful Triumph 2000 saloon into production along with a timely Spitfire sporting car range. Leyland went on to purchase the Rover and Alvis companies in 1967 and with an effective take-over of Austin/Morris in the following year, Triumph became the combine's premier marque. It was a commitment that culminated in the arrival of the Triumph TR7 sports car that sold against the ageing but respected in-house MGB. The Abingdon-based M.G. company had built on the gains of the 1930s to spearhead Britain's export drive in the early post-war years. The archaic T Series two-seater had been eventually replaced by the more up-to-date MGA in 1955, and in 1962 came the outstandingly successful MGB.

The 1960s was a period of great success for M.G. but its re-investment programme was geared to the fortunes of its corporate parent in a decade when BMC was suffering from a fall in profitability. With the arrival of Leyland's Triumph-orientated management, Canley rather than Abingdon tended to get what funds were available for a corporate sports car and the outcome was the controversial TR7 which lost money throughout its six troubled years of manufacture. Meanwhile M.G., probably one of Britain's most famous marques, was allowed to wither away. The MGB soldiered on until 1980 after which the world-famous Abingdon factory

was closed. However, the M.G. name has been revived on the new and highly acclaimed Austin Metro, Maestro, and Montego models which ensures that the illustrious initials will not disappear. Triumph, by contrast, has been discontinued by the re-structured BL cars.

The fuel crisis
The Arab-Israeli war in 1973, the resulting fuel crisis and downturn in the world economy all contributed to British Leyland suffering from an acute cash crisis at the end of 1974 and the firm was nationalized the following year. Lord Stokes, as he had become in 1969, departed and successive managements endeavoured to implement the subsequently discredited Ryder Report on British Leyland, commissioned by the British government in 1974. Not surprisingly when Michael Edwardes took over as Leyland's chairman late in 1977 corporate morale was at a low ebb. Sir Michael – he was knighted in 1979 – undertook radical surgery on the company's management and met union agitators head on. A new model programme was implemented of which the Austin Metro of 1980 was the first example, and it was followed by the equally well-received Maestro. With the appointment in 1980 of John Egan as Jaguar's first chairman for five years, the illustrious firm, at that stage haemorrhaging millions of pounds annually, was revived and its return to the private sector now seems certain. Casualties were major cutbacks in manufacturing plants and a much reduced workforce. The Morris marque disappeared from the group's cars at the end of 1983 though it will continue on commercial vehicles.

The 1973 oil crisis also triggered a difficult time for the small independents and recent years have seen a re-structuring of both the Aston Martin and Lotus companies, and both have diversified into offering their unique and very individual areas of expertise to industry. Even Rolls-Royce, maker of 'The Best Car in the World', has suffered its fair share of financial upheavals. The original company went bankrupt in the wake of the RB 211 aero engine debacle in 1971 and was nationalized. The car division was subsequently offered for public floatation and in 1980 came a merger with the Vickers engineering group.

Of the ten famous British marques considered in this book, three are no longer manufactured. By the year 2000, how many will have survived?

ABOVE LEFT **1984 Lotus Excel.** *The Excel is a radically re-engineered Eclat which employs the same chassis but with revised rear suspension and transmission and brake components, courtesy of Toyota. The front-mounted engine is Lotus's own four-cylinder twin overhead camshaft 2.2-litre unit.*

LEFT **1984 Montego.** *A recent offering from BL is the Austin Montego, a further essay on the transverse engine/front-wheel-drive theme and much more than 'a Maestro with a boot'. The engine options are 1.3 and 2 litres, and there is also a new 1.6-litre S Series overhead camshaft unit. The model has been conceived with a firm eye on the company fleet market, as well as for the family motorist.*

For definitions of engineering and other technical terms in the text and captions, refer to the Glossary, pages 252–3.

ASTON MARTIN

An illustrious sports car line born in the 1920s. After the Second World War, it went on to win Le Mans and today the rugged V8 is Britain's fastest production road car.

The origins of Aston Martin, one of Britain's oldest sporting marques, reach back to pre-First World War days.

It was in 1914 that Old Etonian Lionel Martin built a car in which he competed in the Aston Clinton hill climb, thus giving birth to the famous name. A keen motor sport enthusiast, he was a partner in the London-based Bamford and Martin garage which held an agency for Singer cars. Taking a rather pedestrian 10 hp model, Martin, with the aid of his foreman Jack Addis, proceeded to improve and tune it so that it was capable of 112 km/h (70 mph) rather than its traditional 64 km/h (40 mph). Martin successfully campaigned the little car in rallies and hill climbs and before long the firm began to receive orders for replica versions. However, rather than produce a Singer-based car Martin decided to design a completely new vehicle powered by a proprietary 1400 cc side-valve Coventry Simplex engine with Wrigley gearbox and axles. The chassis would be a conventional affair with

ABOVE **1922 Aston Martin 'Green Pea'**. *This car began life as Count Zborowski's entry in the 1922 French Grand Prix. Afterwards it had its twin overhead camshaft engine removed, a side-valve unit fitted and was subsequently twice re-engined. It was discovered in the late 1950s by Neil Murray, who totally restored it and refitted an 'original' side-valve engine.*

LEFT **The service department**, *Newport Pagnell, in 1976.*

three-quarter rear elliptic springs. While awaiting delivery of the chassis, Martin took one of these engines and installed it in a 1908 Isotta Fraschini chassis. It was after successfully running this Italian special at Aston Clinton, Buckinghamshire that Lionel decided to call his car an Aston Martin, though the outbreak of the First World War later in 1914 temporarily put paid to the project.

After the war, Robert Bamford decided to opt out of the partnership, so Martin took over the firm and began work on the design of a new car. He was rejoined by Jack Addis, his old foreman, and assisted by Robb, a draughtsman who had been involved in the design of the pre-war Coventry Simplex engine; they pushed ahead with a new Aston Martin. By 1923 the car was in production. It bore similarities to the pre-war model and had a 1487 cc side-valve four-cylinder engine and remained in production until 1925. This was a sporting model, but there was also a short-wheelbase touring version.

However, there were more exciting projects in the pipeline. Addis produced a special short-chassis car called *Bunny* aimed at the race track where it soon made a name for itself, though a more potent version with a single overhead camshaft engine was less successful. At about the same time the Polish Count Louis Zborowski, who had already created the famous *Chitty-Chitty-Bang-Bang*, asked Aston Martin to produce an advanced racing car with a twin overhead camshaft four-cylinder engine for him to use at the 1922 French Grand Prix which that year was staged at Strasbourg. Two cars were run at the event but soon retired, and the handsome and expensive power unit was successfully used in subsequent cars and racing motor boats. Although the Polish Count had financed that particular exercise to the tune of £10,000, Lionel Martin is rumoured at this time to have spent well in excess of £100,000 on Aston Martin, a not inconsiderable sum, and a small fortune by 1920s' standards.

By 1924 Martin had produced around 50 cars but his own finances were becoming rapidly depleted and he looked around for someone else to help shoulder the financial burden. The firm's saviour, albeit temporary, was Lady Dorothy Charnwood, who supplied £10,000 to bail the company out and her son, the Hon. John Benson, joined Martin and his wife on the board of directors. Benson, who had read engineering at Oxford, designed yet another costly twin overhead camshaft engine which was exhibited at the make's motor show début at Olympia in 1925 but the fiscal writing was on the wall because within weeks of the show closing a receiver was appointed. Lionel Martin severed his connection with the company and left to pursue the family granite-quarrying business.

Aston Martin for sale
So Aston Martin was put up for sale and there was a surprising amount of interest generated with offers coming from a variety of sources including Vauxhall and the Bristol Aeroplane Company and across the English Channel from Donnet et Zedel in France. However, the eventual buyer was William Somerville Renwick who paid £3600 for the company. It was while Renwick had been employed at the Coventry-based Armstrong Siddeley company that he had met up with Augustus Cesare Bertelli, who was to be responsible for the design of every Aston Martin from 1926 until his departure from the firm in 1937.

Bertelli, who had been born in Italy, was brought up in Cardiff, his family having emigrated to Wales in 1894. On leaving school at the age of 14, Bertelli briefly returned to his native Italy and for a short time worked in Fiat's experimental department under the famous Felice Nazzaro. But he later returned to Britain because, by all accounts, football, a game he loved, was prohibited on Sundays! Italy's loss was Britain's gain because on the outbreak of the First World War Bertelli was already involved with the Graham White Avi-

ation Company, whose works was at Hendon, Middlesex. There he also designed an unconventional rotary engine but was prevented by his terms of employment from putting it into production.

So, at the end of the war, Bertelli moved to Birmingham having been invited to join the Enfield Alldays company, who already had a rather strange rear radial-engined car under development, and intended to use it to cash in on the expected post-war car boom. Bertelli pointed out that the design was wildly impractical and came up with a far more conventional 10 hp car, but a few radial-powered models were built. Tragically, Bertelli's design came too late because it made its début at the 1921 Motor Show, the year the post-war boom collapsed. Then Alldays and Onions, who owned the company, found itself in financial hot water and decided to liquidate the motor car side of its business. So Bertelli lost his job and became a freelance engineering consultant, working around Birmingham and Coventry for such firms as Rover, Armstrong Siddeley and Coventry Simplex.

TOP **May 1922 record attempt in 'Bunny' at Brooklands.** *Clive Gallop checks the front wheel and an overalled Sammy Davis looks at the engine. Katherine Martin is alongside him, while Lionel Martin refuels the car. Ten world records were to fall.*

ABOVE **'Bunny' at Brooklands.** *Bugatti enthusiast B.S. Marshall is at the wheel.*

ABOVE RIGHT **Grand Prix Aston Martin.** *This car was assembled by Aston Martin after the 1922 French Grand Prix and raced in 1923 by Zborowski and Gallop.*

RIGHT **1922 French Grand Prix.** *Count Zborowski at the wheel of one of the two 1½-litre Aston Martins entered. Both retired with magneto drive trouble.*

Bertelli then had the good fortune to be given a free hand to design a new car by millionaire Woolf Barnato, who was later to own the Bentley company, which the magnate was to manufacture. Three Bertelli cars were built at Barnato's mansion at Lingfield, Surrey and were entered in the 1923 Brooklands 200-Mile Race, but they did not achieve expectations and were clearly in need of further refinement.

Meanwhile the election of the first Labour Government in 1923 alarmed Barnato, who hastily departed for the more convivial United States of America. Bertelli was left only with the right to produce the cars under his own name, but fate took a hand because during his visits to Armstrong Siddeley's factory at Parkside, Coventry he had met up with engineer William Renwick. 'Bill' Renwick had just inherited the family fortune and he proposed that Bertelli join him in a venture to produce a motor car. However, 'Bert', as he was to

become universally known, had experienced more corporate cul-de-sacs than most and realised that Renwick did not have sufficient funds at his disposal. What he did consider to be a practical proposition, however, was for the pair to produce a proprietary engine that could then be sold to any manufacturer who wanted it, rather in the same way that Lionel Martin had purchased Coventry Simplex units just prior to the First World War.

The firm of Renwick and Bertelli therefore set up a small machine shop in Kings Road, Tyseley on the southern outskirts of Birmingham and there they jointly designed a four-cylinder 1½-litre single overhead camshaft engine, a sensible decision as most contemporary proprietary units were low cost side-valve fours. Bertelli still had one of the old Enfield Allday chassis at his disposal and it was fitted with the new engine, the resulting car being christened the *Buzz Box*. There followed many thousands of miles of trials to prove the engine's reliability and it was at about this time that Renwick and Bertelli received an approach from the Hon. John Benson of Aston Martin, then in receivership. So the two partners travelled to London to view the garage in a Kensington mews where the Aston Martin cars were assembled. But Bertelli realized that the greatest asset was the Aston Martin name, so Renwick put up the money to buy the firm and the duo moved south and to a new factory at Feltham, Middlesex, where Whitehead aircraft had been manufactured during the First World War. Machine tools were installed and a coach-building department established which was run by Bert's

BELOW LEFT **1930 International.** *A fine example of a four-seater version. Note the filler for the dry sump lubrication system just ahead of the radiator.*

RIGHT **1931 Team Car, chassis LM7,** *one of three financed by H.J. Aldington of Frazer Nash fame. It won its class in the 1931 TT race driven by Major C.M. Harvey and also ran at Le Mans. It was subsequently sold to Morris Mortimer-Goodall, who was also co-opted for the firm's 1933 Le Mans sortie and thus it ran twice at the Sarthe circuit. In recent years, it has been restored by former Aston Martin apprentice and now marque historian Inman Hunter, with the assistance of Les Wigmore.*

BELOW RIGHT **1933 1½-litre** *competing in a contemporary hill-climb event.*

brother Harry (Enrico), who had already produced bodies for the short-lived Enfield Allday venture. It subsequently became a separate company and E. Bertelli Ltd would produce coachwork for other makes in addition to Aston Martin though it remained Feltham based.

Bertelli takes over

Using the *Buzz Box* as his starting point, Bertelli designed the first of a new generation of Aston Martins that made their motor show début at Olympia in 1927 and were to form the basis of all subsequent models of the inter war years. The 66 x 99 mm, 1481 cc engine ensured that the car would be a lively performer and thus followed in the marque's sporting traditions as laid down by Lionel Martin. The three-seater sports version was a particularly attractive offering with low, purposeful bodywork, while large brake drums revealed the need for good stopping power as the car was capable of over 128 km/h (80 mph). But behind the scenes there had been a personality clash between Bill Renwick and John Benson, the latter having stayed on after the reconstruction, and both subsequently left the company. Renwick later went to M.G. and worked on the R-type of 1935.

So Bertelli soldiered on during the worst years of the Depression, triggered by the 1929 Wall Street Crash, and finances were always unstable and remained so until 1932. Money came from a variety of sources during this period. S.C. Whitehouse, a Harrow garage proprietor, provided funds as did Nigel Holder and Straker of Aston Martin distributors Kensington Moir and Straker. Then finance came from ex-Vauxhall managing director Percy Kidner and in 1931 there was a brief liaison with H.J. Aldington, who produced Frazer Nash cars. Yet another distributor, Lance Prideaux-Brune was an Aston Martin provider in 1932 but later that year the company was bought outright by Newcastle shipping tycoon Sir Arthur Sutherland for his son R. Gordon Sutherland, who shared the firm's joint managing directorship with Bertelli.

Aston Martin competes at Le Mans

Despite this precarious financial background, Aston Martin cars were making their all too distinctive marks in sporting

events. The make made its Le Mans début in 1928 and, though the cars did not complete the race, with the exceptions of 1929, 1930 and 1936, they were to appear at the Sarthe circuit every year until 1964, an unrivalled achievement for a British car manufacturer. The cars also regularly appeared at the Brooklands track, chalking up a fifth place in the 1928 Double Twelve race and Bertelli achieved a fourth in the same event in 1930. The following year saw a class victory in the TT and an Aston Martin came fifth in that year's Le Mans 24-hour classic. In 1932 the marque again achieved a fifth placing, and the Rudge Whitworth cup. The car was significant because it incorporated a proprietary gearbox and rear axle which Bertelli had introduced as a cost-saving exercise in place of specially designed units.

There followed the successful Le Mans model in 1932 which was succeeded in 1934 by a Mark II version. In 1935 Aston Martin achieved a third place at Le Mans, its best position at Sarthe of the inter war years. The firm's other successful competitive theatre was the Tourist Trophy race at Ulster and in 1934 Aston Martin won the team award with lightened 177 km/h (110 mph) cars. These successes paved the way for the legendary Ulster Aston Martin, one of the truly great British sports cars of the 1930s. But despite this good progress a rift developed between Bertelli and Sutherland, and in 1937, Bert, who was then at work on a 2-litre model developed from the 1½-litre cars, resigned from the company. He thereafter severed his connection with the motor industry and became a keen farmer and successful pig breeder.

Sutherland wanted to broaden Aston Martin's appeal and

LEFT AND BELOW **1934 Mark II saloon**. *A magnificently restored example, the 1½-litre overhead camshaft engine is readily apparent. It was originally designed by Renwick and Bertelli as a proprietary unit. Provided by Nigel Dawes Collection, owner D.J.E. Proffitt.*

RIGHT **1934 Ulster**, *named after the firm's TT successes.*

FAR RIGHT **Feltham 1935**. *Charles Brackenbury (foreground) with Le Mans entry, and Bertelli behind. Journalist Gordon Wilkins is on the right.*

BXV 102

the new 2-litre car went into production in 1937. It was cheaper and simpler than the earlier 1½-litre and, in retrospect, the magic was somehow lost. Nevertheless the new cars sold better than their predecessors which allowed Claude Hill, who took over from Bertelli, to begin work on a new generation of Aston Martin cars. Hill, whose associations went back to Renwick and Bertelli days in Tyseley, had a far more theoretical approach to car design than his predeces-sor and, although Bert's 1½-litre cars had been well produced, potent and of great aesthetic appeal, they were heavy and, by European standards, outdated designs.

First came a rather odd-looking saloon, nicknamed *Donald Duck*, in 1938, with a box section chassis made from electrical conduit. Later the same year followed the C type, with cowled radiator and more modern bodywork which concealed square section steel tubing. It was his experience with

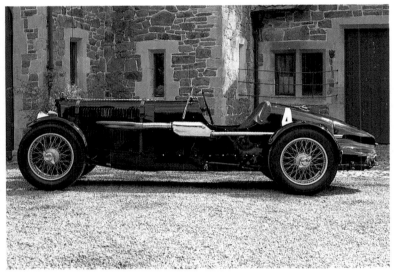

these two cars that permitted Hill to progress to the Atom saloon, which was completed just prior to the outbreak of the Second World War in 1939. In the 1930s designers recognized that independent front suspension, which was gaining in popularity, required a chassis as rigid as possible to work effectively, so Hill built up a strong frame of square and rectangular tubing. Thus he was able to install the Gordon Armstrong cantilever variety at the front, while conventional half elliptics were used at the rear. The four-door saloon body also flew in the face of previous Aston Martin practice. Although initially powered by the proven overhead camshaft 2-litre engine coupled to a Cotal electric gearbox, the car was eventually fitted with a pushrod unit of the same capacity designed by Hill. During and after the war Hill and Gordon Sutherland covered over 160,000 km (100,000 miles) in the Atom which the latter regarded as having 'lots of power in a small package'.

ABOVE **1940 Atom saloon**. *This prototype ran throughout the war, hence the nearside restricted headlamp.*

RIGHT **1948 DB1**. *This actual car featured on Aston Martin's 1948 Motor Show stand. Only 15 DB1s were built.*

DAVID BROWN STEPS IN

During hostilities, Aston Martin was involved in the production of aircraft parts and, although in reasonable shape with the coming of peace, Sutherland recognized that he did not possess the financial resources to develop the Atom concept. So after 15 years' ownership, Sutherland put an advertisement in *The Times* newspaper offering Aston Martin for sale. There it was seen by David Brown, chairman and managing director of gear manufacturers David Brown and Son of Huddersfield, who had diversified into tractor production just prior to the outbreak of the Second World War. So, early in 1947, Brown visited Feltham to find that the company largely consisted of a rented factory, the Atom saloon and the Aston Martin name. He drove the Atom, was impressed by its roadholding, but regarded it as underpowered and then decided to buy the company for £20,000. Work was soon under way improving the Atom, which mostly involved strengthening its chassis, and this eventually emerged as the DB1 of 1948. Brown was insistent, however, that it be an open rather than closed car which was much more in the marque's sporting traditions.

But it was not long before Brown bought another car company for, in 1948, he paid £52,500 for Lagonda who, like Aston Martin, had developed a wartime prototype but had yet to put it into production. The firm had started life in the back garden of Wilbur Gunn's house in Staines, Surrey. An American by birth, Gunn had borrowed the Lagonda name from a business run by his brother-in-law back in Springfield, Ohio which was the Shawnee Indian name for Buck's Creek from where his family hailed. Initially motorized bicycles were produced and cars followed in 1906 but finances were seldom sound and the firm was finally put up for sale in 1935. Although Rolls-Royce was keen to buy the company it was lawyer Alan Good, who headed a consortium that bought Lagonda for £67,500.

Good brought in W.O. Bentley, who had been unhappily employed by Rolls-Royce following the Derby company's take-over of Bentley Motors in 1931, and he became Lagonda's technical director. With Bentley came a small team of Rolls-Royce designers and draughtsmen headed by Stewart Tresillian and it was they who were largely responsible for the 1938 V12 Lagonda intended as a challenge for Derby's Phantom III, also V12 powered. With the coming of the Second World War it soon became obvious that the post-war market was going to be more cost conscious than elements of the pre-war one had been, so during hostilities Bentley designed a new 2.6-litre twin overhead camshaft six-cylinder engine which was subsequently mounted in a chassis boasting all independent suspension and finally revealed to the public early in 1947. But by this time Alan Good was

tiring of his motoring interests and David Brown, who had just bought Aston Martin, was urged by Bedford Lagonda distributor Tom Scratchard to buy the company.

Initially Brown was put off by Lagonda's size but, after driving one of the post-war prototypes, was very much attracted by the potential of the twin cam six-cylinder engine. Although there were offers from Rootes and Jaguar these fell by the wayside in the face of gloomy economic forecasts from Chancellor of the Exchequer Stafford Cripps, leaving the field clear for Brown. So within the space of about a year he became the owner of two of Britain's most famous motoring marques. The deal, however, did not include Lagonda's Staines factory and Brown recognized that future production would have to be concentrated at the Aston Martin works at Feltham.

The arrival of the DB1

It was in September 1948 that the first Aston Martin of the David Brown era, retrospectively titled the DB (for David Brown) 1, appeared but at £2331 there were few takers and only 15 were produced by the time output ceased in May 1950. The car had a multi-tubular chassis with a coil spring and wishbone/torsion bar independent front suspension. Under the bonnet was Claude Hill's 1970 cc pushrod four, also proven in the Atom. The DB1 was soon showing its competitive mettle and a racing version took the chequered flag in the 1948 Spa 24-hour race. There were more successes to follow. In 1949 three special cars were built using a shortened DB1 chassis and distinguished by streamlined bodywork. Two were powered by the Hill pushrod engine but the third used the Bentley 2.6-litre Lagonda unit. Combining Hill's chassis with Bentley's engine resulted in a potent package which was effectively the Aston Martin DB2, which replaced the DB1 in 1950. David Brown had also inherited Frank Feeley, who had styled the V12 and post-war Lagonda and it was he who was responsible for the DB2's stylish GT bodywork, though the model was also available in coupé form. But Claude Hill, understandably disappointed that a six-cylinder version of his pushrod design was not to be used in the new Aston Martins, left the company.

From January 1951 the DB2 was available with a 125 bhp Vantage engine, a 20 bhp improvement over the standard unit. It was replaced in October 1953 with the DB2/4 with improved rear seating but, as it was 76 kg (168 lb) heavier than its predecessor, engine capacity was increased to 2.9 litres from 1954 after the 2.6-litre Vantage engine had initially been carried over from the earlier model. These cars had

ABOVE **Sir David Brown**, *who owned Aston Martin from 1947 until 1972.*

BELOW **1952 DB2**, *the first twin cam-engined model.*

ASTON MARTIN DB2 (1950–3)	
Number built **Approx 409**	
ENGINE	
No. of cylinders	**Six**
Bore/stroke mm	**78 × 90**
Displacement cc	**2580**
Valve operation	**Twin ohc**
Compression ratio	**6.5:1**
Induction	**Twin SU carburettors**
BHP	**105**
Transmission	**Four-speed**
CHASSIS	
Frame	**Square section tube**
Wheelbase mm	**2514**
Track – front mm	**1371**
Track – rear mm	**1371**
Suspension – front	**Independent**
Suspension – rear	**Trailing arm, coil**
Brakes	**Hydraulic drum**
PERFORMANCE	
Maximum speed	**175 km/h (109 mph)**

bodywork by Mulliners of Birmingham, but for 1956 came a Mark II version with coachwork by Tickford of Newport Pagnell, Buckinghamshire. This was because Standard Triumph, as Mulliners' largest customer, had secured exclusive rights to the firm's body output, so Aston Martin, along with Alvis, Daimler and Sunbeam, had to look elsewhere. In March 1957 came a further development of the theme, the DB Mark III, with front disc brakes, which was produced until July 1959. In addition Lagonda cars were also manufactured, albeit in much smaller quantities, the 2.6-litre car entering production in 1949. Output continued until 1958 but the marque was briefly revived in 1962/4 with the arrival of the DB4-based Rapide four-door saloon with de Dion rear axle.

Competition successes of the 1950s

David Brown was intent on building on the racing success of the late 1940s and in 1950 John Wyer was appointed Aston Martin's competitions manager. A trio of DB2s was pressed into service and at Le Mans that year succeeded in achieving fifth and sixth places and also winning the Index of Performance award. Yet another recruit to the Feltham factory was Professor Eberan von Eberhorst, responsible for the C type Auto Union grand prix cars of pre-war days, who had come to Britain from Cisitalia in 1949 to design the Jowett Jupiter sports car. It was he who laid out Aston Martin's purpose-built sports racer, the DB3, the first example appearing at the end of 1951. Its chassis echoed Auto Union practice being tubular with a front suspension by trailing links and torsion bars, while a de Dion rear axle was employed. The 2.6-litre twin cam six was modified to produce 140 bhp, a 35 bhp improvement over the contemporary DB2 road car. However, in 1952 the engine's capacity was upped to 2.9 litres.

As the first car was not completed until later than anticipated, a pair of DB2s was recruited to make up the numbers. That model proved its worth in the 1952 Mille Miglia when examples finished first and second in class and in 12th and 13th overall placings. It was not until the Production Car Race at Silverstone that the DB3s really got into their stride, finishing in second, third and fourth places. DB2s were again used at the Grand Prix de Berne but the new Mercedes-Benz 300SLs were proving their worth and Aston Martins finished in fourth and fifth places. Both DB3s failed at Le Mans but Aston Martin succeeded in winning the Nine Hours Race at Goodwood, despite one of the cars being destroyed in a spectacular pits fire.

During the winter of 1952/3 the DB3 was extensively redesigned with the intention of reducing its weight. The resulting DB3S appeared at Le Mans in 1953 but failed to find its form. Despite this there was a second place and a class win at Sebring and a fifth in the Mille Miglia. Even better was an outright win in the British Trophy Race in the Isle of Man. Yet further 1953 victory laurels came with the *Daily Express* Silverstone race and the Goodwood Nine Hours, with another Aston Martin in second place. A TT first and second rounded off a successful season. The following year was less successful though there was a one-two-three placing at the International Sportscar Race at Silverstone. It was also a year that marked the appearance of a new Feltham-designed $4\frac{1}{2}$-litre Lagonda but this latter-day V12 failed to mirror the achievements of its distinguished pre-war predecessor.

Nineteen fifty-five started better with a seventh Monte Carlo Rally placing and a class win for a DB2/4. A third place was achieved in the British Empire Trophy Race while there was a one-two win in the *Daily Express* Silverstone. The TT produced a fourth and there was yet another victory in the Goodwood Nine Hours. Le Mans saw the best Aston Martin performance for years with a DB3S taking second place behind a D-type Jaguar in an event marred by a tragic accident and the death of 81 spectators which prompted the withdrawal of the Mercedes-Benz team. Although the DB3S

had proved its worth, Aston Martin pressed ahead with a successor, the DBR1, initially featuring a new $2\frac{1}{2}$-litre twin cam engine with dry sump lubrication mounted in a multi tubular chassis. Girling disc brakes were fitted and a de Dion rear axle featured. The model was soon at Le Mans in 1956 but it was running at the $2\frac{1}{2}$-litre limit set for prototype models. The older DB3S repeated the previous year's result by following in the wheel tracks of Jaguar's legendary sports racing D-type into second place. This was the last year the model was fielded competitively by the factory. Other 1956 successes included a fourth at Sebring, a Goodwood victory while Aston Martin again won the *Daily Express* event at Silverstone. European results were distinguished by a second place at Spa, a third at Chimay and a second at Rouen and Le Mans.

The DBR1 moved centre stage in 1957 but at Le Mans all three works cars retired leaving only a French-entered DB3S to uphold Feltham laurels by achieving an 11th overall placing. The cars were in better form for the Belgian sports car race with Aston Martin taking first and second positions. There followed a victory in the Nürburgring 1000-Kilometre race and yet more success nearer home in the *Daily Express* Silverstone event. During 1958 Aston Martin again scored at the Nürburgring while the marque achieved a one-two-three placing at the Goodwood-staged Tourist Trophy. Le Mans went less well with all DBR1s retiring, though the Whitehead brothers took a DB3S into a creditable second place behind a Ferrari, which had led the race since lap 3.

Nineteen fifty-nine was to prove a golden year for Aston Martin when the marque won the International Sports Car Championship, the only occasion, before or since, that this accolade has been received by a British manufacturer. There was a win at the International GT race at Silverstone and, more significantly, a third win at the Nürburgring. But the crowning event came at Le Mans with a DBR1, driven by Roy Salvadori and Carroll Shelby, at last taking the chequered flag with another in second place. The season was rounded off with first and fourth placings at the TT, which secured the coveted championship for Aston Martin after which the firm announced that, like Jaguar had done four years previously, it was intending to retire from racing.

Also worthy of mention was a Grand Prix Aston Martin which made its competitive début at the International Trophy

ABOVE **1953 DB3S**, *pictured at that year's Tourist Trophy race at Dundrod, driven by Pat Griffiths and Peter Collins. Although it suffered from a water leak throughout, it went on to win at an average of 131.50 km/h (87.71 mph).*

RIGHT **1958 Le Mans**. *The team of DBR1s entered by Aston Martin. Race number 2 was driven by Moss and Brabham, 3 Brooks/ Trintignant, 4 Salvadori/Lewis-Evans. All failed to complete the race.*

FAR LEFT **1958 Tourist Trophy, Goodwood**. *Jack Brabham pictured in the DBR1 he shared with Roy Salvadori which was subsequently placed second. DBR1s scored a hat-trick at the event with Moss/Brooks first and Shelby/Lewis-Evans third.*

INSET LEFT **Cars being prepared for Le Mans in 1959**. *In the foreground is the Moss/Fairman DBR1 which dropped out of the event with engine trouble, with the winning Salvadori/Shelby car behind; photographed at the Aston Martin base at La Chartre.*

ABOVE **1959 DBR4**. *This $2\frac{1}{2}$-litre Formula One racing car ran in 1959 and 1960; a rather heavy traditional single-seater, it was outclassed by a new generation of lighter rear-engined cars.*

ABOVE LEFT **1959 Le Mans**. *Victory at last for Aston Martin: the winning DBR1 which took the chequered flag at 181.14 km/h (112.56 mph). Another DBR1 took second place.*

race at Silverstone in 1959 when it achieved second place. In their initial form the cars were designated DBR4 but the early promise was not maintained despite a team of four being prepared. Both entries failed to finish in the Dutch Grand Prix and in the British GP a sixth placing was achieved. It was the same story at the Italian event at Monza when the single-seater Aston managed tenth position. The cars were more powerful and lighter when they appeared for the 1960 season but they achieved little success in this DBR5 form except in Australia where, being tailored to conform to the local 3-litre formula, one came second in the 1960 Grand Prix. This was not a championship event but the $2\frac{1}{2}$-litre formula for which the cars had been built ran out at the end of 1960 and these rather heavy, traditional cars were rendered obsolete by a new generation of $1\frac{1}{2}$-litre lightweight rear-engined models which dominated 1961 grand prix events.

Not that this was quite the end of the competitive Aston Martin story by any means. DBRs finished third and ninth at Le Mans in 1960 and, although five cars appeared at the Sarthe circuit in 1961, none finished. A 'Project' GT, 212, was a works entry in the 24-hour classic in 1962 but it did not finish and 215 enjoyed even less success the following year. Nineteen sixty-four witnessed the last Aston Martin entry, but the lone DB4 failed to make much impact.

Enter the DB4

In the meanwhile time was running out on the range of road cars, the engine of which dated back to the war years, while the body lines had been first laid down in the late 1940s. A completely new Aston Martin, the DB4, that appeared at the end of 1958, was therefore especially welcome. With its DB5

and 6 successors, which remained in production until 1970, it was to prove the most popular range of Aston Martins ever built and represented both an aesthetic and performance triumph for the small company. The DB4 had a platform chassis, and the trailing arm independent front suspension that had featured on practically all post-war Astons was replaced by a wishbone and coil spring layout. A live rear axle was employed with suspension provided by coil springs and located by a Watts linkage and radius arms. The all-aluminium engine was also new but followed in the traditions of the earlier cars by being a twin overhead camshaft six and of 3.6 litres capacity. It had been designed by Aston Martin's own Tadek Marek and had received a competitive début at Le Mans in 1957 under the bonnet of DBR2, though it did not complete the course. Unfortunately for Aston Martin in 1958 the limit for engine capacity in sports car championship regulations was set at 3 litres, hitherto it had been unlimited, which debarred the power unit from use in further championship events.

But it was the decision of John Wyer, who had become the firm's general manager in 1956, to go to Italy for the styling of the new model's bodywork that raised the DB4 a visual head and shoulders above those of its contemporaries. Touring of Milan was responsible for the superbly styled GT bodywork which employed the company's Superleggera form of body construction. In translation the word means *Super light* and featured a superstructure of small diameter steel tubes welded to the main platform, with such items as the windscreen, rear window and angled sections for the door hinges attached directly to it. This skeleton was then clothed with light alloy body panels, the resulting structure being light and extremely rigid. Although Touring had been responsible for the construction of the prototype DB4, Aston Martin obtained a licence from the Italian coachbuilders to replicate the Superleggera body structure. The cars were not built at Feltham but at Newport Pagnell, Buckinghamshire, as David Brown had purchased the Tickford coachbuilding company in 1955 to ensure continuity of body supplies, and Aston Martin production was transferred there. However, the firm's competitions department remained in Middlesex until it too closed down in 1964.

ABOVE **DB4 GT**. *Built between 1959 and 1963, only 75 were produced. Lighter than the standard DB4, the GT also had a 136-litre (30 UK gallon) fuel tank along with lightweight Borrani wheels. The engine featured a 12-plug cylinder head, and Weber carburettors were standardized.*

RIGHT **1962 DB4 GT Zagato**. *Perhaps the ultimate DB4, just 19 were built between 1959 and 1963. Chassis were supplied to the Italian Zagato styling house and then returned to Newport Pagnell for completion. Top speed was 241 km/h (150 mph) plus.*

The new car turned the scales at 1397 kg (3080 lb), which was almost the same weight as the DB Mark III, eventually phased out in the summer of 1959. However, the DB4 was much faster with a top speed of around 225 km/h (140 mph), and with such impressive performance a livelier GT version was inevitable. This had a shorter chassis, while the engine was fitted with a 12-plug cylinder head and Weber, rather than SU carburettors, Girling in place of the standard car's Dunlop all-round disc brakes, and lightweight wheels. Built at the same time, between late 1959 and mid-1963, was the ultimate DB4, the Zagato-bodied GT, 100 kg (220 lb) lighter than standard and capable of over 241 km/h (150 mph). These cars, purposely rounded and bumperless, were bodied in Italy and a few left-hand-drive versions remained there, but most returned to Britain. Engine specifications were similar to the GT but the engine boasted a slightly higher compression ratio and was consequently marginally more powerful. A mere 19 Zagato DB4s were produced, compared with 75 GTs and 1110 standard cars.

Yet a further high performance version of the DB4 appeared in 1962. This was the Vantage, the car's chassis number carrying the SS for Special Series prefix and high compression engine which boosted output to 260 bhp, compared with the DB4's original 240. There were also minor styling changes at the same time when the basic model received faired-in headlights in line with the GT. Another variation followed in 1963 when the Vantage was offered with the GT's engine, the resulting model being known as the Vantage GT.

In its original form the DB4 experienced a variety of teething troubles, namely clutch and gearbox shortcomings and overheating as a result of owners using the newly opened M1 motorway as a test track to see how fast their new cars would go. These problems were largely overcome with the arrival of the DB5 in October 1963. Engine capacity was upped to 3.9 litres and an automatic gearbox was introduced as an option, though a few DB4s had been so equipped. Electric windows were standardized and an air conditioning system also became available at extra cost. At the end of 1963 the David Brown-built gearbox, which had initially been offered with overdrive on the model, was replaced by a five-speed German ZF unit. It seems that the parent David Brown and Sons was rather better at building tractor gearboxes than car ones! It was a special version of the DB5 that was used in the James Bond film *Goldfinger*, complete with bullet-proof rear screen, special over riders for ramming, ejector seat, retractable scything hub caps and rotating number plates. Aston Martin received valuable publicity from the film and produced a further two replica cars worthy of 007 himself. There was also a very exclusive estate car version of the DB5.

By the time DB5 production ceased, in October 1965, a total of 1025 cars had been sold, making it only marginally less successful than its predecessor. It was replaced by the DB6, a mechanically similiar car, but lengthened in response to owners' demands for more rear seat space for their children. Aston Martin took the opportunity to revise the car's interior trim, and the instrument panel was improved and the dials enlarged. Externally the car was instantly identifiable by a distinctive rear spoiler, though the optional power steering was a less obvious improvement. In July 1969 came a Mark II version with larger tyres and flared wheel arches to accommodate them. The interior trim was again improved and an electronic fuel injection system offered as an optional extra. The model continued in production until November 1970. The DB6 had proved to be the most popular model yet built with 1575 sold of which 245 were Mark IIs. Before leaving the DB5/6 series, mention should be made of the open Volante model, introduced on the DB5. These exclusive vehicles were built in relatively small numbers with only 37 DB5s and 150 DB6s sold. There were, in addition, a further 38 DB6 Mark II Volantes.

DB5. *Externally similar to the DB4, the DB5, introduced in late 1963, had a 4-litre engine and continued in production until 1965. A total of 1025 was built.*

William Towns's DBS

By the mid-1960s Touring of Milan had, alas, ceased trading so the new Aston Martin, the DBS with de Dion rear axle, was conceived in house at Newport Pagnell by William Towns. Visually it was a worthy successor to the earlier Touring-styled cars and had been planned to receive a new Tadek Marek-designed aluminium V8 engine. Unfortunately it was not ready at the time of the car's announcement in October 1967, so the DBS was initially offered with the DB6's six-cylinder engine and transmission. It was not until the spring of 1970 that the DBS received the long-awaited 5.3-litre V8 giving this heavy car – it turned the scales at 3920 kg (8640 lb) – a top speed of over 233 km/h (145 mph). Aluminium wheels in place of wires identified the car and the model was redesignated the DBS V8. Power steering was a standard fitment while transmission could be either a ZF manual or a Chrysler automatic.

But early in 1972, 25 years after he purchased Aston Martin, Sir David Brown (as he had become in 1968) found that he could no longer continue to carry the burden of a loss-making company. So, in February, he sold out to Company Developments, a property concern, who took over the firm's shares for £100 and its debts, then standing at around half a million pounds, for £1. There followed a six-week hiatus while the company was reconstructed and the staff rationalized. In May a mildly face-lifted V8 appeared though no longer with the DB prefix, the first Aston Martin not to carry the famous initials since 1948. The V8 had a revised front end with two headlamps rather than four. The car was also offered in Vantage form, with the faithful twin cam six under its bonnet. Production continued until July 1973 and with it went the twin overhead camshaft six-cylinder engine that had served the company so well since it had appeared in the DB4 of 1958. From there on all Aston Martins would have V8 engines.

In August 1974 Lagonda was briefly revived as a model rather than marque but only seven examples of this long-wheelbase four-door version of the V8 were built.

FAR LEFT **1971 DBS V8**. The William Towns-styled DBS first appeared in 1967 and was six-cylinder engined until 1970, when a 5.3-litre V8 was fitted. With many detail modifications this car is, in essence, still in production today.

LEFT **Alan Curtis**, an Aston Martin director from 1976 and joint chairman, with Peter Sprague, from 1977 until January 1981.

BELOW **1974 Aston Martin Lagonda**. Lagonda was revived as a model name for this long-wheelbase four-door version of the V8. Only seven were built between August 1974 and May 1976.

BOTTOM **1967 Lola Aston**. One of two cars powered by an experimental Aston Martin V8 entered for Le Mans in 1967. Both retired with engine trouble.

ASTON MARTIN V8
(1970 to date)
Number built **Still in production**

ENGINE		CHASSIS	
No. of cylinders	V8	Frame	Platform
Bore/stroke mm	100 × 85	Wheelbase mm	2641
Displacement cc	5340	Track – front mm	1498
Valve operation	Twin overhead camshaft per bank	Track – rear mm	1498
		Suspension – front	Independent
Compression ratio	8.3:1, 9:1	Suspension – rear	De Dion
Induction	Four twin-choke Weber carburettors	Brakes	Hydraulic disc
BHP	Not disclosed	PERFORMANCE	
Transmission	Four-speed	Maximum speed	233 km/h (145 mph)

However, Company Developments' involvement with Aston Martin was destined to last a mere 23 months for in December 1974, William Willson, its chairman, appointed a receiver and the firm's future was again in jeopardy. But it was six months later, in June 1975, that the company's new owners emerged. They were George Minden, a Canadian restaurant owner, and Peter Sprague, a youthful American who had built up a reputation for salvaging troubled companies; both, significantly, were already Aston Martin owners. However, production was not re-started until nine months later following the creation of Aston Martin Lagonda (1975) Ltd. A new recruit for the board of directors was Alan Curtis, whose interests ranged from property development to flying and he later became Aston Martin's chairman.

A new Lagonda

The restructured company pushed ahead with an ambitious new project, an Aston Martin Lagonda four-door saloon, which made its sensational début at the 1976 Motor Show at London's Earls Court. Using the V8's engine, drive line with manual or automatic gearbox and suspension, stylist William Towns came up with a striking and utterly individual design. Chief engineer Mike Loasby was responsible for the car's mechanical layout, the chassis being based on the long-wheelbase version of the DBS which had been employed on the shortlived V8-based Lagonda.

Production of the prototype had been undertaken at great speed, William Towns having begun work on it in February 1976. This was a mere eight months before the Motor Show and, although Towns had been employed by the firm from 1966 to 1968, he had subsequently set up in business on his own account. Inside the low saloon – it was only 130 cm (51 in) high – the trimming was discreetly luxurious with traditional leather used extensively. But the instrumentation was a space-age confection as the intention was to make extensive use of computer-assisted electronic displays. The driver was confronted by a black perspex sheet but when the ignition was switched on it was intended that the dials and read-out

light up, rather in the manner of an electronic calculator. Such vital information as speed and engine revolutions were indicated by the use of gas plasma dials with changes from miles to kilometres per hour being possible at the turn of a switch. That the Lagonda was very much a car of the electronics age was mirrored by the touch-sensitive electrical switches, the idea coming from Mike Loasby after he had encountered a lift in a London hotel so equipped!

The Lagonda's price was expected to be in the £20,000 region, though a 1977 start date proved to be over ambitious and the first car was handed over to its owners, the Marquis and Marchioness of Tavistock of Woburn Abbey, in April 1978. The car's top speed was around the 209 km/h (130 mph) mark and there were minor changes to the suspension and the car's ride height. The seats could be adjusted for rake, tilt and height with a computer providing a memory so that individual setting could be recalled. The car's front doors had electrically operated windows but the rear ones were fixed, a not unusual state of affairs on a car with air conditioning, such as the Lagonda boasted. The revolutionary in-strument panel was simplified somewhat on the production cars. The price had risen to £32,620.

Yet another William Towns design appeared in 1980 when Aston Martin revealed its gull-wing doored Bulldog, a one-off vehicle to show the world that the firm was very much back in business. Engineering director Mike Loasby was responsible for the mechanical layout, the Aston Martin V8 engine being mounted amidships. But later in 1980 the company again changed hands though this time the new owners were already shareholders. Victor Gauntlett was chairman of Pace Petroleum and a keen old-car enthusiast, while Tim Hearley's company was C.H. Industrials which emerged from the old Coventry Hood and Sidescreen Company and was a supplier of original equipment to the motor industry. Gauntlett became the firm's executive chairman at the end of 1980 and decided on a further string to the Aston Martin bow by establishing a new company, Aston Martin Tickford, to sell the company's expertise to the motor industry. It was Tickford who was responsible for the special Lancia Hi-Fi model and the luxurious Frazer version of the Austin Metro.

The Nimrod at Le Mans

Even more exciting was the Nimrod-Aston Martin. Nimrod Racing Automobiles, and completely independent of the factory, was founded in 1981 by Gauntlett, Robin Hamilton, who had competed at Le Mans in an Aston Martin during the four previous years, and Peter Lavanos of the firm's American sales company, though the latter's involvement was of brief duration. Hamilton had already been thinking in terms of a car for the World Endurance Championship and in May 1981 Eric Broadley of Lola Cars was commissioned to produce a high performance car to qualify for Group C regulations. Notable features of this mid-engined design included a duplication of ignition and fuel sources, a stylized Aston Martin 'grille' built into the front of the car and a statutory rear flat undershield. An aluminium and dural monocoque was employed, and the car was so designed that the removal of only four bolts meant that the entire rear section could be detached. This contained the engine, transmission and suspension, and replacement took only 30 minutes to effect.

Nimrod Racing Automobiles spent over half a million pounds on the project for the team's ambition was clear cut: to win the Le Mans 24-hour race, thus reviving those heady memories of 1959. Although factory involvement had ceased in the early 1960s, in 1967 two Lolas had entered the race powered by Aston Martin's new V8 then under development but both cars dropped out with engine trouble. The 1982 Le Mans challenger would employ the by now proven V8, tuned to 550–600 bhp and consuming fuel at the rate of 43.5 litres/ 100 km (6.5 mpg). In all, five Nimrods were eventually built and the first two appeared at the Sarthe circuit. Hamilton's car retired after about four hours while a second car entered by Lord Downe finished in seventh position having attained a fourth place earlier in the event. With later successes to its credit this car was eventually placed third in the 1982 World Endurance Championship. In 1983 the same car ran at Silverstone, Brands Hatch and Spa though the previous year's Le Mans achievement was not repeated.

A programme of refinement continued with Aston Martin's road cars. A high performance Vantage version of the long-running V8, with front air dam and rear spoiler, had arrived in 1977 and the following year the V8 appeared in open form, with power-operated hood, which revived the Volante name. In 1979 there was a restyled bonnet with smaller engine bulge and interior improvements. Late in 1983 the Lagonda saloon was offered with revised wheels, new safety bumpers and under spoilers. Interior refinements included restyled seats giving extra support, and opening rear windows were introduced while there were also revisions to the futuristic instrument console. Individual air conditioning for rear passengers followed soon after.

Aston Martin's ownership again changed in September 1983 when Pace Petroleum's share in the company was sold to Automotive Investments, owners of Aston Martin Lagonda of North America, the firm's American importers, but C.H. Industrials retained its interest in the firm. However, in February 1984, Automotive Investments acquired the rest of Aston Martin's shares, while Victor Gauntlett remains as chairman of this illustrious company.

FAR LEFT **1978 Aston Martin Lagonda**. *This sensational William Towns-styled luxury saloon is powered by the current Aston Martin 5.3-litre V8 engine. The magnificent interior will be readily apparent. Price is £42,498.*

LEFT **Victor Gauntlett**, *Aston Martin's current chairman, who took up the post in January 1981. Previously, in 1972, he had founded Pace Petroleum which was acquired by the Hays Group in September 1983.*

ASTON MARTIN LAGONDA	
(1976 to date)	
Number built	Still in production
ENGINE	
No. of cylinders	V8
Bore/stroke mm	100 × 85
Displacement cc	5350
Valve operation	Twin ohc
Compression ratio	9.5:1
Induction	Four twin-choke Weber carburettors
BHP	Not disclosed
Transmission	Automatic
CHASSIS	
Frame	Platform
Wheelbase mm	2921
Track – front mm	1498
Track – rear mm	1498
Suspension – front	Independent
Suspension – rear	De Dion
Brakes	Hydraulic disc
PERFORMANCE	
Maximum speed	209 km/h (130 mph)

RIGHT **Nimrod Aston Martin**. *Robin Hamilton's car pictured at Le Mans 1982. It retired after about four hours racing.*

AUSTIN

Today's Austin Metros, Maestros and Montegos are stylish modern products, yet Herbert Austin's models were robust but dated cars. It was Leonard Lord's arival in 1938 that rejuvenated the firm and Longbridge subsequently became the centre of the British motor manufacturing industry.

Created in the pre-First World War era, in the 1920s and '30s Austin was second only to Morris as the country's largest vehicle producer. In the late 1940s Austin became Britain's largest car maker and grew to even greater importance during the years of the British Motor Corporation. The marque became exclusively front-wheel drive during the ill-fated Leyland years, and today Austin is the re-structured car company's quantity production flag holder with the success-ful Metro, Maestro and Montego models.

Herbert Austin (1866–1941) was born in Little Missenden, Buckinghamshire. His father was a farmer and when Austin was a youngster the family moved to Yorkshire where Austin senior, like William Morris's father, became a farm bailiff. Herbert attended Rotherham Grammar School and soon dis-played a talent for drawing. Consequently he decided on an architectural career but his interest in mechanical matters resulted in a change of course and his parents secured a

LEFT **Austin 40 hp York Landaulette**. *A typical Longbridge product of the Edwardian era, solid and dependable with coachwork produced in-house. The 5843 cc model was built between 1907 and 1913, a total of 152 being manufactured.*

BELOW **1913 10 hp 'Coquette'**. *This was the most popular of Austin's pre-First World War models; 1879 were produced between 1913 and 1915. Provided by the Patrick Collection.*

provisional acceptance for an apprenticeship with the Great Northern Railway. But before young Austin could take it up the family received a visit from his mother's brother, who had earlier emigrated to Australia and was on a short visit to Britain. Herbert was convinced by his uncle of the prospects that existed 'down under' and returned to the antipodes with him. While there he made the acquaintance of Frederick York Wolseley, an Irish immigrant and brother of the famous soldier, Field Marshal Sir Garnet Wolseley. Frederick Wolseley produced mechanical sheep shearing equipment and Austin joined him in the venture, later returning to Britain in 1893.

Once back in his native country as Wolseley's general manager, Austin looked about for a factory in which to manufacture sheep shearing equipment and in 1895 he found a works in Birmingham that served his purpose. It was soon after his arrival there, probably in 1896, that Austin designed his first car based on the contemporary French Leon Bollée. The idea was not proceeded with but Wolseley car production proper began in 1900 when Austin-designed models, with old-fashioned horizontally mounted engines, were produced. However in 1905 Austin left the company that had been purchased by the Vickers engineering combine, having walked out following a disagreement and was then sacked.

The start of Austin cars

So in mid 1905, 38-year-old Austin, accompanied by three colleagues, climbed into a little $7\frac{1}{2}$ hp Wolseley and set off to look over a disused printing works known as White and Pykes, at Longbridge, about 11 km (7 miles) south of Birmingham and alongside a branch of the Midland Railway. For Austin had decided to go into business on his own account and he settled on Longbridge as his manufacturing base. He

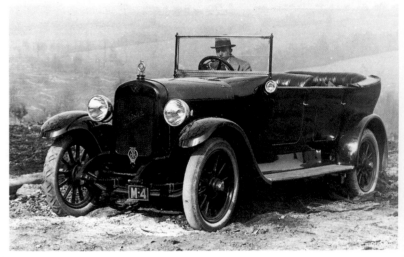

attended the 1905 Crystal Palace Motor Exhibition armed only with a set of drawings of his proposed car and before long he was in production offering a wide range of models. By 1914 Austin had become one of Britain's leading car manufacturers.

The Longbridge factory rapidly expanded during the 1914–18 war and with the coming of peace Sir Herbert (knighted 1917) dispensed with all his previous models and in 1919 introduced a massive 3.6-litre Twenty which was very American in concept. It was clearly unsuited for the British market, so he hastily scaled down the design and produced the successful 1.6-litre Twelve in 1921. The firm had, however, taken a financial mauling, a receiver was appointed in April, and the company did not begin paying dividends again until 1929.

It was against this troubled financial background that in 1921 Austin conceived the idea of introducing a new small car. The result was the famous Seven of 1922 and was destined to span the inter-war years. Its success lay in the fact that it was a large car scaled down and not a crude design that was typified by many small cars of its day. Ironically it was not Austin who was responsible for the Seven's all-important four-cylinder engine but an 18-year-old draughtsman, Stanley Edge, who worked at Longbridge, but was seconded to Austin's home, Lickey Grange, in the winter of 1921–22 to help design the car. The dogmatic Austin was determined to produce a small car with a two-cylinder engine and had in mind something on the lines of the noisy and rough air-cooled Rover Eight. Edge, however, had different ideas and with his technical knowledge and direct approach he was

able to convince Austin that a small four could be produced for about the same price as a twin, and would have overwhelming practical and marketing advantages. The car with its four-wheel brakes, an unusual feature for the day, went into production in 1922, the original 696 cc engine soon being increased to 748 cc. The car sold well throughout the 1920s but production really picked up in the following decade, peaking in 1935 when 27,280 left Austin's Longbridge factory, output continuing until 1939 by which time over 290,000 had been built.

In 1927 Austin introduced a fashionable six-cylinder model, the 3.4-litre Twenty, though the earlier four-cylinder car remained available for a time. Just as the Twelve was created by scaling down the four-cylinder Twenty so his next model, the 2.3-litre Sixteen of 1928, was based on the six-cylinder Twenty design. The small six-cylinder engine gained popularity in the early 1930s and Austin's contribution was the 1½-litre Twelve Six, hardly his most successful model. A far better seller, by contrast, was the 1932 Ten, well suited to the decade and it remained in production, in facelifted form, right up until 1947. The faithful Twelve, which had received an enlarged 1.9-litre engine and wider track in

TOP **1933 Austin Seven**.
By then the model had been in production for ten years and was still selling strongly. It was to remain available until 1939, after a 17-year production run.

ABOVE **1929 Seven** (left) and **1928 Twelve**, *Austin's best-selling models of the 1920s. The family resemblance is readily apparent.*

RIGHT **Leonard Lord** *(1896–1967),*
who joined Austin from Morris
in 1938 and post war ran BMC
from 1952 until 1961.

FAR RIGHT **1931 Ulster TT**.
Cooke's supercharged Seven is
in the foreground, with
Goodacre in a similar car (37).
The event was won by M.G.

BELOW **1932 Ten**. *Longbridge's*
best-seller of the 1930s remained
in production until 1947.

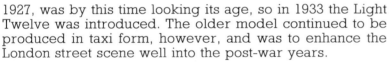

1927, was by this time looking its age, so in 1933 the Light
Twelve was introduced. The older model continued to be
produced in taxi form, however, and was to enhance the
London street scene well into the post-war years.

Leonard Lord arrives

Austin had dragged his feet in introducing an Eight, Ford's
pace-setting model having appeared back in 1932.
Longbridge's answer did not arrive until 1939 by which time
Lord Austin's 'heir apparent', Leonard Lord, was already
making his mark on Austin affairs. (Austin received his peerage in 1936.) Leonard Lord's appointment was of crucial
importance not only for the firm but also for the future history
of the British motor industry. Leonard Percy Lord (1896–
1967) had been educated at Bablake School, Coventry,
served an apprenticeship with Courtaulds and then, during
the First World War, moved to the Coventry Ordnance
Works. Later he went to Daimler and in 1922 he joined
Hotchkiss's Coventry factory which was then absorbed in
producing engines for William Morris's fast-selling Bullnose.
The following year, in 1923, Morris bought the firm and Lord
left his drawing office job to become a machine tool engineer. It was at this time that general manager Frank
Woollard was achieving production miracles, with fully
machined and drilled Bullnose engine blocks being produced at the rate of one every four minutes. This flow line
production system was only taken up by the American motor
industry after the Second World War and the rest of the
automotive world then followed suit.

In 1927 Leonard Lord moved to the Wolseley company
which had just been drawn into the Morris orbit. There he
was responsible for putting the overhead camshaft Morris
Minor engine into production along with its cheaper side-
valve successor. Morris, obviously impressed by Lord's

abilities, appointed him managing director of Morris Motors in 1933 at a time when the firm was in some disarray. There he was responsible for initiating a £300,000 re-investment programme designed to make the plant one of Europe's most up-to-date car factories. Lord also brought some sense of order to Morris's rambling model range and the Eight, produced in response to Ford's best seller, hit the production jackpot as the most successful British car of the decade. Unfortunately Lord clashed with Lord Nuffield, Morris having received his peerage in 1934, and in the summer of 1936 he stormed out of Morris Motors, later threatening to take the place apart 'brick by bloody brick'. Two years later, in 1938, he joined Austin, Morris's arch rivals, and set about re-vitalizing Longbridge's well-made but rather old-fashioned products.

Austin in competition
Before leaving the inter-war years, reference should be made to Austin's competition successes in the 1920s and '30s which were mostly achieved with the lion-hearted Seven. In 1922, the year of its appearance, a prototype achieved a third in class in the Shelsley Walsh hill climb. The following year, in 1923, a Seven was taken to the Cyclecar Grand Prix at Monza, Italy, won the event and had the distinction of being the first British car to compete there. A Seven came second in class in the 1923 200 Mile Race at Brooklands, while Gordon England took a series of 750 cc records.

By 1924 Gordon England had produced his 120 km/h (75 mph) Brooklands Super Sports model and won his class in that year's 200 Mile Race at the track, repeating the feat in 1925 and 1926. Further factory-sponsored record breaking followed, mainly at the French Montlhéry circuit.

The Austin factory began to produce works racers towards the end of the decade and in 1929 a team competed in that year's TT, four supercharged Sevens achieving 3rd, 4th, 16th and 19th places. A Seven also won its class at that year's 500 Mile Race at Brooklands, the first staging of the event. The Double Twelve of that year saw a Seven win its class, though the following year the side-valve cars were strongly challenged by the more efficient overhead camshaft M.G.s, but in 1932 the small Austin won the 750 cc class in the 1932 British Empire Trophy race. It was during that year that Austin employed Tom Murray Jamieson, who had made his mark with his own potent Seven at Brooklands, to look after Longbridge's special racing cars.

In 1933 Sevens won the team prize in the International Trophy race and were second in class at the German Avus circuit. There followed many Austin/M.G. battles on the race track but in 1935 the Abingdon company withdrew from competition leaving the 750 cc class to Austin. By this time, however, Austin, recognizing the limitations of the Seven's 1922 side-valve design, gave Jamieson the go ahead to produce a purpose-built 750 cc racing car. The resulting

single-seater, which resembled a scaled down grand prix car, was powered by a four-cylinder twin overhead camshaft supercharged unit of 744 cc. It had been conceived to attain the stupendous feat of achieving 12,000 revolutions per minute, although throughout the cars' racing career they seldom exceeded 9000 rpm. The car's chassis was a straight-forward channel section frame while the suspension – transverse leaf at the front and quarter elliptics at the rear – loosely followed Seven practice.

LEFT **1933 supercharged, streamlined Seven.** *This was Murray Jamieson's first car for Austin, taking records at Montlhéry track in 1933, pictured with L.P. Driscoll, Brocklands, 1934.*

BELOW **1936 Austin twin cam racer.** *This supercharged car of 744 cc was designed by Murray Jamieson, assisted by W.V. Appleby and Tom North.*

The cars took a little time to find their form but in 1937 they won the Junior Trophy at Donington, the Crystal Palace Trophy held at the south London circuit, and the Brooklands-based Imperial Trophy. The cars did even better in 1938 when they won the British Empire Trophy at Donington and were placed second in the Nuffield Trophy there, and also performed well in the Shelsley Walsh and Prescott hill climbs. Tragically Murray Jamieson did not live to see his little car's full potential. He had left Austin in 1937 to join the ERA racing concern and was killed while spectating at Brooklands in May 1938.

Only one car – there was a team of three built – ran in 1939 and it won the Imperial Trophy race at Crystal Palace. During their racing career, the twin cam Austins took no less than 19 international class records, while the car's all-time class best at Brooklands was 195.05 km/h (121.2 mph), only about 32 km/h (20 mph) slower than the track's fastest-ever car, the Napier-Railton of 24 litres which was over 32 times the little Austin's capacity!

Austins post-war

Aircraft, trucks and ambulances were produced at Longbridge during the Second World War and Leonard

Lord wasted little time in announcing Austin's first post-war model in September 1944, well before hostilities had ceased. This was the Sixteen, basically the Austin Twelve for 1940, but fitted with a 2.2-litre overhead valve four-cylinder engine. It was Longbridge's first car to employ overhead valves; hitherto rather dated side valves had sufficed. The remaining Eight, Ten and Twelve models were carried over from pre-war days and looked it. Yet another overdue update was an independent front suspension system which appeared on the big 4-litre Sheerline saloon of 1947. Later the same year the A40, with a new overhead valve 1200 cc four-cylinder engine, replaced the Eight, Ten and Twelve. Like the Sheerline the A40 employed an independent front end but retained a separate chassis rather than the increasingly popular unitary construction.

TOP **Tom Murray Jamieson** *(1905–1938), Brooklands, 1937.*

ABOVE **1946 Austin 16**, *featuring Longbridge's first ohv unit.*

RIGHT **1937 Austin Ten**. *This was the top year for Ten production; 35,000 were made during the twelve months. It slumped the following year.*

The following year, in 1948, came the A135 Princess, with similar mechanics to the earlier Sheerline but with aluminium coachwork by Vanden Plas, Austin having taken over the famous North London coachbuilder in 1946. Further new Austins arrived during the year. There was the A70 Hampshire, county names having been initiated by the two-door Dorset and four-door Devon A40, powered by the Sixteen's engine, and that model was discontinued early in 1949. It was

in that year the power unit found its way, in 2.6-litre over-bored form, into the A90 Atlantic drophead coupé intended for sale in America. It was followed a year later by a fixed-head coupé version. The model was not a success, however, but its engine found a home in Donald Healey's new 100 sports car (see page 61). Nineteen fifty-one saw the Hampshire replaced by the A70 Hereford and there was also a sports version of the A40 introduced at the same time and produced, in small numbers, by Jensen Motors.

There had been no small Austins since the demise of the Eight in 1947 but this state of affairs was rectified in 1951 by the arrival of the 800 cc A30. Not only did the model represent Longbridge's first foray into unitary construction but its new engine was destined for a long production life, its derivatives still powering the Mini and Austin Metro. The A40 Devon was replaced by the re-styled A40 Somerset in 1952, a year that saw the rival Austin and Morris companies combine to form the British Motor Corporation with Leonard Lord in charge, and its headquarters at Longbridge.

The A40 was face-lifted again for the 1955 season, the Cambridge being offered in A40 (1200 cc) and A50 (1489 cc) forms. At the same time the A90 Westminster, with similar styling, appeared with a new 2.6-litre six-cylinder engine replacing the A70 Hereford. In mid 1956 came a high performance version of the A90, the twin carburettored A105 and that year's Motor Show featured a re-styled Princess, the not dissimilar Sheerline having been discontinued in 1953. Also the A30's engine capacity was increased to 948 cc for 1957 and re-designated A35.

Nineteen fifty-seven saw the arrival of a livelier version of the A50, the resulting A55 remaining in production until 1958. It was also during the year that the 1489 cc Metropolitan made its appearance on the British market. Austin had been producing this Nash model for American Motors since 1953 though for US markets. It remained available until 1961.

The first really new car to appear since the creation of BMC arrived in 1958, both companies having previously seen through projects too far advanced prior to the merger to be halted. This was the 948 cc A40 though, significantly, the styling hailed not from Longbridge but the Italian Farina concern and dramatically anticipated the current hatchback look by its apparent absence of a boot. Farina was also responsible for a new be-finned corporate four-door saloon in 1959 which was destined to carry BMC marque names; the badge engineering era had arrived. Austin's contribution was the 1489 cc A55 Cambridge and later, in 1959, came the A99 Westminster powered by an enlarged 3-litre six.

AUSTIN A40 (1958–67)	
Number built 340,000 (approx)	
ENGINE	
No. of cylinders	Four
Bore/stroke mm	62 × 76; from 1961 64 × 83
Displacement cc	948, 1098
Valve operation	Overhead pushrod
Compression ratio	8.3:1, 8.5:1
Induction	Single SU carburettor
BHP	34 at 4800, 48 at 5100 rpm
Transmission	Four-speed
CHASSIS	
Construction	Monocoque
Wheelbase mm	2120
Track – front mm	1206
Track – rear mm	1193
Suspension – front	Independent wishbone and coil
Suspension – rear	Half elliptic
Brakes	Hydraulic
PERFORMANCE	
Maximum speed	114 km/h (71 mph)

TOP **Austin A30.** *Longbridge's post-war small car introduced for 1952; its 803 cc engine was upped to 948 cc for 1957, re-designated A35, and remained in production until 1962.*

ABOVE **1952 A40 Somerset.** *The 1200 cc A40 Devon, introduced in 1948, was updated in Somerset form in 1952; in 1954 it was replaced by the similarly designated but larger Cambridge.*

LEFT **Farina-styled A40 of 1958–67.** *A Mark II version with 1098 cc engine, replacing the 948 cc unit, appeared in 1961.*

ABOVE RIGHT **1958 A95 Westminster.** *A six-cylinder, 2639 cc Austin produced until 1959.*

FAR RIGHT **Sir Alec Issigonis** *(born 1906), knighted 1969; creator of the Mini.*

Conception of the Mini

Yet the really major event of 1959 was the arrival of the revolutionary transverse engine/front-wheel-drive, all independent suspension Mini. It was designed by Alec Issigonis, who 11 years previously had seen his Morris Minor acclaimed at its appearance at the 1948 Motor Show. The Mini not only represented a major shift in engineering commitment for BMC but it has gone on to change the course of small car design throughout the world. It is consequently the most technically influential car in the history of the British motor industry and, significantly, is still in production.

Alec Issigonis was born in Smyrna in Turkey in 1906. His father though of Greek descent was a British subject and a marine engineer, while his mother was Bavarian. The Issigonis family fled to Britain in 1922 in the wake of a Greek/Turkish bloodbath though Alec's father unfortunately died on the voyage at Malta. After completing an engineering course at the Battersea Polytechnic young Issigonis joined the Rootes Group drawing office in Coventry. In 1936 he moved south to Morris Motors at Cowley and later, during the war, he began work on a design, codenamed Mosquito, which emerged as the Morris Minor in 1948. By 1952 Issigonis was on the move again, this time to Alvis and there he designed a spacious five-seater saloon, powered by either a $3\frac{1}{2}$-litre V8 or a 1750 cc four and using an interconnected suspension system. Eventually Alvis decided not to proceed with the design and 1956 saw Alec Issigonis back in the BMC fold, based at Longbridge.

His first project for the Corporation was a rear-wheel-drive saloon that bore a visual resemblance to the front-wheel-drive 1100 of 1962. Then, in 1957, it was decided to set this project aside and in March Issigonis was given the go-ahead to design a proper small car in the wake of the cheap economical bubble cars that swarmed over Britain's roads following on from the 1956 Suez Crisis.

Just before he left Morris in 1952 Issigonis had completed the designs of an experimental front-wheel-drive Minor with its engine/gearbox mounted transversely. He was thus attracted to the space-saving advantages of a car driven by its front wheels. Yet to have perpetuated this layout for a small car would have resulted in a disproportionately wide vehicle, and clutch plate replacement might have presented problems. He solved the difficulty by positioning the gearbox *underneath* the power unit, effectively in the engine's sump, so the transmission shared the same oil. With this revolutionary compact package attained, Issigonis then turned his attention to the car's bodywork, having an unprecedented 80 per cent of the remaining space for the car's occupants. The resulting vehicle, measuring only 3.04 metres (10 feet) from bumper to bumper, was a triumph of functional packaging. Only two major modifications had to be made to the design during the Mini's evolution. In an effort to prevent carburettor icing the engine had to be turned 180 degrees, removing the instrument from its forward location. Also sub-frames were introduced as they were demanded by the Moulton independent rubber suspension units and no doubt cut down interior noise somewhat.

The Mini appeared in August 1959 and was rightfully hailed as the design triumph it represented, and the rest of the world has since followed in the Mini's transverse engine/front-wheel tracks. The cheaper Austin version, named the Seven in memory of Longbridge's famous baby, cost £496 but the title was discontinued in 1961. (There was also a more expensive Morris Mini Minor version.)

John Cooper's Surbiton, Surrey company had won the Formula One Grand Prix manufacturers' championship in 1959 and 1960 with its pioneering rear-engined cars. Cooper, therefore, suggested to Issigonis the wisdom of producing a faster version of the Mini, incorporating his company's name. The result was the twin-carburettored, disc-braked 997 cc Mini Cooper, which appeared in 1961, with the 1071 cc Cooper S following two years later.

Yet a further development on the front-wheel-drive theme was the 1964 Austin version of the top-selling 1100 that had carried the Morris badge since its announcement two years previously. Hydrolastic interconnected suspension was applied to the Mini range from late 1964, though the original rubber units were re-introduced from 1969 onwards, and in 1969 the Austin and Morris prefixes were dropped. The Mini had well and truly grown up. There was another variation on the front-wheel drive/transverse engine theme, the strong, roomy but ungainly 1800 of 1964, produced until 1975.

The big Farina saloons remained in production for most of the 1960s. There was the 1622 cc engined A60 of 1962, continued until 1969, while the six-cylinder A99's power was increased and the car renamed A110 Westminster the same year; it continued to be available until 1968. An upmarket version, which took the Vanden Plas marque name, was the 3-litre Princess of 1960 and was produced until 1964. It was replaced by the Rolls-Royce engined Princess Four Litre R, with automatic transmission and power steering, which remained in production until 1968. There was also the Three Litre saloon introduced for 1968, sharing the same engine as the controversial MGC (see page 198 of M.G. section) and, surprisingly, rear-wheel driven, but only around 10,000 were made before output ceased in 1971.

It had been in 1968 that BMC was taken over by Leyland Motors, which already controlled the Triumph, Rover and Alvis companies. However, the 1969 Maxi was a BMC design with rear hatchback and a new 1½-litre four-cylinder overhead camshaft engine. The following year came a 1750 cc engine option and improved rod actuated gear change. The model, after a shaky start, soon acquired a good reputation and remained in production after a 12-year manufacturing run, until 1981.

The mighty Mini Cooper

The Leyland take-over saw the virtual close down of the corporate competitions department which had enjoyed an unprecedented period of success during the 1960s. The competitive potential of the Mini had not escaped rally and racing enthusiasts and 1961, the year of the lively Cooper's announcement, saw Sir John Whitmore win the British Racing and Sports Car Club's championship in a Mini Minor. However, as far as the works was concerned, the model's first really big win did not come until 1963 when a Mini Cooper S won the ten-day Tour de France Rally. Nineteen sixty-four began well with Paddy Hopkirk taking a Mini to its first Monte Carlo Rally victory, while the recently introduced 1275 cc

RIGHT **1964 Monte Carlo Rally**. *The winning Mini Cooper S of Paddy Hopkirk and Henry Liddon. Other Minis finished in fourth and seventh places, and BMC also took the team prize.*

BELOW **1959 Austin Seven**. *This version of the Mini was so named in honour of its famous pre-war predecessor. It sold for £496, which was £40 cheaper than the Morris Mini Minor version announced simultaneously. It continued in its original 848 cc form until 1980. A 998 cc version arrived in 1968 and is still in production.*

MINI COOPER	
(1961–4)	
Number built 25,000 (approx)	
ENGINE	
No. of cylinders	Four
Bore/stroke mm	62 × 81
Displacement cc	997
Valve operation	Overhead pushrod
Compression ratio	9:1 (optional 8.3:1)
Induction	Twin SU carburettors
BHP	55 at 6000 rpm
Transmission	Four-speed
CHASSIS	
Construction	Monocoque
Wheelbase mm	2032
Track – front mm	1212
Track – rear mm	1104
Suspension – front	Independent wishbone and rubber spring
Suspension – rear	Independent trailing arm and rubber spring
Brakes	Hydraulic, front disc
PERFORMANCE	
Maximum speed	136 km/h (85 mph)

version won the Tulip on its first entry in the event. There was yet another Monte Carlo win for the Mini Cooper in 1965 and the little front-wheel-drive cars also chalked up victories in that year's Circuit, Geneva, 1000 Lakes and RAC rallies. It was a year in which BMC won 17 international rallies and there had been 116 other awards on road and track, mostly achieved by Mini Coopers.

The 1966 Monte saw a sensational one-two-three Mini win but all were disqualified on a technicality. Nevertheless the BMC babies went on to win the Circuit, Tulip, Scottish, Polish and 1000 Lakes events. In 1967 the previous year's disqualifications were avenged at Monte Carlo with yet another Mini win and there were further successes throughout the European rally scene. Unfortunately by 1968 the Minis were becoming outclassed by the twin cam Ford Cortinas. None the less there were third, fourth and fifth places in the Monte Carlo Rally and there was a second in the Scottish, third in the Tulip, while there were fourths in the 1000 Lakes and RAC, both events which in the past had witnessed Mini victories.

The robust 1800 saloon had indulged in record-breaking activities in 1967 and, rather surprisingly, one finished second in the London–Sydney marathon event of 1968. That to all intents and purposes was the end of the works career of the front-wheel-drive car in rallies and races though private owners continued to campaign their Minis. However, Leyland re-activated the Abingdon-based competitions

department in 1975 to field a team of TR7s which are dealt with in the Triumph section of this book.

With the departure of the Three Litre in 1971, Austin became exclusively a front-wheel-drive marque. The popular 1100 acquired a 1300 engine option for 1968 and the model was discontinued in 1974. It had been replaced the previous year by the Allegro, with Hydragas suspension and a range of 1100, 1300, 1500 and 1750 cc engines: output continued until 1982. For 1975 there was a new wedge-shaped 18-22 range available with the pushrod 1798 cc four formerly used in the 1800 model discontinued the same year, and an overhead camshaft six-cylinder 2.2-litre version of the Maxi unit that had previously powered the Morris/Wolseley Six of 1972–5. Originally introduced in Austin and Morris forms, later in 1975 the marque names were dropped and the Princess title introduced. These two models continued until 1978 when the O Series overhead camshaft 1700 replaced the 1800 engine and a further 2-litre version on the same theme joined the Princess range. These options remained until 1982 when Austin was re-introduced to the cars as a marque name and the now Ambassador model benefited from styling improvements and the introduction of a hatchback. The six was discontinued but the two remaining overhead camshaft units remain in production at the time of writing.

The Mini had survived all the corporate upheavals of the late 1960s and 1970s. The Cooper's capacity was upped from 977 to 998 cc in 1964 while the S went from 970 to 1275 cc the same year and remained available until 1971 when the model was discontinued: the new Leyland management had decided to end royalty payments to firms outside the corporate orbit. The original 850 cc Mini was also joined by a 998 cc version in 1968 and, like the earlier car, was available in saloon and Countryman estate versions. The 1970 model year saw the arrival of the Clubman version with its redesigned angular front end. It was 998 cc powered and there was a 1275 cc front-disc-braked GT, intended to replace the soon-to-be-dropped Cooper. In 1976 the Clubman range

received an additional 1098 cc engine option, as fitted to the Allegro, and all versions were discontinued in 1980. The same year the 850 cc model was dropped, having been produced in this capacity since 1959, though there had been improvements in 1970 with the arrival of wind-up windows and concealed door hinges.

The 998 cc Mini fared rather better. Updates were mostly confined to the interior trim and in 1980 the cheaper City 1000 was introduced taking over from the discontinued 850 cc version. This was followed by the City E (for economy)

version in 1982 while the luxurious Mayfair appeared later in the year. In 1983 there was the limited edition Mini Sprite powered by the 998 cc Metro engine with extended wheel arches and side decals.

The aforementioned Metro, a stylish update on the Mini theme, with hatchback, was introduced in 1981. Initially available in 998 cc form it was soon joined by a 1275 cc version, while an M.G.-badged variant of 1982 also used the larger capacity power unit.

The success of the Metro was followed by the four-door Maestro, also with hatchback, in 1983. It was offered with two engine sizes, a 1275 cc pushrod unit, while a 1.6-litre version used a new R Series overhead camshaft four. Meanwhile a larger 'stretched' Maestro appeared in spring 1984 and was named Montego. With such a strong line-up, the fortunes of the Austin marque look brighter than they have done for many years.

ABOVE LEFT **Austin Allegro.** *The Mini and 1100 transverse-engine front-wheel-drive theme was continued in this model; introduced in 1973, it remained in production until 1982.*

LEFT **Ambassador.** *This car began life in Austin and Morris forms in 1975 and was re-designated Princess for 1976. It was face-lifted in 1982, again became an Austin, and finally ceased production in 1984.*

ABOVE **Austin Metro.** *BL's top seller. Introduced in 1980, this hatchback perpetuates the now global Mini configuration.*

RIGHT **Maestro** *joined the Metro in 1983, a front-wheel-drive car with 1275 and 1598 cc engine options. There are also Vanden Plas and M.G. versions of this popular hatchback.*

AUSTIN METRO (1980 to date)	
Number built **Still in production**	
ENGINE	
No. of cylinders	Four
Bore/stroke mm	64 × 76, 70 × 81
Displacement cc	998, 1275
Valve operation	Overhead pushrod
Compression ratio	9.6:1
Induction	Single SU carburettor
BHP	44 at 5250, 63 at 5650 rpm
Transmission	Four-speed
CHASSIS	
Construction	Monocoque
Wheelbase mm	2250
Track – front mm	1279
Track – rear mm	1271
Suspension – front	Independent wishbone Hydragas
Suspension – rear	Independent trailing arms Hydragas
Brakes	Hydraulic, front disc
PERFORMANCE	
Maximum speed	135 km/h (84 mph), 137 km/h (85 mph)

AUSTIN HEALEY

With a stylish two-seater aimed at the buoyant American sports car market, Donald Healey joined forces with the British Motor Corporation in 1952 to create the Austin Healey marque.

Although Austin Healey lasted for only 17 years it is still remembered on both sides of the Atlantic as one of the truly great British sporting marques.

Two men were responsible for the Austin Healey's creation in the early 1950s: Donald Healey, with a wealth of experience in the motor industry and competitive driving behind him, and Leonard Lord, head of the British Motor Corporation, who was looking for a sports car to sell in the rapidly expanding American market.

Donald Mitchell Healey is a Cornishman, born in 1898 in the seaside village of Perranporth. Fred, his father, ran the local Red House general store and was later a building contractor. From his earliest days, young Healey was fascinated by mechanics and in the first instance it was the newfangled aeroplane that captured his imagination. One of his most vivid childhood memories is being taken to Dover by his father to see the monoplane which Louis Blériot had used to

ABOVE **Donald Mitchell Healey** *(born 1898) pictured, appropriately, in a left-hand-drive Austin Healey 100, conceived for sale in the expanding American sports car market.*

LEFT **Targa Florio**. *The Sicilian road race has long been a favourite Austin Healey stamping ground. The 3000 of Hawkins and Makinen is shown here in the 1965 event when they finished second in class.*

cross the English Channel in 1909. On leaving Newquay College Healey, not surprisingly, took up an apprenticeship with the Sopwith Aviation Company which had just opened a factory at Kingston-upon-Thames, Surrey. Donald joined them in 1914 but the First World War started later in the year and young Healey wanted to see some action. So in 1915 he added two years to his age – he was 16 at the time – and joined the Royal Flying Corps. The following year he gained his wings, though his time with the RFC was destined to be short-lived because he was invalided out of the service in 1917 after his aeroplane had been hit by allied anti-aircraft fire in France. He therefore returned to Britain and joined the Aeronautical Inspection Department where he served for the remainder of the war.

With the ending of the First World War in 1918, Healey decided to return to his native Cornwall, as Sopwith was convinced that there was little future in building aircraft and had gone over to manufacturing ABC motorcycles. Once back in Perranporth Healey decided to go into the motor trade and built the Red House Garage alongside his parents' shop. His father had been an enthusiastic motorist in pre-war days when he had run a 1907 Panhard, so young Healey was no stranger to automobiles, and he learnt more about them when he drove an RFC Crossley during the war. Not content with working on other people's cars Donald started running his own and in 1922 he played a formative role in the creation of the Truro and District Motor Club. Its first hill climb was held on a public road and Healey put up fastest time of the day at the wheel of a 30 hp Buick. The medal he received was his first competitive motoring award.

Soon afterwards Healey acquired an ABC, with its distinctive flat twin engine, on which he managed to achieve close on 106 km/h (66 mph) in a Truro club event. This whetted his

appetite for competition further afield and in 1923 Donald entered the Motor Cycling Club's London to Land's End Trial, but the ABC's engine seized and he had to retire. In 1924 Healey, by then driving a 10 hp Ariel, managed to get the trial organizer to divert the event off the main road through Perranporth so as to take in a local hill! That year Healey met Victor Riley of the famous Coventry car company, who was destined to become a life-long friend and Donald bought a Riley Redwing for the 1924 trial, but the car caught fire on the way to the start. So he dashed the 64 km (40 miles) or so back to Perranporth, collected his trusty ABC, which did not miss a beat throughout, and won his first MCC medal.

Donald Healey continued to compete in rallies and trials, and raced at Brooklands track, winning his first medal there in 1925. However, in 1929 he shot to international fame when he took part in the Monte Carlo Rally, driving a Triumph Super Seven; a small car of only 833 cc and hardly the most suitable of vehicles. Healey was supposed to start at Riga in the Baltic but heavy snow forced him to Berlin and he arrived at Monte Carlo two minutes outside the qualifying time. No

throughout the 1930s and in 1939 the fiscal pot boiled over, a receiver was appointed and the firm sold to Thomas Ward, a Sheffield-based engineering and steel-making combine. Healey as general manager stayed on after the Triumph collapse and negotiated the sale of the works to carburettor manufacturers H.M. Hobson. He remained there for a short time but then moved to Humber and armoured car development, though he still found time to join the Royal Air Force

LEFT **Donald Healey** *upholding British honours in the 1931 Paris-Nice Rally in a Riley Nine. He won his class in the event.*

BELOW LEFT **1936 Monte Carlo Rally**. *Donald Healey in a Triumph Dolomite, running in 2.4-litre unsupercharged form, was the first British car home and was placed eighth. His co-driver was Lewis Pearce.*

RIGHT **The Riley-engined Healey**. *The Healey was produced in chassis form only, with Elliot saloon and Westland tourer offered as factory options until 1950. From thereon the respective styles were refined by Tickford and Abbott. In addition, the chassis was available to a variety of coachbuilding establishments.*

doubt spurred on by this near miss, in 1930 Healey again entered the event in the same car and finished seventh. His was the first British car home.

Monte Carlo win

In 1931 Healey changed his car and drove a rather more suitable 4½-litre Invicta, even though its handling terrified him. He started in Norway, hit a telegraph pole in Sweden which pushed the rear axle out of true (he had to saw through a brake rod to free it), and he completed the event on three brakes and a misaligned axle and won. Healey drove an Invicta again the following year and managed a second place, once more being the first British entrant to reach Monte Carlo. He was less lucky in 1933 when he crashed after trying unsuccessfully to avoid a runaway horse sledge in Poland.

It was in that year that Victor Riley asked Healey to manage a team of cars for the Alpine Rally, Donald having joined the Coventry firm in 1931. He did not remain there long and moved to the nearby Triumph company as experimental engineer and later was appointed to the post of technical director. Not surprisingly, in the 1934 Monte Carlo Healey drove a Triumph Ten and after experiencing mud, floods and fog managed yet another second place. Soon after joining Triumph, Healey was responsible for conceiving that fabulous extravagance, the Triumph Dolomite, a straight-eight supercharged sports car with twin overhead camshafts, closely modelled on the contemporary 8C Alfa Romeo. However, with a £1225 price tag there were no takers, though Healey entered one in the 1935 Monte Carlo Rally but crashed at a level crossing in Denmark. In 1936 he drove another Dolomite and finished eighth.

During his time at Triumph Donald Healey was responsible for the overall conception of a more conventional Dolomite and developments of the Gloria range of cars. Unfortunately Triumph's finances had seldom been stable

Volunteer Reserve where he held the rank of Squadron Leader in charge of the Warwickshire Air Training Corps.

It was while he was at Humber that Healey met up with James Watt, an old friend who had been on Triumph's sales staff in 1934–8. Healey was keen to go into car manufacture on his own account and a specification that Watt wrote in 1942 shows that the duo was considering a 10 hp model intended to compete with Rover and Sunbeam-Talbot in the motoring market place. The pair then approached Ashley Ward, of Thomas Ward, who owned the old Triumph company in the hope that they might buy it, but by this time Standard's Sir John Black had shown an interest in the moribund firm and eventually bought it for £75,000.

By this time Healey had changed his model strategy and began thinking in terms of a car in the spirit of the old 4½-litre Invicta though rather smaller and with better handling! But like the Cobham product it would have to be capable of 160 km/h (100 mph). Two more Humber employees were recruited to the embryo design team: stylist Ben Bowden, who had previously worked for Farina, and A.C. 'Sammy' Sampietro an Italian engineer, whose motor industry experience embraced Maserati and Alfa Romeo and who in later years became chief engineer of the American Willys Jeep.

Healey obviously was not in a position to manufacture his own engine so he approached Sir Miles Thomas of the Nuffield Organization and asked whether they would supply him with the 2½-litre Riley engine, the combine having purchased the Coventry firm in 1938. Although the power unit employed two side-mounted camshafts, usually associated with engines of relatively low efficiency, it boasted many attributes of a high-performance twin overhead camshaft engine but without its cost or complication, and in six-cylinder form had been the basis of the ERA racing car of the 1930s. Thomas readily responded to Healey's overtures and with his engine supply assured work could begin on the design of the first Healey car.

Help came from Peter Skelton, a director of Westland, the Humber distributors in Hereford, and initially activities were concentrated there, but in the summer of 1945 the small team moved to the corner of Benfords' former concrete mixer factory at The Cape, Warwick, owned by Wally Allen, a former Triumph director. It was in these inauspicious surroundings that the prototype Healey took shape and the car was revealed to the motoring press early in 1946.

The new Healey

This first car had an open four-seater body made by Westland and its chassis was fitted with a sophisticated trailing arm independent front suspension system that Donald Healey reckons must have been the most expensive used on any car at the time! Under the bonnet was the proven Riley engine with power conveyed to the rear axle via a torque tube. Coil springs provided the suspension medium front and rear. In addition to the open car there was also a saloon built by Samuel Elliot of Reading, Berkshire, who specialized in the manufacture of shop fittings. Ben Bowden had sketched these body shapes on the walls of his dining room and then traced the originals. But the cars were expensive, the saloon selling for £1597, £31 more than the roadster which was priced at £1566. In December 1946 Donald Healey took one of the new saloons to Italy where it reached 168.34 km/h (104.6 mph) on the Milan-Cosmo *autostrada* making it the fastest British closed car of its day. As demand for the new cars built up, production was soon outgrowing the confines of the Benfords premises and a new works was established nearby for the cars' construction.

However, times were hard in those early post-war years; the government was directing car manufacturers to export their products to earn valuable foreign currency and gearing vital steel supplies to export achievement. For Healey this meant America and from the mid-1940s onwards Donald Healey became a regular trans-Atlantic traveller. He also continued his competitive forays gaining valuable publicity for his cars in the process. In 1948 he entered a Westland roadster in the famous Italian Mille Miglia rally, the first occasion he had taken part in the event, and despite hitting a dog at 120 km/h (75 mph), which burst his tyre, he managed a ninth place and was the first British car home. The following year's run was less eventful and Healey achieved a creditable fourth placing.

Unfortunately for the Donald Healey Motor Company, at the beginning of 1948 a new £10 flat rate of road tax was introduced, instead of the payment being geared to the RAC-assessed horsepower of a car's engine. But to offset the loss of revenue on large capacity cars, vehicles costing over £1000 were subjected to a swingeing 66.6 per cent purchase tax rate, which was double the original levy. The price of the Healey therefore soared. In an attempt to beat the £1000 price ceiling, Healey introduced the cost conscious two-seater Silverstone model for £975. Styled at Warwick by Len Hodges, the bodywork was produced by the Coventry-based Abbey Panels. The Silverstone proved a popular club racer and 105 were built in 1949 and 1950. Less successful was the contemporary slab-sided Sportsmobile which was for export only and a mere 23 were built. It preceded the Silverstone by about six months, having been announced towards the end of 1948 and remained available until early in 1950. It was a genuine four-seater and also offered a big boot. Undoubtedly its looks weighed against it!

1950 Silverstone. *The clean body lines were accentuated by the headlamps mounted within the radiator cowl and the windscreen that retracted into the bodywork; the cycle wings were detachable for racing. In April 1950 the original D specification chassis was replaced by the E type, after 51 cars had been built. The later variety is readily identifiable by the bonnet air intake.*

HEALEY SILVERSTONE
(1949–50)
Number built 105

ENGINE		CHASSIS	
No. of cylinders	Four	Frame	Box
Bore/stroke mm	80 × 120	Wheelbase mm	2344
Displacement cc	2443	Track – front mm	1371
Valve operation	Overhead pushrod: twin underhead camshafts	Track – rear mm	1346
		Suspension – front	Independent trailing arm/coil spring
Compression ratio	6.9:1	Suspension – rear	Coil spring
Induction	Twin SU carburettors	Brakes	Hydraulic
BHP	106 at 4800 rpm		
Transmission	Four-speed	PERFORMANCE	
		Maximum speed	177 km/h (110 mph)

The trans-Atlantic Nash Healey

The most popular Warwick model of its day was the Nash Healey with 506 built between 1950 and 1954, and a larger factory was constructed near the original in which to build it. The car came about largely by chance. Donald Healey was on one of his regular visits to America on board the *Queen Elizabeth*. One of his hobbies is photography and he chanced to get into conversation with George Mason, president of the American car company Nash Kelvinator, who had a stereoscopic camera (a device in which two pictures are combined into one). Mason asked Healey down to his cabin to talk photography when it emerged that Donald was on his way to General Motors in the hope that the American company would supply him with Cadillac engines for use in the Healey. Mason offered one of his own engines and the Nash Healey was born. Bodies were initially produced by Panelcraft in Coventry but later Farina in Turin took over the work. Engines and gearboxes were sent to Warwick from America where they were then fitted to their chassis. Later these running chassis were despatched to Italy for their bodywork and so on to America, a continental merry-go-round that continued until the Nash Healey ceased production in 1954. Healey was the first to recognize that this was not the most efficient way to build a motor car. There were also changes being made to the British-bodied cars with the Elliot saloon and Westland roadster being replaced, from 1951, by coachwork courtesy of Tickford and Abbott respectively.

However, there was little doubt that America represented the largest potential market for Healey's products and in 1951 he embarked on a fact-finding tour of that continent. He returned with the recognition that what was required was a faster, lighter and, above all, cheaper car than he had been producing hitherto. He faced the fact that, unless he could produce such a model, he would very likely go out of business. Money was also tight and the firm had been set up on around £20,000 provided by Donald and his father.

The greatest challenge to the handbuilt Healey came from the stylish and potent XK120 Jaguar which by 1952 cost £1759 against a Healey, with a six-cylinder Alvis engine option in Britain, which cost a pricey £2490. But Healey recognized that there was a sports car market between the M.G. TD and XK120 and it was there that the new car was aimed.

Birth of the 100

His first requirement was a new engine in place of the heavy and dated Riley unit. With great discretion he approached the Austin Motor Company's Leonard Lord, so as not to jeopardize his supply of engines from the rival Nuffield Organization. After carefully studying the market he had come to the conclusion that the overhead valve engine used in the Austin A90 Atlantic would form an ideal basis for his sports car engine. This particular unit had a rather interesting life in that it had started out as a wartime project intended to power a British version of the Jeep. With the re-starting of car production in 1945, Austin fitted the engine in its pre-war Austin 12, re-naming it the 16. In mid-1948 the 2.2-litre engine was also used in Longbridge's new FX3 taxi and at the end of the year it found a new home in the A70 saloon being fitted with a new steering column-change gearbox.

The 16 was phased out early in 1949 and at about the same time a new model – the A90 Atlantic intended for sale in America – appeared powered by an over-bored version of the 16 engine, increasing its capacity to 2.6 litres. But the Atlantic was not a success. Only about 15,000 convertibles were produced before output ceased at the beginning of 1951, though a sports saloon version limped on until the autumn of 1952. Lord, no doubt pleased to have a customer for his redundant engines, agreed to Healey's request and also supplied steering gear and front suspension units from the same source, but the coil springs and dampers were peculiar to the sports car.

Donald, who had been joined by his engineer son Geoffrey in 1950, burnt much midnight oil at the Healey home at Barford, near Warwick, designing the new car, work beginning in the winter of 1951. It was built up around a new chassis, underslung at the rear to permit a low body line. The A90 engine dictated the bonnet height but as the gearbox had been intended for use with a column gear change the selector mechanism was at the side rather than at the top of the box. This was ideal for left-hand-drive cars for the American market, the prototype being so equipped, but when offered in right-hand-drive form a cranked lever was necessary. Barry Bilbie completed the final drawings while the crucially important styling to Healey's brief was undertaken by Gerry Coker, who had joined the Warwick firm

LEFT **Healey Alvis**. *This was Healey Motor Company's answer to the Jaguar XK120, with a 3-litre, six-cylinder Alvis engine. Styling was similar to that of the Nash Healey and was produced in Birmingham by Panelcraft. However, the model was expensive at £2490, and only 25 examples of this Sports Convertible were produced between 1951 and 1953.*

RIGHT **1956 Austin Healey 100M**, *with distinctive louvred bonnet and securing strap. Produced in 1955 and 1956 the 100Ms were modified from production cars by Healey at Warwick, the engine being tuned to produce 110 bhp instead of 90 developed by the standard 100. A total of 1159 100Ms was produced. It had a top speed of around 164 km/h (102 mph).*

from Humber in 1950. When the chassis was completed it was road tested by Healeys father and son and then delivered to the Newport Pagnell Tickford company for fitment of its bodywork. As a styling exercise the offside rear wing incorporated a fashionable fin, but fortunately this was removed from the finished product, and the completed body was then sprayed a sensational ice blue.

The 1952 Motor Show, due to open on 22 October, was looming but when the car was completed and road tested the Healeys realized that the top gear ratio was too low. As a higher ratio back axle was not available, an overdrive unit

was introduced which took the top speed over the 160 km/h (100 mph) mark. Donald Healey then drove the prototype to the Jabbeke-Aeltre motorway in Belgium and *Autosport* magazine obtained a mean maximum speed, judged on two runs, of 170.67 km/h (106.05 mph). But Healey felt that the car was capable of more. Back home in Warwick further adjustments were made to the carburettors and plugs and it was returned to Belgium where it clocked a sensational 178 km/h (111 mph). Then the car was returned to Britain for its Motor Show début.

The Healey 100, so called to indicate its 160 km/h (100 mph) top speed, weighed just 889 kg (1960 lb), compared with the contemporary Healey's 1168 kg (2575 lb) and was to sell at £1326 which was a staggering £1167 less than the Riley-engined car. This was because the new 100's basic price was £850, well below the £1000 threshhold and therefore not liable for double purchase tax. Although the 100 looked low, fast and purposeful Healey disliked the radiator grille with its pointed top, so he had the car's front end disguised with potted plants for the motor show launch!

AUSTIN HEALEY 100M			
(1955–6)			
Number built 1159			
ENGINE		**CHASSIS**	
No. of cylinders	Four	Frame	Box
Bore/stroke mm	87 × 111	Wheelbase mm	2286
Displacement cc	2660	Track – front mm	1244
Valve operation	Overhead pushrod	Track – rear mm	1289
Compression ratio	8.1:1	Suspension – front	Independent wishbone and coil
Induction	Twin SU carburettors	Suspension – rear	Half elliptic
BHP	110 at 4500 rpm	Brakes	Hydraulic
Transmission	Three-speed with overdrive		
		PERFORMANCE	
		Maximum speed	164 km/h (102 mph)

ENTER THE AUSTIN HEALEY

Nevertheless, one visitor was greatly impressed by what he saw. During 1952 the Austin and Morris companies joined forces to form the British Motor Corporation and Leonard

Lord was at its head. On seeing the 100, Lord immediately asked Healey to his hotel to talk about the car. His proposal was that BMC should rename it the *Austin* Healey, reduce the price and mass produce it. When Healey conceived the 100 he had been thinking in terms of making it at Warwick at the rate of around 20 cars a week, so he was surprised and delighted by the proposal. He readily agreed and then and there Austin Healey, a new marque, was born.

What Healey did not know was that Lord had conducted an unofficial design competition for a corporate sports car for the American market, though none of the participants knew they were taking part! Knowing of the Healey's existence, he had commissioned prototypes from in-house M.G. and also from Frazer Nash and Jensen. But it was the Healey that got his seal of approval to fill the vital gap between M.G. and Jaguar in the all-important two-seater trans-Atlantic market. Significantly this sales vacuum had not escaped Standard Triumph's Sir John Black and what was to emerge as the TR2 sports car also made its début at Earls Court in 1952.

It was then a matter of turning the one-off Healey 100 into the mass production Austin Healey. Tickford, who specialized in hand-crafted coachwork, was quite unable to cope with the projected 100 cars a week that Leonard Lord was aiming for. So the wooden master jig that the firm had built to produce the first body was transferred to the West Bromwich Jensen company, who had made the Austin A40 Sports of 1950–51 for Lord. Jensen would build the car using panels economically produced by Boulton and Paul who manufactured them on a 'rubber' press hitherto used for making aircraft fuselages. The West Bromwich firm would also paint and trim the cars which would then be transported to Austin's Longbridge factory for fitment of their engines and gearboxes.

As the Jensen/Austin assembly was not scheduled to start until the summer of 1953, 20 pre-production cars were produced by Healey at Warwick for promotional purposes. One was displayed at the International Motor Sports Show in New York where the Austin Healey 100 was lauded as the International Motor Show Car of 1953. It was a good start. In addition, a batch of Special Test cars was built up, designed

for competition work. Although they closely resembled what was to be the production car, they had light alloy bodywork and even special aluminium bumpers. The engines were also carefully assembled by Austin and used a robust crankshaft borrowed from their diesel engine. Larger SU carburettors were fitted, and a strong gearbox, courtesy of a London taxi cab, featured. One of these cars was displayed at the Geneva Motor Show in March 1953.

Meanwhile, detail modifications had been made to the design. The front of the car was slightly modified to raise the height of the headlamps in view of new lighting regulations and the top of the radiator grille was smoothed out in accordance with Donald Healey's wishes. There were changes to the steering gear, while 27.9 cm (11 in) brake drums from the Austin A70 replaced the 25.4 cm (10 in) ones used on the prototype. The A90 engine was unchanged though the gearbox was modified as a three-speed unit with overdrive operating on the top two gears. The car was priced at £1063 and continued in production, with minor modifications, until mid-1955.

ABOVE LEFT **Donald Healey** *in the streamlined and supercharged Austin Healey 100 at Bonneville, Utah, USA, in 1954. The car achieved 310.2 km/h (192.74 mph) over the flying kilometre, which was a disappointment because the team was aiming for over 320 km/h (200 mph). The special body for this car was styled by Gerry Coker and then refined following testing in the Armstrong Whitworth wind tunnel at Whitley, near Coventry.*

ABOVE **1954 Sebring 12 Hour Race**. *Effectively the prototype of the 100S, this car, driven by Lance Macklin and American George Huntoon from Florida, was placed third overall in the race and first in class, being robbed of outright victory by valve gear trouble. It provided Austin Healey with valuable publicity in the USA, and the model was marketed as the 100S (for Sebring) in 1955.*

LEFT **1955 100S**. *Only 50 of these cars were produced by the Healey Motor Company in Warwick during 1955. The louvred bonnet, distinctive radiator grille and Dunlop all-round disc brakes identify it. The 132 bhp engine had an aluminium Weslake cylinder head. Over half the output of the 100S (26) was exported to America: a further 18 were sent elsewhere abroad, with only six remaining in Britain.*

Record breaking

With Donald Healey's established reputation in competitive events, the 100 was a natural vehicle for these activities which gained the marque valuable publicity. Nineteen fifty-three, the year of the model's introduction, saw Utah, USA play host to a modified 100 which covered the flying mile at 229.5 km/h (142.6 mph), coupling this with a run of 197.80 km/h (122.91 mph) for 12 hours. Austin Healey made its Le Mans début in 1953 with 100s placed 12th and 14th and second and third in their class. The American Sebring race of 1954 brought a well-deserved third place for a Warwick-prepared Special Test 100, effectively a prototype for the 100S, of which more later. There were more records in 1954 when Utah was again the venue. This time a supercharged 100 took the flying mile at 309.99 km/h (192.62 mph) and set up impressive 12- and 24-hour runs. Sebring proved to be another Austin Healey happy hunting ground in 1955 when a 100 was placed sixth overall and achieved one-two-three class successes and, after two unsuccessful years, a first and second in class in that year's Mille Miglia. It was much the same story in 1956 with a Sebring third in class and a second class placing in the Italian rally. On home ground two 100s were first and second in class in the *Autosport* production sports car championship.

A special low production version of the model, the 100S (S for Sebring) was announced at the end of 1954. The car mirrored the specification of the Special Test 100 which had achieved a third place at Sebring earlier in the year. A standard chassis was retained though fitted with larger shock absorbers, while Jensen produced a special light-alloy body shell. The car's front end was revised to feature a new, smaller radiator grille and there was a shallow perspex windscreen. Usually the 100S was finished in smart blue and white livery. Under the louvred bonnet the 100's engine benefited from a new alloy Weslake cylinder head which resulted in its power being raised from the standard car's 90 to 132 bhp. Greater performance required improved stopping power and the S was fitted with Dunlop disc brakes all round, while a 90-litre (20 UK gallon) petrol tank rounded off an impressive competition specification. Such specialized requirements did not lend themselves to mass production methods so the cars – there were just 50 of them made in 1955 – were built at Warwick with practically all examples finding homes across the Atlantic.

In August 1955 the original 100, which carried the factory designation BN1, was replaced by a mildly modified version. BN2 was almost virtually identical to its predecessor, for the main changes were mechanical. The 100's three-speed gearbox was replaced by a four-speed unit with overdrive on third and top gears. At the same time the rear axle was changed to a Morris unit in the interests of BMC rationalization. There was also a 100M version of this BN2 specification but unlike the 100S, with its special aluminium body, which was Warwick built, the 100M was a standard car, completed at Longbridge and then delivered to the Healey works for modification. These changes included engine modifications which increased output to 110 bhp, suspension refinements, and a two-tone paint finish similar to the 100S. A total of 1159 examples was built in 1955 and 1956, but the option was dropped with the arrival of the six-cylinder 100-Six announced in the autumn of 1956.

Six cylinders

The BMC 2.6-litre C Series six-cylinder engine had made its production début in the Austin A90 and Wolseley 6/90 in 1955. The Corporation decided to introduce it in the Austin

AUSTIN HEALEY 100-SIX (1956–9) Number built 14,436	
ENGINE	
No. of cylinders	**Six**
Bore/stroke mm	**79 × 88**
Displacement cc	**2639**
Valve operation	**Overhead pushrod**
Compression ratio	**8.25:1**
Induction	**Twin SU carburettors**
BHP	**102 at 4600; from 1957 117 at 4750 rpm**
Transmission	**Four-speed with overdrive**
CHASSIS	
Frame	**Box**
Wheelbase mm	**2336**
Track – front mm	**1238**
Track – rear mm	**1270**
Suspension – front	**Independent wishbone and coil**
Suspension – rear	**Half elliptic**
Brakes	**Hydraulic**
PERFORMANCE	
Maximum speed	**165 km/h (103 mph)**

RIGHT **Austin Healey 100-Sixes,** *leaving Abingdon in 1959 with MGA Twin Cams behind.*

BELOW **1956 100-Six** *with disc wheels.*

Healey, much to the dismay of the Healey family, on the grounds that the faithful four-cylinder unit was about to be discontinued, but in practice it soldiered on for years powering London taxi cabs. Introduced to the public as the 100-Six and designated BN4 in corporate nomenclature, the model's top speed was almost the same as its predecessor, at around 165 km/h (103 mph). There were obvious external differences with a new radiator grille having horizontal rather than vertical bars, an auxiliary air intake was introduced in the bonnet, while the wheelbase was lengthened by 4.21 cm (1.66 in) to permit the introduction of two small bucket seats behind the driver and passenger for the owner's offspring. In its original form the 100 had featured a folding windscreen but the 100-Six had a more conventional fixed unit. Like their predecessors, the BN4s continued to be completed at Longbridge until the autumn of 1957 when production was transferred to the M.G. factory at Abingdon which from thereon was to be the production centre for all BMC sports cars.

This move coincided with improvements to the engine's cylinder head; the new more efficient six-port unit had the effect of increasing power from 102 to 117 bhp. In 1958 an additional BN6 version of the 100-Six was introduced with a straightforward two-seater layout which reverted to the original 100 theme, though there was no change to chassis length. This continued in production alongside the BN4 until

both were replaced by the Austin Healey 3000 in 1959.

The increase in capacity was inevitable because all BMC cars which used the unit had their capacities increased from 2.6 to 2.9 litres, achieved by increasing the cylinder bore. A stronger clutch and revised gearbox internals coped with the extra power, the engine developing 124 bhp, and the new car was slightly faster than its predecessor with top speed around the 183 km/h (114 mph) mark. In addition, front disc brakes were offered though externally the new model was virtually indistinguishable from the 100-Six with the exception of a small *3000* badge introduced on the radiator grille. The BT7 version saw the 100-Six's two-plus-two seating theme confirmed and there was also a BN7 two-seater.

Frog-eye Sprite

However, by the time the 3000 went into production, another smaller Austin Healey model, the Sprite, was already a year old and was well on its way to making plenty of friends. It had been late in 1956 that Sir Leonard Lord (knighted 1954), in conversation with Donald Healey, told him that he felt there was a need for a small, low-cost sports car in the spirit of the Austin Seven Nippy of pre-war days. Donald's son Geoffrey, along with chassis engineer Barry Bilbie, was largely responsible for the new model which carried the Q type number. Unlike the 100, which boasted a chassis frame, the new small car was a monocoque featuring a layout inspired by the Le Mans-winning D type Jaguar. Most mechanical

components were borrowed from the Austin A35 saloon, namely the engine, independent front suspension and rear axle casing. That model's steering gear was dispensed with as being unsatisfactory, so a Morris Minor rack and pinion unit was pressed into service. For cheapness the rear suspension featured quarter elliptic springs. It was the same need for economy that prompted Donald Healey to think of the bodywork having identical front and rear profiles, but

AUSTIN HEALEY SPRITE	
MARK ONE (1958–61)	
Number built 48,999	
ENGINE	
No. of cylinders	Four
Bore/stroke mm	62 × 76
Displacement cc	948
Valve operation	Overhead pushrod
Compression ratio	8.3:1; optional 9:1
Induction	Twin SU carburettors
BHP	43 at 5200 rpm
Transmission	Four-speed
CHASSIS	
Construction	Monocoque
Wheelbase mm	2032
Track – front mm	1162
Track – rear mm	1136
Suspension – front	Independent wishbone and coil
Suspension – rear	Quarter elliptic
Brakes	Hydraulic drum
PERFORMANCE	
Maximum speed	136 km/h (85 mph)

ABOVE **John Sprinzel** *in his famous 'Sebring' Sprite, shown at Boulogne in the 1959 Monte Carlo Rally. He and Willy Cave came 14th, 3rd in class.*

LEFT **1959 Mark One Sprite**.

TOP **Mark One Austin Healey Sprites** *lined up prior to the 1959 British GP at Aintree, when they were driven by the Formula One drivers. The event proper was won by Jack Brabham in a Cooper.*

the results lacked visual appeal so Gerry Coker came up with a neat and straightforward two-seater with a one-piece forward-opening bonnet fitted with pop-up headlamps. The latter feature proved too expensive for the production cars so the lamps were fixed, giving a distinctive 'Frog-eye' look which provided the little car with much of its personality.

By the time the model went into production in 1958 the Q car had become the Austin Healey Sprite, competitively priced at £678, and was to prove to be the best selling of all the Sprites with close on 49,000 finding buyers before it was replaced by a Mark Two version in mid-1961. This looked an altogether more conventional car as the cheeky bonnet was dispensed with and replaced by a new front end with the headlights transferred from the bonnet to the wings, changes that did not meet with Donald Healey's approval. Simultaneously a badge-engineered M.G. version, which revived the pre-war Midget name, was introduced and built alongside the Austin Healey Sprite on the Abingdon production line. For 1963 the Sprite and Midget were fitted with a larger capacity 1098 cc engine, which increased the weight and lowered the top speed to around 136 km/h (85 mph).

The 3000 Mark Two

We left the Sprite's big brother, the 3000, in its original form and in 1961 a Mark Two version with vertical barred radiator appeared which echoed the old 100 model. Mechanical changes were minimal but power was upped from 124 to 132 bhp, three SU carburettors replaced the two employed earlier, and there were minor modifications made to the camshaft. The Mark Two's duration was a brief one but in late 1961 the model received a revised gearbox along with other BMC users of the C Series engine.

It was in the summer of 1962 that the 3000 experienced the only styling facelift of its eight-year production life. The body lines were not altered but customers benefited from wind-up windows in place of the sidescreen that had featured hitherto, and the hood was improved and thereafter could be readily stowed away when not in use. These changes had the effect of turning the 3000 more into a drop-head coupé than a somewhat spartan roadster and were no doubt intended to broaden the model's appeal. At the same time the two-seater BN7 version was discontinued in view of the lack of demand. There were yet further engine changes with the original two-carburettor layout re-instated and there was another new camshaft.

Austin Healey in competition

In truth the 3000 was beginning to show its years but this did not detract from an impressive competition record that dated back to the 100-Six. It had been in 1956, the year of its announcement, that the Healey team had again returned to the flats of Utah with their record breaker, by this time running in supercharged six-cylinder form, in the hope of breaking the 200 mph (322 km/h) barrier. This proved successful when the car recorded 327.66 km/h (203.6 mph). In 1957 one of the M.G. record breakers, EX 179, though powered by a prototype Sprite engine, averaged 190.11 km/h (118.13 mph) for 12 hours. This was achieved with the car in unsupercharged form, but with the blower added speeds of up to 228.66 km/h (142.08 mph) were managed. Meanwhile on the race track a 100-Six achieved a second in class at the 1957 Sebring 12-hour race, while the model won its price class in that year's Mille Miglia.

The four-cylinder and early six-cylinder cars had a successful enough competition record but the new 3000, introduced in 1959, achieved even greater things and seemed happy in rallies, sports car races and record breaking. Up until 1957 the Healey works at Warwick was responsible for the preparation of competition machinery, but from the following year solely concerned itself with the racing versions. The Abingdon-based BMC Competitions Department thereafter looked after the rally cars and even prepared the occasional Austin Healey for the race track. We should also not overlook the little Sprite and in 1959 a team achieved a one-two-three class win at Sebring. The same year a 100-Six took a class third and was placed fourth overall in the GT race at Silverstone, while the newly introduced 3000 managed a class win in the Oulton Park Gold Cup and an overall third in the *Autosport* championship. That year's rally successes included a 3000 taking second place in the German rally.

Nineteen sixty started well for Austin Healey with a Sprite taking second place in the newly instituted Sebring Four Hour race with only an Abarth outpacing it. The 12-hour event saw the small car chalk up a class win, while its larger 3000 brother took second and third placings in its class. The 3000 was unlucky at Le Mans but the Sprite achieved a class win and 16th overall placing, and also won its class in the Nürburgring 500-kilometre event. The Big Healey (as the 3000 was nicknamed) won the Marathon Rally with another in third place, and was runner-up in the Alpine and second and third in the RAC.

The Sprite again set the pace in 1961 with a second overall placing at the Sebring Four Hour with an Abarth again robbing it of outright victory, while in the 12-hour event Sprites were second and third in class. Other Austin Healey class victories during the year included a second in the Mille Miglia and a one-two-three position in the GT race at Brands

Hatch. The 1961 rally scene was less successful than previous years though the Morley twins won the Alpine, and there was a second place in the RAC and a third in the Acropolis event.

The Warwick company also marketed the lightened GT version of the Sprite which performed so well at the American Sebring circuit. The Sebring Sprite of the early 1960s offered 160 km/h (100 mph) plus performance and was popular with the club racing fraternity.

From 1962 onwards the sensational Mini Coopers moved to pole position in the BMC competitive line-up and the Sprite and 3000 were, to some extent, relegated to secondary events. A privately entered Sprite took a class second in the Nürburgring 1000-kilometre but the Big Healey won the Alpine and there were second and third positions in the RAC.

Nineteen sixty-three started on the right note with the Big Healey winning the GT class in the Monte Carlo Rally and there was a second in that year's Tulip, and the model came fourth and fifth in class at Sebring behind the Ferraris.

Nürburgring was again a happy Sprite hunting ground with a class second in the 1000-kilometre, and the GT race at Silverstone produced a similar result.

Although in 1964 the little cars did not finish at Sebring they won the team prize for having covered the minimum mileage while a 3000 won the Marathon Rally, along with the Austrian Alpine, the GT category in the Tulip and rounded off a good year with a second class placing in the Alpine and a second in the RAC Rally.

These successes represented a high point in Big Healey fortunes as, from 1965, Group Two regulations, which were becoming more widely adopted by rally organizers, did not favour large cars in the GT class but helped the smaller and potent Mini Coopers. Despite this a 3000 took a class second in the Alpine, third at Geneva and a fourth in the Tulip. On the familiar Sebring circuit Austin Healeys big and small did well with the 3000 winning its class and Sprites being placed first and second in theirs. Nürburgring saw yet another Sprite success with a class win in the 1000-kilometre event and a second in the 500-kilometre. Sprites also did well at Le Mans with a class victory and 12th overall placing. In its last RAC Rally appearance, in November 1965, the Big Healey was placed in second position. This was in reality the 3000's last official competitive appearance though the Sprite continued to uphold Austin Healey laurels.

It had been the experience gained in the rally field that resulted in improvements to the 3000's chassis which appeared in the spring of 1964. One of the model's shortcomings had been its poor ground clearance as an underslung chassis was employed. The member was restructured and softer rear springs and twin radius arms were introduced, while a Panhard rod, which had featured since the 1953 100, was dispensed with. These modifications were applied to a Mark Three version of the Big Healey that had been introduced the previous year. Coded BJ8 it looked externally similar to its predecessor but there were cosmetic changes with the introduction of a new wood veneer dashboard along with a central console complete with a useful cubby box. Under-bonnet improvements included yet another camshaft change and modifications to the carburettors and exhaust system. These had the effect of increasing engine power to 148 bhp and the car's top speed to over 193 km/h (120 mph) making the Mark Three the fastest of all the Big Healeys.

The 3000 bows out

Nevertheless by 1967, with demand for the car falling off fast, the Austin Healey 3000 came to the end of its very distinguished line, with the impending American safety regulations – which would have demanded a considerable re-structuring of the car – providing the knock-out blow. One last example was built in March 1968 though to all intents and purposes the model had ceased production at the end of 1967. The Big Healey was no more.

However, a replacement for the Big Healey had been exercising corporate thought throughout the 1960s. There had been the 'Firrere', coded XC 512 by BMC, which was inspired by a Pininfarina coupé built on an Austin Healey 3000 chassis in 1962. Its engine was the 4-litre Rolls-Royce engine from the slow-selling Vanden Plas Princess R, while the suspension was Hydrolastic and borrowed from the Austin 1800 saloon. The Healeys father and son disparagingly referred to the car as 'Fireball XL5' or even 'The Thing' as they found it difficult to believe it was actually being preferred as a sports car. The idea was eventually dropped but not until a million pounds had been spent on tooling.

There was to have been an Austin Healey version of the controversial MGC of 1967 but Donald Healey saw enough of the car's development pangs to request that his name be removed from it. Otherwise the C would probably have been offered with an alternative radiator as the Austin Healey 3000 Mark Four. Healey came up with the idea of fitting the ex-Princess R 4-litre engine to the Mark Three 3000 chassis and a prototype car, with a specially widened body to accommodate the R's rear axle, was built. A further two cars were made by BMC but the ageing chassis and body were limiting factors, the engine was not really happy in a sports car, and the idea did not proceed.

Despite the Big Healey's demise, the Sprite continued to remind the competition that it should not be underestimated on the race track. The little cars set a cracking pace in 1966

ABOVE **Mark Two Austin Healey Sprite** *which dispensed with the cheeky 'Frog-eye' front and incorporated a more conventional profile. The 948 cc engine was upped to 1098 cc for 1963, and it remained in production in this form until 1964.*

LEFT **1967 Mark V Sprite.** *The Lenham Motor Company offered this version in the manner of the works Le Mans cars.*

ABOVE RIGHT **1967 3000 Mark III.** *The fastest – with a top speed of around 193 km/h (120 mph) – and most comfortable of the Big Healeys, this version, the last of the line, was built until 1967.*

AUSTIN HEALEY 3000
(1959–68)
Number built 42,924

ENGINE		CHASSIS	
No. of cylinders	Six	Frame	Box
Bore/stroke mm	83 × 88	Wheelbase mm	2336
Displacement cc	2912	Track – front mm	1238
Valve operation	Overhead pushrod	Track – rear mm	1270
Compression ratio	9:1	Suspension – front	Independent wishbone and coil
Induction	Twin SU; 1961–62 triple SU carburettors	Suspension – rear	Half elliptic
BHP	124 at 4600, 132 at 4750 rpm	Brakes	Hydraulic, front disc
Transmission	Four-speed with overdrive	PERFORMANCE	
		Maximum speed	183 km/h (114 mph) to 193 km/h (120 mph)

with class wins in the Daytona 24-hour, the Sebring Three and 12-hour events and at that old faithful, the Nürburgring 1000-kilometre. In 1967 the Sprite achieved a notable success at Le Mans when one finished in 15th place, averaged 162.36 km/h (100.89 mph), and won the *Motor* trophy for the best and only British finisher. The following year, 1968, saw the by now regular class win at Sebring and yet another Le Mans 15th position but at a slightly lower average speed and another *Motor* trophy. It was perhaps appropriate that Austin Healey's official competition career came to an end in 1969 on the American Sebring circuit where the Sprite achieved a one-two-three class win at the scene of so many of its victories.

It had been in January 1968 that BMC, having been renamed British Motor Holdings following a merger with Jaguar in 1966, became the British Leyland Motor Corporation. In came new management, headed by Sir Donald

Stokes, who was intent on discontinuing royalty payments outside the corporate orbit. This meant Healey and with it the Austin Healey marque.

At this time there was only the Sprite in production, though, of course, the M.G. Midget had started life as a Warwick design. The small Austin Healey had received updates during the 1960s. For the Mark Three model, introduced in the spring of 1964, the original rear quarter elliptic springs were replaced by the more traditional half elliptics, while sliding windows and a new facia featured. For 1967 there was a Mark Four version with more powerful 1275 cc engine increasing the car's maximum speed to the 149 km/h (93 mph) mark.

The agreement between Healey and BMC's successors was thus curtailed in December 1970 but some *Austin* Sprites were produced in 1971 and the last car was built in July. The M.G. Midget, however, soldiered on for another eight years, the final example being built at the end of 1979.

The Jensen-Healey

Most of Jensen's revenue had come from the Big Healeys but when discontinued in 1967 the company was forced to fall back on its low production, high-cost Interceptor. There followed a restructuring, with Kjell Qvale, a wealthy Californian car distributor, obtaining a majority share in Jensen, with a view to producing a sports car to take over from where the Austin Healey 3000 had left off, and Donald Healey became the Midland firm's new chairman. Initially the car was to have been Vauxhall engined but the American-orientated Jensen-Healey, announced in 1972, was powered by a Lotus twin overhead camshaft unit (see Lotus section) Unfortunately there were mechanical and body problems and output only lasted four years.

Meanwhile, an energetic and enthusiastic Donald Healey continues to keep in touch with car clubs the world over who still venerate and cherish the cars that bear his name.

BENTLEY

W.O. Bentley's sports cars brought Britain glory in the 1920s, refinement with the Rolls-Royce takeover, and post-war the winged B is still one of the country's most respected makes.

ABOVE **W.O. Bentley** *in one of the 3-litres prepared for the 1922 Tourist Trophy race in the Isle of Man, with mechanic Leslie Pennel. They finished in fourth place.*

LEFT **1929 Supercharged 4½-litre Bentley.** *The engine of Tim Birkin's illustrious single-seater which lapped Brooklands at 222.02 km/h (137.96 mph). The blower relief valves feature prominently on the engine's inlet manifold. The model later went into production but had a patchy competition record.*

The Bentley is for many the epitome of British vintage sports cars and its five victories at Le Mans in the 1920s remain an evergreen memory. Since 1931, when Rolls-Royce bought the firm, it has nurtured this sporting ambience which is today perpetuated by the turbocharged Bentley Mulsanne, providing an echo of past glories.

Walter Owen Bentley (1888–1971) was born into the comfortable circumstances of a London middle class family, the youngest of nine children. Although motor cars were making their first appearances in Britain as young Bentley grew up, he took little interest in them, for steam locomotives were his great interest and he was intent on becoming a railway engineer. One of his governesses had a nephew who was an apprentice with the Great Northern Railway (G.N.R.) at Doncaster, Yorkshire and, by the age of eight, young Bentley knew that this was what he wanted to do. His walks with this particular governess always tended to veer towards the northern outlets of London's Primrose Hill tunnel where, at appointed times, the *Flying Scotsman* express could be seen emerging from the blackness! After prep. school, W.O. (as he was always called) attended Clifton College, Bristol, which he enjoyed, though he disliked most lessons with the exceptions of physics and chemistry. It also allowed him to pursue his great and consuming passion for the game of cricket, which was to last throughout his life.

It was during a holiday, just prior to taking up his G.N.R. apprenticeship, that Bentley made his first acquaintance with the internal combustion engine. The family was on holiday in Scotland and he had occasion to travel in a Daimler bus which, he later recalled, was fitted with a crude hot tube ignition system. The journey, however, failed to leave much impression. He was fully committed to the glories of steam.

So in 1904, at the age of 16, W.O. Bentley entered the workshops of the Great Northern Railway. Yet soon afterwards, while he was on week-end leave in London, he purchased a Quadrant motorcycle as he was already consuming the pages of *The Motor Cycle* magazine with enthusiasm. W.O. took his 'bike back to Doncaster on the train but it soon occurred to him to ride it the 264 km (164 miles) back to London, a feat he accomplished much to the astonishment of his family. Before long he was competing in motorcycle trials all over the country and he took part in a London-to-Edinburgh run in which he gained a gold medal. His next machine was a more powerful Quadrant and in 1908 he graduated to a two-cylinder Rex on which he competed in London-Plymouth-London and Land's End trials, on both occasions receiving gold medals.

Bentley was getting more ambitious and in 1909 he entered his new Rex in the Tourist Trophy race at the Isle of Man but had the misfortune to crash. By 1910 he had become a regular competitor at Brooklands, the motor racing circuit having opened two years previously. After the Rex he transferred his allegiances to the American Indian on which he successfully competed in the Kop Hill climb. Spurred on by this success he again entered the TT but retired after getting a puncture. The Indian was finally exchanged for a Riley car. It may come as little surprise to learn that, after completing his five-year apprenticeship in 1910, W.O. Bentley decided that a career in railways might provide rather limited horizons.

Four wheels take over

He therefore wrote to E.M.P. Boileau, who was on the staff of *The Autocar* and with whom he was acquainted. As a result, 22-year-old Bentley was given an introduction to a Mr Greathead, general manager of the National Motor Cab Company based in London's Hammersmith, where he became assistant to the firm's second in command. Bentley left after two years, in 1912, as he had invested £2000 in the company of Lecoq and Fernie, who imported the French D.F.P. car to Britain. He was later joined by H.M. Bentley, his chartered accountant brother, who contributed a similar sum. The original partners were effectively bought out and the firm renamed Bentley and Bentley with showrooms in Hanover Street in London's fashionable West End. W.O. moved into an old coachhouse in New Street Mews, just off Baker Street, rented from coachbuilders J.H. Easter, who did work for the firm.

The Bentley brothers' predecessors had made little effort to promote the D.F.P. in Britain, so W.O. decided to gain valuable publicity by entering the car in competitive events. He drove the 2-litre 12-15 model in hill climbs, such as Shelsley Walsh and Aston Clinton, and also competed at Brooklands. In a bid to improve the British version of the 12-15, Bentley decided to go over to France to visit the D.F.P. factory in the Paris suburb of Courbevoie. The firm of Doriot, Flandrin et Parant had been building cars since 1906 and at about the time of Bentley's visit was selling about 650 cars a

ABOVE **W.O. Bentley** *in a single-seater DFP, pictured at Brooklands where he gained records and publicity for the marque, snatching records from Tuck's Humber. He covered a flying mile at 144.35 km/h (89.7 mph) in 1913. Aluminium pistons were fitted to D.F.P.s the following year.*

RIGHT **1922 Tourist Trophy.** *W.D. Hawkes in one of the special flat-radiatored 3-litres, pictured in practice at Hillberry.*

BELOW RIGHT **1926 3-litre.** *A Vanden Plas-bodied tourer, once owned by Woolf Barnato.*

year, so Auguste Doriot positively responded to W.O.'s ideas for a sportier 12-15. While seated in M. Doriot's office Bentley noticed a miniature piston on the French manufacturer's desk, obviously produced as a souvenir paperweight by the firm which did D.F.P.'s castings. On enquiry Bentley was informed that the little piston had been cast in aluminium which triggered a thought process in the British engineer's mind. At this time practically all car pistons were made of cast iron but Bentley became convinced that engines would perform better with lighter aluminium ones.

On his return to London he had a set cast of 12 per cent copper and 88 per cent aluminium and fitted them in a standard D.F.P. 12-15. The results were impressive so the pistons were lightened and the car performed even better. Consequently they were fitted to the 12-40 Speed Model D.F.P. which was produced in response to Bentley's French visit. However, the unconventional piston material was not mentioned in the firm's advertisements! In 1914 Bentley entered the TT race which was open to cars of up to 3.3 litres capacity and the 2-litre aluminium-pistoned D.F.P. achieved a creditable sixth position. The cars were also making their mark in record breaking but all these activities were brought to a halt with the outbreak, in 1914, of the First World War.

Bentley's outstanding contribution to the conflict came in 1915 after he had joined the Royal Naval Air Service as a lieutenant. It was in this somewhat unlikely capacity that he designed the BR (for Bentley Rotary) aero engine: this was a great improvement on the French Clerget unit which was his starting point. It was followed by the BR2 of 230 hp which was distinguished by being the most powerful rotary of the First World War. Needless to say both engines employed aluminium pistons and they were stamped with the indelible hallmark that was to typify all Bentley's future designs: that of reliability. Their durability in action, where a mechanical failure might have spelt life or death to a pilot, provided Bentley with an immense source of satisfaction.

Designing the Bentley

With the coming of peace, in 1918, Bentley could have returned to the car agency business but his creative urge was strong and he decided to design his own car, so Bentley Motors was founded in January 1919 to further this end. During the war Bentley had met Humber's chief designer, F.T. Burgess, and he joined W.O. in a similar capacity while Harry Varley was recruited from Vauxhall. It was this trio that set to work to design the first Bentley car in a small upper office in London's Conduit Street. W.O. was keen that his car should be larger than the D.F.P., sporting in character, and it was also conceived with an eye to Continental motoring: Bentley was well acquainted with those long straight French roads during his trips there prior to and during the war.

Bentley opted for an unstressed four-cylinder unit of 3 litres capacity clearly inspired by the 1914 Grand Prix Mercedes engine. By chance one of the cars that had been driven to a sensational one-two-three victory in that year's French Grand Prix happened to be in Britain when war broke out. Its engine was taken to Rolls-Royce at Derby and provided much of the inspiration for Henry Royce's Eagle aero engine. Bentley was also a visitor to Derby during the war years, being deeply involved with aircraft engine design and had an opportunity of studying it there. Thus the Bentley engine closely followed the Mercedes overhead camshaft, four valves per cylinder layout. However, while the German engine featured welded-on water jackets, the Bentley motor was rather more up to date as its cylinders were cast *en bloc* though similarly the cylinder head was integral, a feature of all subsequent engines W.O. designed for Bentley Motors. (The exception was the 1931 4-litre model, for which W.O. was not responsible.)

Once the designs had been completed in Conduit Street,

the parts were subcontracted and the engine assembled in the upper room of the New Street Mews coach-house which Bentley had used in his pre-First World War D.F.P. days. The completed power unit was lowered through a trap door in the floor and bolted into the chassis situated below. Once in position the engine started with a deafening roar much to the chagrin of a hospital matron who informed Bentley that there was an ill patient within earshot. The usually reserved W.O. was unrepentant, feeling that the bark of the first 3-litre Bentley was a happy sound to die to!

The young company now required somewhere to build its cars, so some land was purchased at Oxgate Lane, Cricklewood in north London and a small works was established there. This flew in the face of convention as many motor manufacturers were based in the Midlands with component suppliers readily to hand. Unfortunately it took a little time to get the 3-litre in production and the firm was unable to cash in on the post-war boom that fizzled out at the end of 1920 and it was not until the following August that the first production Bentley was delivered.

The 3-litre was destined to remain available until 1929 and with 1619 built it was to be the most popular of all W.O.'s cars. Although conceived as a sports car many customers insisted on their vehicles being fitted with spacious saloon bodies that rather took the edge off the model's performance. Most 3-litres would reach 112 km/h (70 mph) while a special short chassis sports model, introduced in 1925, was capable of 160 km/h (100 mph).

piston configuration but also the four's noisy camshaft drive was dispensed with and replaced by a far quieter arrangement of connecting rods and eccentrics that have been likened to the connecting rods on the wheels of a steam locomotive. With the 6½-litre, Bentley moved decisively into the Rolls-Royce market place and, like the Derby company, he had always produced his cars in chassis form only with the customer deciding on his own coachbuilder and body style.

The investment required to put the 6½-litre car into production cannot have much helped Bentley's seldom sound finances; in 1924 the company had made a loss of £6,700. Bentley Motors was in need of a substantial injection of capital and, during the winter of 1925/6, W.O. wrote to William Morris, who was then the country's most successful car manufacturer, in the hope that he would put some money into the firm. Although Bentley visited Cowley and gave Morris a run in the new 6½-litre, the latter courteously declined the offer, feeling that he could not manufacture both cheap *and*

BELOW **The Bentley works.** *The rather basic facilities of the works in London's Cricklewood is revealed in this photograph of the engine assembly shop. The fixed-head cylinder blocks will be readily apparent, a feature of all 1920s' Bentleys.*

Six-cylinder model

In order to cater for this lucrative though limited trade soon after the 3-litre entered production, Bentley started work on a new model intended to supplement it. Unlike the first Bentley model, the new car was to have a 4½-litre six-cylinder engine and the prototype, carrying the fictitious Sun name, was completed in 1925. W.O. took it to France for testing, and, by chance, encountered a 7668 cc Rolls-Royce Phantom I, due for announcement in May of that year. An unofficial race ensued and the result was close enough to convince Bentley of the need to increase the capacity of his new car to 6½ litres. It duly appeared at the end of 1925 and, although the new six perpetuated the 3-litre's valve layout, it was both smoother and quieter than its predecessor. This was not only due to its

RIGHT **Le Mans 1924.** *The winning 3-litre, driven by John Duff and Frank Clement. For the first time, Bentleys were protected at Le Mans with guards over the headlamps and below the petrol tank to prevent bombardment from stones, which had damaged the car in the 1923 event. The Bentley's winning speed was 86.55 km/h (53.78 mph). All the other cars were from France.*

expensive cars. So, a Cowley-built Bentley was never made.

Fortunately Bentley's salvation came in the shape of millionaire and enthusiastic racing driver Woolf Barnato, who invested close on £143,000 in the firm, these arrangements being announced in May 1926. This resulted in Bentley having a smart new showroom in Pollen House, Cork Street, London while W.O.'s brother H.M., who had been with him since the outset of Bentley Motors, left the company at this stage and took over the old Hanover Court premises trading under the name of H.M. Bentley and Partners.

Although the 6½-litre car clearly fulfilled a need there was a hard core of customers who believed that the big six had moved away from the original Bentley concept. It was a feeling that E.R. Foden, who had owned both a 3-litre and a 6½-litre – and is otherwise better remembered for his very pedestrian steam lorries – well summed up, when he told W.O. that he 'missed that bloody thump' of a four-cylinder engine. The result was the 4½-litre. It was a virtual re-state-

ment of the 3-litre theme with a similar mechanical layout, but the larger capacity engine ensured that the car remained competitive. Top speed was around 148 km/h (92 mph), though 160 km/h (100 mph) was possible with a high axle ratio. The 4½-litre was to remain in production until 1931. Improvements were also being made to the 6½-litre car. In late 1928 came the faster Speed Six model, recognizable by its parallel-sided radiator, the standard car having a tapered one. Under-bonnet changes included a higher compression ratio and twin carburettors rather than a single Smiths instrument. It was a model that was to give Bentley its fourth victory at the Le Mans 24-hour race, an event with which the marque is forever identified.

Victory at Le Mans

Back in his D.F.P. days W.O. had recognized that successes in the competitions field were the cheapest way of publicizing and thus selling cars, and throughout Bentley Motors's some-

what turbulent existence the racing programme remained sacrosanct. It was in 1922 that a works involvement began with cars, having distinctive flat radiators and high compression engines, running in the American Indianapolis race and the Tourist Trophy event in the Isle of Man. The 3-litre finished 13th in the US event while in the TT the cars were placed second, with W.O. driving one into fourth place while another Bentley was sixth. The following year, 1923, saw the establishment of the Le Mans 24-hour race. It was drawn to Bentley's attention by John Duff, one of the firm's London agents, who managed to get W.O. to agree to the experimental department preparing his 3-litre for the event. Bentley himself was sceptical that the car could survive 24 hours of continuous racing, but the event might have been instituted with the Bentley in mind favouring as it did under-stressed, slow running and, above all, reliable engines.

were thereafter duplicated on racing Bentleys), while the other was damaged after a carburettor fire. The firm was equally unsuccessful in 1926 when all three cars failed to finish the 24-hour run, one driven by *The Autocar's* Sammy Davis, having buried itself in a sandbank only 20 minutes from the end when running in third place.

Nineteen twenty-seven, by contrast, was a sensational year for Bentley at Le Mans. The team consisted of three cars: the first of the new 4½-litres and two 3-litres. One of the latter was known as Old Number Seven, after its racing number from the previous year, and was driven by Sammy Davis and Dr J. Dudley Benjafield. All the cars ran well through the first day of the race, but at about 9.30 pm Leslie Callingham, in the 4½-litre, took the fast double White House curve at his usual 136 km/h to 144 km/h (85 to 90 mph) to find that a Th. Schneider had crashed and was half blocking the road. He

Bentley, who travelled to the Sarthe circuit to watch the event, was surprised and delighted when Duff, as the only British entrant, achieved a creditable fourth place. In 1924 he entered his 3-litre – again it was works prepared – and on this occasion it sported front-wheel brakes and radiator and headlamp stone guards. This time, with Frank Clement as co-driver, Duff managed to win the race and took the chequered flag almost a lap ahead of a Lorraine Dietrich in second place.

By 1925 the event was beginning to attract a more international following with cars from America and Italy as well as Britain. Bentley Motors now decided to enter its own team and two 3-litres were prepared. Unfortunately both dropped out during the race, one with a broken fuel pipe (the lines

ABOVE **Le Mans 1927.** *The d'Erlanger/Duller 3-litre pictured prior to the famous White House crash, one of three Bentleys entered for the race. It was while Duller was at the wheel that he hit Callingham's 4½-litre which had crashed into another car at the corner. However, the Davis/Benjafield 3-litre, although crippled, went on to win the event. It gave Bentley its second Le Mans victory and the marque also triumphed there in 1928–31.*

ABOVE **1928 4½-litre Bentley.** *As the model is usually remembered: in four-seater touring form. However, many examples were fitted with saloon coachwork.*

LEFT **Le Mans 1928.** *The start of the race with two 4½-litre Bentleys of Birkin and Clement leading, followed by Chiron's Chrysler, Barnato in another 4½ (he went on to win) and Zehender's Chrysler. Birkin's car was placed fifth, though Clement's 4½ eventually retired.*

took evasive action, swung to the right to avoid it, went into a ditch and almost barricaded the road on the opposite side. One small car managed to get through the gap but a Bentley, driven by George Duller, could not avoid the 4½ and crashed into it, badly damaging the 3-litre in the process. Sammy Davis, in Old Number Seven, was soon on the scene and, although he had reduced speed by around 32 km/h (20 mph), he could not avoid hitting the rear of the disabled 4½. Fortunately none of the drivers was injured but Callingham's and Duller's Bentleys were damaged beyond repair. Old Number Seven had been luckier and sustained only a broken wheel, bent front axle, wrecked mudguard and headlamp. Fortunately Davis re-started the engine and made his way to the Bentley pits. There it was found that the frame was also bent, which affected the car's braking, but some temporary repairs were carried out and Sammy pressed on, handing over to Dr Benjafield at midnight. By this time the Bentley, with only one working headlamp, was six laps behind the leading French Aries and by the time Davis took over again at 11 am on the following day the gap had been reduced to four laps and the Bentley was in second place. Then at around 2 pm the Aries dropped out with engine trouble and Old Number Seven took the chequered flag to give Bentley its

ABOVE **The 4½-litre Bentley team** *for the 1928 Le Mans race, the first occasion that hoods were not required to be raised, while the upright windscreens were replaced by fold-flat ones. Tim Birkin and Jean Chassagne are in the first car, with Frank Clement and Dr Dudley Benjafield next, and Woolf Barnato and Bernard Rubin in the last one. W O Bentley is on the extreme left of the picture. There was no question of the Le Mans cars being trailered or otherwise transported in those days.*

second Le Mans victory. Later the car, in its be-spattered and damaged state, was returned to London and was man-handled into the Savoy Hotel to take pride of place at a celebration banquet in her honour.

For 1928 Bentley entered a team of three 4½-litre cars when Woolf Barnato and Bernard Rubin took first place and a second car was fifth, the third Bentley having dropped out when it lost its water. The firm was in deadly earnest in 1929 with the new Speed Six as the leading car, which went on to win and with Bentleys in second, third and fourth places having successfully fended off an unexpected challenge from Stutz. It was much the same in 1930 when Speed Six Bentleys took first and second places. The event also wit-

nessed the appearance of two 4½-litre supercharged ('blower') cars, which, weighing two and a half tons apiece, not only consumed tyres at a prodigious rate but eventually withdrew with mechanical trouble.

Birkin's 'Blowers'

The 'blower' Bentley had been a project nurtured by driver Sir Henry Ralph Stanley 'Tim' Birkin, but in the face of considerable opposition from W.O. To supercharge the Bentley engine was to fly in the face of its designer's avowed maxim of reliability, and the 'blower' 4½ did indeed have a patchy competitive career, which may have done the marque's image some harm. Birkin had got Amherst Villiers to produce a special supercharger for the 4½-litre Bentley which was positioned in front of the engine between the dumb irons. He also managed to charm the Hon. Dorothy Paget into financing the project to the tune of £40,000 and a works was established at Welwyn, Hertfordshire in which to build the cars. As Birkin had decided to enter the aforementioned 1930 Le Mans event, 50 cars had to be built to meet the race's regulations. Although both supercharged 4½-litres failed to complete the course, Birkin had the satisfaction of breaking the lap record at 144.34 km/h (89.69 mph). But he managed to gain fourth place in the Irish Grand Prix the month after Le Mans. Even more impressive was Birkin's

second place in the 1930 French Grand Prix at Pau.

Bentleys had, of course, also competed at home as well as abroad. The company's most important successes were staged at Brooklands of which the Double Twelve race was the most significant. These were two 12-hour runs, as overnight events were not permitted at the Weybridge circuit. In 1929 a Speed Six just lost to an Alfa Romeo on handicap, though Bentleys were first and second in the 500 Mile Race later in the year. A Speed Six also took the chequered flag in the 1929 Six Hour Race while the same car was driven into second place, by Glen Kidston, at the Irish Grand Prix.

Nineteen thirty was the last season for the works cars and the year began well with Speed Sixes taking first and second places in the Brooklands Double Twelve. Bentleys also competed in the 500 Mile Race at the track with Dr Benjafield and Eddie Hall averaging 180.44 km/h (112.12 mph) for second place. In 1931 a Barnato-entered Speed Six won the event with Jack Dunfee driving.

The Bentley Boys

Reference has already been made to some of the famous 'Bentley Boys'. They represented a social and racing élite of which Woolf Barnato, known to his friends as Babe, was probably the best known. His grandfather, Isaac Isaacs, grew up in London's East End and his son Barnett, who changed his

TOP **1930 Speed Six Bentley.** *This magnificent Gurney Nutting coupé was delivered to Woolf Barnato in June 1930. By all accounts he sketched the profile on the back of an envelope and told the coachbuilders to get on with it!*

ABOVE **The Bentley Boys at Le Mans 1927.** *Left to right: Frank Clement, Leslie Callingham, Baron d'Erlanger, Woolf Barnato (at rear), George Duller, W.O. Bentley (at rear), Sammy Davis and Dudley Benjafield, with the latter duo's winning 3-litre on the right.*

name to Barnato, emigrated to South Africa and made his fortune in the Kimberley diamond fields. Woolf Barnato inherited much of his father's business canniness and as Bentley's chairman he naturally kept a stable of 4½, 6½, Speed Six and 8-litre cars. Barnato loved a challenge and on one occasion, while cruising at Cannes, a friend wagered that he could not beat the famous Blue Train back to Britain. He responded immediately, set off from the South of France in his 6½-litre Bentley and drove right across the country, caught the boat to Dover and was in London four hours before the boat train arrived. In W.O.'s opinion he was also Bentley's best driver and his record confirms this with no less than three Le Mans wins, in 1928, 1929 and 1930.

Another driver at the very core of the Bentley establishment was the stuttering baronet 'Tim' Birkin, whose enthusiasm for the supercharged 4½-litre Bentley incurred W.O.'s displeasure. An outstanding driver, he won Le Mans once for Bentley, sharing the winning Speed Six with Barnato in 1929, and again in 1931 in an Alfa Romeo. He later set down his racing reminiscences in the suitably titled *Full Throttle* and died at the early age of 37 in 1933 after contracting an infection from a burn on a hot exhaust pipe.

Very much in the Birkin mould was Glen Kidston, a former naval officer, who co-drove with Barnato to give Bentley its last Le Mans win in 1930. He was also an enthusiastic aviator

LEFT **Tourist Trophy at Ards, Belfast, 1930.** *Start of the 3- to 5-litre class, with Bertie Kensington Moir (2) and Dr Benjafield/Jean Chassagne (3) in 'Blower' 4½s entered by the Hon Dorothy Paget. Behind is Eddie Hall's privately entered unsupercharged 4½. Kensington Moir and Hall were placed 11th and 12th respectively.*

RIGHT **1930 Double Twelve race.** *The Barnato/Clement 6½-litre Bentley on the Brooklands Members Banking, with time-keepers' bus in the background. It went on to win at 139.49 km/h (86.68 mph), with another 6½-litre, driven by Davis and Dunfee, in second place. It was an event that was begun on the Friday and completed on the Saturday, with the winning Bentley taking the chequered flag at 8 pm.*

and had some narrow escapes in daring aircraft exploits. He died in South Africa after setting up a new flying record between London and Cape Town. Then there was Bernard Rubin, a friend of Barnato's, who shared the winning 4½-litre with him at Le Mans in 1928. All four, Barnato, Birkin, Kidston and Rubin, had adjoining flats in Grosvenor Square in the heart of London's Mayfair. Not surprisingly its south-east side became known as 'Bentley Corner' as there were usually up to a dozen green Bentleys parked there. Then there were also socializing and impromptu parties at the Ritz, Claridges and Grosvenor...

However, not all the Bentley Boys belonged to this inner charmed circle as they had to work for a living. Sammy Davis, sports editor of *The Autocar*, was a journalist who had worked for its publisher, Iliffe, since 1912 and, after enlisting in the Royal Naval Air Service during the First World War, joined *The Autocar* in 1919 and remained there until 1950. Jack and Clive Dunfee were also well respected Bentley drivers. Their father, Colonel Vickers Dunfee, was well known in the City of London and his sons drove in Britain and on the Continent. Tragically Clive died when his 8-litre Bent-

ley went over the top of the Brooklands banking during the 1932 500 Mile Race.

A man who shared the driving seat with the saddle was George Duller, who was introduced to the Bentley circle by Barnato. He was a successful steeplechaser and was responsible for the 4½-litre model's first win at the Grand Prix de Paris race at the Montlhéry circuit in 1927. Another somewhat unlikely 'Bentley Boy' was the unmistakably balding figure of Dr J. Dudley Benjafield, later a Harley Street consultant, who partnered Sammy Davis in Bentley's celebrated 1927 Le Mans victory following the débâcle at the White House. He had the distinction of being Bentley's first 'outside' driver and ran both a lumbering 3-litre saloon and a dashing two-seater.

With the demise of Bentley Motors in 1931, the Bentley Boys dispersed. Things would never be quite the same again...

1930 6½-litre Bentley. *This Gurney Nutting coupé for 'Bentley Boy' Glen Kidston pictured with appropriately august background. The following year Bentley Motors was no more.*

The magnificent 8-litre

It had been in 1930 that Bentley had announced perhaps his greatest model, the 8-litre, which was also Britain's largest capacity production car. The decision to go ahead with this new model was no doubt influenced by the fact that the firm had recorded the only substantial profits of its 12-year existence in 1929 when a figure of £28,647 was announced. The 8-litre was basically an enlarged version of the 6½-litre car, the larger capacity being achieved by increasing the size of the engine's cylinder bore. The block was also turned around 180 degrees on the 8-litre so that the carburettors were on the same offside as their accelerator pedal, thus simplifying the controls. However, the chassis was new, lower than hitherto and available in two lengths. Also specially designed for the new model was the gearbox, which, unusually, was split down its centre to permit the use of large bearings, so adding to the car's overall smoothness and silence. Fitted with elegant coachwork, the 8-litre, with a top speed of around 167 km/h (104 mph), was the ultimate grand tourer which could have conveyed its owners in speed and comfort across Europe to winter in Cannes or Monte Carlo.

Unfortunately for Bentley it was just this clientele who were first to feel the effects of the catastrophic collapse of the Wall Street Stock Market in 1929. Bentley Motors recorded a small £1023 loss in 1930 but the following year the figure had spiralled to a record £84,174. It was with these mounting losses in mind that the firm's management decided to overrule W.O. Bentley's wishes and introduce the cheaper 4-litre model with a Ricardo-designed overhead inlet/side exhaust engine and a detachable cylinder head. It was a slow seller and the last of the 50 built was not sold until 1933, two years after the old Bentley company's demise.

Rolls-Royce take-over

It was in this rapidly deteriorating atmosphere that, in June 1931, Bentley's managing director, J.K. Carruth, wrote to Rolls-Royce suggesting an amalgamation of the two concerns but, after due consideration, the Derby firm felt that there was little advantage in such an arrangement. The following month Carruth was appointed receiver by Barnato while, a few days later, Patrick Frere acted in a similar capacity for the London Life Association, a major shareholder. In September 1931 Bentley Motors went into voluntary liquidation.

However, since the end of July, W.O. and a small team of designers had been at work on the plans of a new car for the Napier company. This respected Acton-based firm had built cars until 1924 but had withdrawn from the market to concentrate on their successful aero-engine business. They were keen to re-enter the field and the projected Napier Bentley would have resembled a scaled down 8-litre with a

BENTLEY 8-LITRE (1930–2)
Number built 100

ENGINE		CHASSIS	
No. of cylinders	Six	Frame	Channel
Bore/stroke mm	110 × 140	Wheelbase mm	3657 (short), 3962 (long)
Displacement cc	7982		
Valve operation	Overhead camshaft	Track – front mm	1422
Compression ratio	5:1, 5.5:1	Track – rear mm	1422
Induction	Twin SU carburettors	Suspension – front	Half elliptic
BHP	200, 225	Suspension – rear	Half elliptic
Transmission	Four-speed	Brakes	Mechanical

PERFORMANCE
Maximum speed 167 km/h (104 mph)

TOP RIGHT **1931 Bentley 8-litre.** *W.O.'s last magnificent model of which 100 were built. This saloon has coachwork by H.J. Mulliner.*

FAR RIGHT **1932 8-litre.** *This four-seater tourer was delivered the year after Bentley Motors was liquidated.*

RIGHT **1931 4½-litre.** *Originally fitted with Vanden Plas open four-seater bodywork, it was restyled in 1936 by Cooper Bodies of London using the Triumph Gloria Flow-free saloon as inspiration.*

capacity of 6¼ litres. This proposed alliance had been made public by August 1931 though the announcement in the motoring press underlined that no formal agreement had been concluded. Patrick Frere had reached agreement that Napier pay £84,000 for the Bentley assets.

Meanwhile, these plans were causing concern at Derby where Rolls-Royce was concerned that its old rival Napier would challenge its own Phantom II, so the British Equitable Trust was assigned the task of bidding for the company as it was felt that the Rolls-Royce name would have ensured a tough counter bid from Napier. By November the price of Bentley's assets had risen with Napier agreeing to pay £103,675 but the sale had to be ratified by a court. This was duly convened but the judge informed Napier that the Trust had offered more money and required sealed bids to conclude the matter. Napier offered £104,775 while the Trust's figure was over £20,000 more at £125,265 and, indirectly, Rolls-Royce became owners of Bentley Motors.

W.O. Bentley, after staying on with Napier for a short time, joined Rolls-Royce first at their Conduit Street showrooms, and later became responsible for the Continental testing of the existing Rolls-Royce cars and the new Bentley model then under development. Not surprisingly he was unable to assume a design role and when the Lagonda company came under new management in 1935 and asked W.O. to join them as technical director he jumped at the chance. He therefore left Rolls-Royce in January 1936 and established himself at Lagonda's Staines factory where a number of ex-Bentley employees joined him. There a V12 model was produced intended as a challenge to the Rolls-Royce Phantom III.

The first Rolls-Royce built Bentley made its appearance in 1933. This 3½-litre model was born from a supercharged cheaper Rolls-Royce, code-named Peregrine, that never reached production and while the power unit was dispensed with the chassis was retained for the new Bentley. The production engine, however, was the Rolls-Royce 20/25 unit but with higher compression ratio and, to underline the model's sporting flavour, two SU carburettors. This 144 km/h (90 mph) car remained in production until 1936 when it was replaced by a 4¼-litre model which used the 25/30 Rolls-Royce engine, with similar modifications, as its power source.

BENTLEY 3½-LITRE (1933–6)	
Number built 1191	
ENGINE	
No. of cylinders	Six
Bore/stroke mm	82 × 114
Displacement cc	3669
Valve operation	Overhead pushrod
Compression ratio	6.5:1
Induction	Twin SU carburettors
BHP	110
Transmission	Four-speed
CHASSIS	
Frame	Channel
Wheelbase mm	3200
Track – front mm	1422
Track – rear mm	1422
Suspension – front	Half elliptic
Suspension – rear	Half elliptic
Brakes	Mechanical with servo assistance
PERFORMANCE	
Maximum speed	148 km/h (92 mph)

FAR LEFT **1936 Bentley 3½-litre.** *This was the first model to be produced by the Rolls-Royce company following its acquisition of Bentley Motors in 1931. The engine was similar to that used in the Rolls-Royce 20/25.*

ABOVE **1934 3½-litre.** *The drophead coupé coachwork is by James Young of Bromley, Kent.*

LEFT **1939 Bentley Corniche.** *This prototype was styled by Rolls-Royce's Ivan Evernden, who worked with Van Vooren of Paris. It crashed during testing in France and was left at Dieppe, later to be destroyed by bombing.*

That the competitive Bentley spirit had not been totally extinguished was highlighted when Eddie Hall decided to enter a 3½-litre car in the 1934 Tourist Trophy race and received Rolls-Royce backing for his effort. He achieved a creditable second place, repeated the feat in 1935, and victory again eluded him in 1937 but on this occasion his entry was 4¼-litre engined. The indefatigable Hall used his car at Le Mans after the war when he was placed eighth in the 1950 event. This was not the only post-war Bentley Le Mans entry as H.F.S. Hay ran a pre-war streamlined saloon, of which more anon, in 1949 when he was placed sixth, though in 1951 he finished in 23rd place.

Meanwhile, the mainstream Bentley models continued to evolve. It was intended that in 1940 the 4¼-litre car would be replaced by the Mark V but only 11 were built before the war put paid to the project. The model had coil and wishbone independent front suspension, the first on a Bentley, and a stronger chassis than its predecessor. Although the 4257 cc six-cylinder overhead valve engine shared a similar capacity to its 4¼-litre predecessor, it had more in common with the Rolls-Royce Wraith that had succeeded the 25/30 in 1938. A

few cars were built in 1940 and some were used by dignatories during the war years of which the most notable was Air Chief Marshal Sir Arthur Harris, head of Bomber Command, who ran a Park Ward bodied coupé.

The Corniche crashes

Also worthy of mention is an experimental Mark V, named the Corniche, and fitted with a striking four-door saloon body which dispensed with the traditional radiator grille and replaced it with a stylish cowl. Integral headlamps and concealed door hinges were other noteworthy and progressive features. This car was the culmination of a project that had begun back in 1938 when Walter Sleator, manager of Rolls-Royce's Paris office, commissioned a Van Vooren-bodied streamlined 4¼-litre Bentley for Nicky Embiricos, the Greek racing driver. It differed radically from the more conventional English bodied Bentley having a cowl in place of the usual Bentley radiator, integral headlamps and no running boards. Also it weighed 1574 kg (3470 lb) which was around 336 kg (740 lb) lighter than the more standard products. The car had been conceived for high speed Continental touring and also came into its own on the newly opened German *autobahns*. Top speed was around 189 km/h (118 mph) and fuel consumption was not excessive. In 1939 the car was brought to Britain and Captain George Eyston drove it at Brooklands, where he averaged over 183 km/h (114 mph) for a full hour. Rolls-Royce was sufficiently impressed by these figures to go ahead with a production version of the design, the intention being that Park Ward would be responsible for the construction of the distinctive bodywork.

This was styled by Rolls-Royce's own Ivan Evernden, who worked in conjunction with Van Vooren's M. Paulin and the car was subsequently bodied in the French capital. A Mark V chassis was used but the engine was an experimental 4257 cc overhead inlet/side exhaust six-cylinder engine, a layout that was used in Rolls-Royces and Bentleys post-war.

While the car was undergoing testing in France it crashed and was then removed to Dieppe in a badly damaged state prior to its shipment to Britain. Unfortunately the outbreak of the Second World War in 1939 prevented the car from being moved and during hostilities it received a direct hit on the quay at Dieppe and was totally destroyed. However, the original Embiricos car that inspired it thankfully survived and was run at Le Mans by Hay in the post-war years, while Rolls-Royce revived the Corniche name for the luxury version of the Silver Shadow/Bentley S Series in 1971.

It was during the war years that a new approach to the manufacture of Rolls-Royce and Bentley cars began to evolve. As chronicled on page 253, experimental engineer William Robotham recognized that the firm must move into the era of pressed steel bodywork rather than rely on low production hand-crafted methods. Perhaps wisely it was decided that Bentley, rather than Rolls-Royce, should reflect this more realistic approach to car production and work was put in hand for the development of a Mark VI saloon.

BENTLEY MARK VI (1946–52)	
Number built **4946**	
ENGINE	
No. of cylinders	**Six**
Bore/stroke mm	**88 × 114; from 1951 92 × 114**
Displacement cc	**4257, 4566**
Valve operation	**Overhead pushrod**
Compression ratio	**6.4:1**
Induction	**Twin SU carburettors**
Transmission	**Four-speed**
CHASSIS	
Frame	**Channel**
Wheelbase mm	**3048**
Track – front mm	**1441**
Track – rear mm	**1492**
Suspension – front	**Coil spring/wishbone**
Suspension – rear	**Half elliptic**
Brakes	**Front hydraulic, rear mechanical with servo assistance**
PERFORMANCE	
Maximum speed	**153 km/h (95 mph), 163 km/h (101 mph)**

ABOVE **1948 Mark VI Bentley.** *Although most Mark VIs had standardized saloon bodywork, it was also available for bespoke coachwork, as this drophead coupé shows.*

LEFT **Mk VI production line.** *After World War 2, Bentley and Rolls-Royce production was transferred from Derby to a former Merlin aero-engine factory at Crewe. This 1947 photograph shows Mark VI models, with Pressed Steel four-door bodywork, undergoing completion.*

FAR RIGHT AND RIGHT **Bentley Continental.** *This model was introduced on the R type in 1952 and continued with the S type of 1955–59, as featured on the immediate right.*

THE POST-WAR BENTLEYS

With the ending of the Second World War in 1945, car production was transferred to a former Merlin aero-engine factory at Crewe that the firm had managed during hostilities. The Mark VI Bentley, planned during the war, and introduced in 1946, represented a significant 'first' in that, instead of being produced in chassis form only, it was offered with standard bodywork by Pressed Steel though the Mark VI was also available for bespoke coachwork. The chassis was basically the same as employed on the pre-war Mark V, while the engine was a 4.2-litre overhead inlet/side exhaust six. This was increased to 4½ litres in 1951 and two years later, in 1953, came the R type identifiable by its larger boot, with production continuing until 1955. Also significant was the Rolls-Royce Silver Dawn of 1949, initially an export only car and effectively a Mark VI Bentley with a Rolls-Royce radiator as the Bentley name was relatively unknown in the all-important American market. But it is of relevance because it foreshadowed a merging of the Bentley and Rolls-Royce marques that finally occurred in 1955.

Styling Continental
Meanwhile a Bentley far more in the make's pre-war traditions appeared in 1952. This was the R Type Continental, a stylish two-door coupé with gently sloping streamlined tail, built by coachbuilders H.J. Mulliner. It was not only considerably lighter than the standard saloon but there were underbonnet changes to the engine's compression ratio, carburation and exhaust system. These all combined to push the car's top speed up from around 160 km/h (100 mph) to about 193 km/h (120 mph). This made the Continental the fastest production four-seater in the world and although, in the first instance, it was an export only model, it later became available on the British market. In 1954 the Continental's engine capacity was increased to 4.9 litres and output continued for a further year by which time 207 examples had been built. Its S type successor sold 388.

In 1955 the Bentley and Rolls-Royce marques became fully integrated with the arrival of a new four-door Pressed Steel saloon. The Bentley version was the S Type while in Rolls-Royce form it was titled the Silver Cloud. The chassis was new and the 4.9-litre version of the long-running six had been foreshadowed in the R Type Continental of the previous year. A Continental S Type, with coachbuilt bodywork, was also available though mechanical changes were confined to a higher rear axle ratio and modest engine improvements. Automatic transmission featured on both models but, in the latter instance, a manual gearbox was available until 1957.

In 1959 came the externally similar SII/Silver Cloud II though with a new 6.2-litre aluminium V8 engine and power steering. The Continental chassis only differed from the standard one in having a higher axle ratio and larger tyres. The arrival of the SIII/Silver Cloud III in 1963 saw the introduction of a distinctive and fashionable twin headlight layout, while a more powerful V8 featured, boasting a seven per cent increase in output. Although a Continental version was still listed it was basically a coachbuilt Bentley with marginally improved performance. Thereafter this Bentley disappeared from the range because the SIII's T series successor was a monocoque, making a coachbuilt body option less easy to accomplish.

BENTLEY CONTINENTAL R TYPE (1952–5) Number built 207		
ENGINE		**CHASSIS**
No. of cylinders	**Six**	Frame **Channel**
Bore/stroke mm	**92 × 114; from 1954 95 × 114**	Wheelbase mm **3048**
		Track – front mm **1435**
Displacement cc	**4566, 4887**	Track – rear mm **1479**
Valve operation	**Overhead pushrod**	Suspension – front **Coil spring/wishbone**
Compression ratio	**7:1, 7.25:1**	Suspension – rear **Half elliptic**
Induction	**Twin SU carburettors**	Brakes **Front hydraulic, rear**
BHP	**137**	**mechanical with servo**
Transmission	**Four-speed; from 1954 automatic optional**	**assistance**
		PERFORMANCE
		Maximum speed **185 km/h (115 mph)**

circuit, thus reviving memories of the 1920s. The new car carried over the 6.7-litre V8 of its predecessor though there were radical improvements to the independent rear suspension system. An external difference that was peculiar to the Mulsanne was the curved front bumper – the Spirit's was almost straight – though the traditional Bentley radiator lacked its familiar winged 'B' motif.

A latter day 'Blower'

The marque's famed sporting reputation was further underlined in 1982 with the arrival of the Mulsanne Turbo which echoed the memory of the supercharged 4½-litre of yore. There was, significantly, no Rolls-Royce equivalent. Work on the project had begun in 1974 and there was a one-off version of the Silver Shadow produced by Broadspeed the tuning specialists. (It is interesting to note that should the Spirit have been turbocharged, a further 35 bhp would have been required to achieve the same performance as the Bentley due to the relatively poor aerodynamics of that classically in-

ABOVE LEFT **The T Series** *was the Bentley equivalent of the Rolls-Royce Silver Shadow, introduced in 1965. This is the Series 2 version, which appeared in 1977, with new protective rubber bumpers, rack and pinion steering and suspension refinements.*

LEFT **Bentley Corniche.** *The two-door saloon and convertible version of the Silver Shadow/ T Series Bentley became models in their own right in 1971 with the arrival of the Corniche, reviving a projected pre-war Bentley name. Increased engine power and a re-styled facia also featured.*

This car represented a major milestone for the Crewe company as the Bentley T Series/Rolls-Royce Silver Shadow embodied monocoque construction, all independent suspension and disc brakes. A sophisticated specification was completed by an ingenious hydraulic self-levelling system. The 6.2-litre V8 was basically a carry over from the previous model. Air conditioning was standardized in 1969 and the engine's capacity was increased to 6.7 litres in 1970. The following year, 1971, saw the two-door saloon and convertible versions replaced by the Corniche, which was also available in Bentley form and the work of Mulliner Park Ward, though the closed version was discontinued in 1981.

With the appearance of the improved T2/Silver Shadow in 1977 there were changes to the front suspension, steering and a re-designed facia. Despite these improvements there was an erosion of the model's Bentley identity with the removal of the name from the engine rocker box covers and facia panel, so that only the radiator, hub caps and boot lid badge differentiated it from the Rolls-Royce Silver Shadow.

It therefore came as an agreeable surprise that the Bentley version of the new 1981 Rolls-Royce Silver Spirit was not, as previously, given a rather anonymous type letter but was named the Mulsanne, after the long straight on the Le Mans

spired radiator shell!) By the time the Bentley Turbo made its appearance, its V8 engine developed about 300 bhp, a 100 more than the standard Mulsanne. The Garret AiResearch turbocharger is driven by the exhaust gases from both banks of the V8 at 0.5 kg/cm (7 lb per square inch) which force feeds air through a single four-choke Solex carburettor.

This has the effect of pushing the car's top speed up from the 191 km/h (119 mph) mark to 217 km/h (135 mph) with improved acceleration to match. The Mulsanne Turbo is only identifiable by its painted radiator though beneath the surface there are tougher drive shafts and the engine's torque converter studding has been strengthened to cope with the extra power. The type of tyres is also peculiar to the model. Thus the Mulsanne and its stylish and impressive Turbo derivative are the current Bentley products costing £55,240 and £61,744 respectively.

You may have to be wealthy to buy a modern Bentley but W.O.'s 8-litre of 1930 was also aimed at an exclusive and discerning clientele. The current Bentleys therefore perpetuate this theme and also demonstrate that the marque's sporting pedigree has not dimmed over the last half century since the big green cars from Cricklewood took the chequered flag at Le Mans.

1982 Bentley Mulsanne Turbo. *This model, introduced in 1982, is externally identifiable by its painted rather than plated radiator shell. However, once the bonnet is raised the mechanical differences become apparent (below), while the interior conforms to the usual high standards associated with the cars from Crewe. Top speed is about 217 km/h (135 mph). It is a concept in the spirit of the 'Blower' Bentleys of the 1920s.*

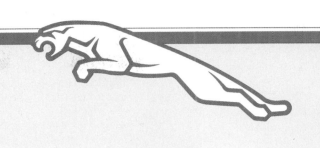

JAGUAR

Britain's greatest post-war marque, Jaguar offered style and performance at a sensationally low price, while the classic sports cars triumphed at the Le Mans 24-hour race.

1954 Jaguar D type, *pictured above, driven by Mike Hawthorn in the 1955 International Trophy race at Silverstone in which he was placed fourth; and the same car today. Provided by Martin Morris.*

The story of Jaguar concerns a company that started in a shed in 1920 and went on to produce the 'Best Car in the World'; it centres on one man, an inspired stylist named William Lyons. His personality was stamped on everything the company made and in 1956 he received a knighthood for his services to the British motor industry. Although it was cars that brought lasting fame to the name Jaguar, the company's roots lay in motorcycle sidecars. These were products of the fertile imagination of William Walmsley, an English coal merchant's son who built his first sidecar at his family home in Stockport, Cheshire, in 1920. It was a wonderful-looking device, shaped like a cigar and unlike anything seen before. By 1921, his family had moved to the seaside resort of Blackpool in Lancashire, where Walmsley continued to make sidecars behind their new home. His activities quickly attracted the attention of a young neighbour, William Lyons. Although only 20 years of age, Lyons was determined to succeed in big business. Walmsley was not so concerned, but nevertheless they went into partnership to produce sidecars in quantity, backed by their respective fathers. They chose the name Swallow for their business, as Lyons was already firmly of the opinion that the name of animals and birds known for their speed and grace presented the ideal image for their company.

Business expanded rapidly when the Swallow Sidecar Company was set up in 1922, although to keep down overheads Lyons made sure that it did so with the minimum of staff. Soon the partnership was occupying three separate workshops in Blackpool and was big enough to exhibit at the Motor Cycle Show at London's Olympia in 1923. This led to the establishment of a chain of Swallow dealers. At that time Walmsley and Lyons shared equal authority in the direction of the company although Lyons usually appeared in public as spokesman, mainly because of Walmsley's rather retiring nature. He was a brilliant stylist, however, and Lyons learned much from this man, ten years his senior. Between them they also showed exceptional ability at keeping down costs, not by skimping but by adopting efficient methods of using labour and materials. Sidecar building tended to be a rather seasonal occupation, however, and by 1926 the rapidly expanding company was considering moving into car bodies, for which there was a demand all the year round. In addition, it was obvious even at that date that the car had more of a future than the motorcycle. With this in mind, the

LEFT **Swallow sidecar**. *A Rover motorcycle, with one of the original Swallow sidecars, produced by William Walmsley in Blackpool, who went into partnership with William Lyons in 1922. Provided by Jaguar Cars Ltd.*

BELOW **1939 SS100**, *William Lyons's most memorable pre-war car, combined great beauty with high performance on road and track. This example, with its original interior and colour, was provided by the Nigel Dawes Collection.*

firm was renamed the Swallow Sidecar and Coachbuilding Company in 1926.

New, larger premises were acquired to bring the whole operation under one roof in Blackpool and more skilled workers taken on from factories in the English Midlands, which was already the centre of Britain's motor industry: labour was highly mobile in those days of rising unemployment. In January 1927, Lyons persuaded Stanley Parker, a dealer in Bolton, Lancashire, to supply him with a new Austin Seven chassis. So the first Swallow-bodied Austin was built, largely as a result of the efforts of Cyril Holland, a coachbuilder who had been hired from the Midlands.

Sidecar production built up to around 100 a week and continued through 15 distinct models until 1929 as car bodies began to occupy more of the partners' time. This situation, together with a serious lack of space, led Lyons to search for a new, far larger factory in the Midlands.

The move to Foleshill and the first SS cars

Eventually an old ammunition factory was taken over at Foleshill, Coventry, and the firm moved lock, stock and barrel in 1928, taking many workers with it, and recruiting many more locally. Standard and Wolseley chassis also received Swallow bodies before Lyons and Walmsley became car manufacturers in their own right with the SS1 of 1931.

The chassis of the new car was made by one of the existing suppliers, Standard, but it was available only for Swallows, so the resultant product was a distinctive car in its own right, rather than just a special body on a chassis shared with another company. Exactly what the initials SS stood for is still open to conjecture, but it is often assumed that they meant Standard Special. The first SS1 was a long, low, rakish fixed-head coupé with the option of six-cylinder Standard engines of 2054 cc or 2552 cc. At the same time, a smaller, four-cylinder coupé was introduced with a 1006 cc engine, called the SS2; but it was the SS1 that captured everybody's imagination because of its outstanding styling and extraordinarily low price of just over £300.

The founding of SS Cars Ltd

Demand for the new SS cars was such that production of the other Swallow-bodied cars was run down in 1932 and ceased in 1933 as the SS1 and SS2 ranges were increased to include tourers and, in 1934, saloons. At the same time, Lyons formed a new company called SS Cars Ltd to handle his burgeoning brainchild. However, other people did not feel so happy about SS cars. They sniped at them, saying they were not nearly as fast as they looked, although a couple of SS1 tourers had done well in the 1933 Alpine Trial. Lyons took such criticism to heart, and started a quest for more power to ensure his cars lived up to their appearance. Initially, larger engines, of 2143 cc and 2663 cc for the SS1 and 1343 cc and 1608 cc for the SS2, were fitted in 1934. Walmsley was not happy with the way things were going and resigned at the first annual general meeting.

The first results of Lyons's bid to improve the performance of SS cars were seen in work performed on the 2.6-litre engine by the brilliant freelance gas-flow expert, Harry Weslake. The new unit was a great improvement on the old and it was used at first as a special lightweight two-seater version of the SS1, called the SS90 because it was good for 90 mph. This beautiful short-wheelbase vehicle was to be the forerunner of one of the most spectacular sports cars made before the Second World War. No sooner had the SS90 been introduced in March 1935 than a gifted young engineer, William Heynes, was lured from Humber to coordinate the new engineering department: a vital step in Lyons's plan to become self-sufficient and not dependent on others for his mechanical components. This illustrates another Lyons gift: his flair for recruiting talented subordinates.

One of Heynes's first tasks was to help revise the by now complex SS range for 1936: its most important car was to be a new four-door saloon powered by a Weslake overhead-valve conversion on the 2.6-litre engine, which boosted its output from 70 bhp to 105! A smaller version used the existing 1.6-litre unit from the SS2. The SS90 was to continue as the SS100 with the overhead-valve engine taking its performance past the 160 km/h (100 mph) mark and a 3½-litre engine followed for 1938. The SS1's touring body was fitted to the new saloon's chassis to cover that body option. Lyons intended the new range to last at least as long as the SS1 and SS2 and gambled on dramatically low prices to encourage volume sales: only £385 for the saloon, which even experts estimated to be worth twice as much! Such a new range also deserved a distinctive new name and, after consultation with advertising agents, Lyons decided on that of an animal renowned for its grace and speed: Jaguar.

By the end of 1938, production was running at the rate of more than 5000 cars a year and the time was ripe for further expansion. Brooklands race tuning ace Wally Hassan was taken on as chief experimental engineer under chief engineer Heynes, as Lyons started thinking about a new engine all of his own. Plans for that had to be shelved, however, as war intervened in 1939 and SS Cars went over to aircraft and prototype work. It was late in the war, during routine civil defence duties at the factory involving watching for fires, that Lyons, Heynes, Hassan and chief engine designer Claude Baily began dreaming up the new unit: a mass-produced twin overhead camshaft engine.

ABOVE **1936 SS1 Airline saloon.** *The looks were there but so was a six-cylinder side-valve Standard engine, of 2.1 or 2.6 litres. Provided by BL Heritage and Jaguar Cars Ltd.*

The post-war export drive

When the war was over in 1945, the initials SS – which had been for ever tainted by their association with Hitler's Nazi corps – were dropped to be replaced by, simply, Jaguar. Lyons also managed to buy the Standard tooling to continue production of the 2.6-litre and 3.5-litre engines. A 1.8-litre engine introduced in 1938 was still available from Standard, so the post-war range was launched substantially as before,

with three engine capacities, in saloon and drophead forms. The SS100 was dropped to avoid complication. Left-hand-drive versions of these cars, known retrospectively as the Jaguar Mark IVs, were introduced from August 1947 with a special eye on the United States. Although they cost nearly twice as much as their pre-war equivalents, they were still very cheap by post-war standards, and sold well.

Meanwhile Heynes and company had been busy developing the new engine and an ingenious independent front suspension system to improve the car's ride and handling. The new engine was so revolutionary that it could not be put

BELOW **1950 Mark V**. *Available in saloon and drophead coupé form, this model retained the Standard-derived sixes of 2.6 or 3.4 litres. It boasted a new chassis with torsion bar/wishbone independent front suspension. Provided by Classic Cars of Coventry, owner P.J. Masters.*

BELOW RIGHT **XK120s in action**. *Peter Walker leading Stirling Moss in a works car in the 1951 Silverstone Production Car race. Moss went on to win.*

into volume production immediately, but was introduced in a sensational new sports car, the XK120, in 1948. The XK120 used a shortened version of a new chassis with the independent front suspension that was intended for a new saloon, the Mark VII, which is described later. (It was designated the Mark VII, rather than Mark VI, to avoid confusion with Bentley's rival Mark Six.) Such was the complexity of the body for the Mark VII that it could not be put into production until 1950, and in the meantime its chassis was used on an interim model, the Mark V, which replaced the Mark IV Jaguars in 1948. The Mark V was available only with the old 2.6-litre and 3.5-litre engines, and used bodywork developed from the Mark IVs. Like all the other Jaguars before, it sold successfully, but the world was waiting for the new Jaguars.

THE EXCELLENT XKs

The XK120 that was unveiled at the London Motor Show in 1948 was the sports car that had everything: a roadster body more beautiful than anything even Jaguar had produced before; an immensely strong chassis that had taken years to develop; and an engine so sophisticated that it looked as though it should have graced a Grand Prix racer rather than a sports car costing only £988! This was not only the first pure-bred Jaguar engine, it was also the world's first mass-production engine with twin overhead camshafts and hemispherical combustion chambers. Such technical sophistication had only been seen before in racing cars costing a great deal of money and produced only in very small quantities. Lyons, who was the inspiration behind the engine, gambled once more on its staying in production for so long that the tooling and development costs would amount to only a tiny sum on each engine. But even he could not have guessed that the XK unit would be so successful that it would still be powering Jaguars into the 1980s!

The genesis of the XK engine
When this unit was still in the design stage during the wartime fire-watching sessions, even engineers as experienced and adventurous as Heynes, Hassan, Baily and Harry Mundy doubted whether it would be possible to produce a twin overhead camshaft engine for a passenger car. They recognized the advantages of such a layout in that it produced tremendous power, but pointed out that it carried penalties: these engines tended to be very noisy because long chains or trains of gears were needed to drive the camshafts; they were difficult to make, which inevitably meant that they cost more, and were potentially less reliable; and they were far from easy to service. But Lyons would not settle for second best and insisted that he must have a 'twin cam'; what is more, it also had to look good! Once they had expressed their

reservations, Heynes, Hassan, Baily and Mundy worked with a will that resulted in the sensational six-cylinder in-line XK unit that produced no less than 160 bhp from 3442 cc. They had the assistance of Harry Weslake, who was to help extract even more power from the engine as time went on. With bores of 83 mm, the XK engine had a relatively long stroke of 106 mm, which gave it impressive torque. The XK engine's power was enough to propel the 1320 kg (2912 lb) car at more than 190 km/h (120 mph), hence the designation XK120.

A rather 'graunchy', but very reliable Moss four-speed manual gearbox was used in a shortened version of the Mark V saloon's ladder-design chassis. This used conventional half-elliptic leaf-spring rear suspension with a live axle, and Heynes's new independent front suspension, which employed wishbones and torsion bars parallel to the chassis

JAGUAR XK120 (1948–54)		
Number built 12,055		

ENGINE		CHASSIS	
No. of cylinders	Six	Frame	Box
Bore/stroke mm	83 × 106	Wheelbase mm	2591
Displacement cc	3442	Track – front mm	1295
Valve operation	Twin overhead camshaft	Track – rear mm	1270
Compression ratio	8:1, 7:1 or 9:1	Suspension – front	Independent wishbone/torsion bar
Induction	Twin SU carburettors	Suspension – rear	Half elliptic
BHP	160 at 5000, 180 at 5300 rpm	Brakes	Hydraulic
Transmission	Four-speed	PERFORMANCE	
		Maximum speed	201 km/h (125 mph)

sides. His inspiration was the *traction avant* Citroën.

At first the XK120 had an aluminium two-seater roadster body, built in the old manner on an ash frame because Lyons did not envisage making many of these cars. He saw them principally as a mobile test bed for the engine and an advertisement for his planned Mark VII saloon, which would use the same unit in the longer Mark V chassis. The great expense of assembling the giant presses and tools needed for all-steel body construction could be justified only if a large number of cars was to be produced. As it happened, there was such a demand for the car that he had to do just that, although it took until 1950 to tool up for the first all-steel XK120. The demand had been set off, first by the car's spectacular appearance and incredibly low price – there is some evidence that Lyons initially saw it as a loss leader – and, secondly, by a demonstration for the doubting Thomases that it really was capable of the performance claimed when test driver 'Soapy' Sutton managed 213.4 km/h (132.6 mph) with a mildly modified version before astonished journalists on the Jabbeke motorway in Belgium in May 1949.

The first customer cars – mostly for export – left Foleshill in July 1949, a month before three were entered in the new Silverstone Production Car Race. It was Britain's first big motor race since the war in which production cars could be compared, and two of the XKs, driven by Leslie Johnson and Peter Walker, left the field standing. Johnson, who won at Silverstone, went on to perform impressively in America before receiving a new works-supported XK120 in company with Walker, Wisdom, veteran Italian racing driver Clemente Biondetti, and rallyman Ian Appleyard, whose successes with an SS100 included a Coupe des Alpes in the

Alpine Rally. Appleyard had special connections with the factory because, apart from being a Jaguar dealer, his crew consisted of his wife, Pat, who happened to be Lyons's daughter! And their car, registered NUB 120, was to become one of the most successful competition Jaguars.

Johnson spearheaded Jaguar's assault on the classic Le Mans 24-hour race in 1950 and took his near-standard car up to third place, leaving many outright racing sports cars trailing, until failing brakes led to an overstrained clutch and eventual retirement. Even though the car did not finish the race, enthusiasts everywhere were extremely impressed by its showing against far more specialized machinery that could not be bought by ordinary people. And Heynes was convinced that, with a special competition version of the XK120, it would be possible to win the 24-hour race. Lyons agreed and authorized the building of the C (for Competition) type, which went on in 1951 to the first of Jaguar's five victories at Le Mans.

The XK120 fixed head coupé

Production of the Mark VII saloon finally started in October 1950, leaving Jaguar's staff free to work on a fixed-head version of the XK120, which was introduced in March 1951. It met the demand for a car as civilized as the Mark VII saloon without sacrificing the performance of the sports car. This new coupé was like the XK120 roadster (to use the American description which has now become universal; Jaguar preferred to call it a super sports) with an attractive steel top, the lines of which bore a close resemblance to those of the Mark VII. The coupé option continued on the subsequent XK140 and 150.

Soon after, Jaguar provided more options in the form of tuning equipment for customers who wanted to use their XK120s (and Mark VIIs) in competition. These consisted chiefly of higher-lift camshafts, higher compression pistons, larger carburettors, stiffer springs and thicker brake pads; they were based on well-tried items used on the C type. These modifications could boost power to 190 bhp.

LEFT **1951 XK120**. *The magnificent lines are shown to good effect. It proved that a sports car could be a civilized form of transport without sacrificing performance and top speed. Provided by Joss Davenport.*

BELOW **The XK120 coupé** *that took nine international records at the French Montlhéry circuit in 1951. The aerial reveals the presence of a two-way radio. Provided by BL Heritage and Jaguar Cars Ltd.*

Demand for the XK120 and the Mark VII was so great that Jaguar was again faced with the old problem: the factory was not big enough. So Lyons started searching for new premises once more and managed to acquire a modern factory used by Daimler to make cars and buses. Daimler had made armoured cars there during the war, but its needs were contracting and in 1951 the firm decided to centralize its operation on the main works at Radford, Coventry. Jaguar was happy to move into the million square feet at Browns Lane, Allesley, on the outskirts of Coventry, which is still the company's home.

Jaguar was still recovering from the move to Browns Lane and it was not until April 1953 that a new car was launched – in this case a drophead coupé version of the XK120, intended to be driven with the hood down only when the weather was really good. This was particularly important because the flatter, fixed-head style windscreen needed with the wind-up windows set up air currents that whipped around the back of the occupants' necks: fine on a good day but not so pleasant on a bad one!

give a similar effect without changing the roof pressing, although the roofline was raised 25 mm (1 in) to heighten the impression of airiness in the cockpit. The extra space liberated in the drophead (which also had a 25 mm higher hood) and fixed-head coupés was used for two tiny rear seats, which made the cars more appealing to families with small children. At a pinch, an adult could squeeze in the back across the seats for short journeys.

The XK140, which was introduced in October 1954, was easily identified because it had similar bumpers to the Mark VII saloon, a development that gave better protection against clumsy parkers, and a different radiator grille with a new cooling system, following complaints about overheating in traffic. It was also a better car mechanically. The special-equipment XK120's engine was used as standard on all XK140s, with a single exhaust to give 180 bhp, or with a high-compression C type head and twin exhausts to give 210 bhp. The standard XK140 was called the XK140M in the United States (because of its 'modified' engine) and the XK140 with a C type head, the XK140MC, following similar, but unofficial,

RIGHT **1960 XK150S**. *The fastest of all the production XKs, this version with a 3.8-litre triple carburettored engine was capable of more than 210 km/h (130 mph), a power unit that was carried over for the E type of the following year. Provided by John Blake.*

FAR RIGHT **1955 XK140**. *This model has more interior room than the 120, and the rack and pinion steering was a great improvement over the earlier model's re-circulating ball unit. More substantial bumpers were also fitted and the radiator has fewer slats. It was introduced in October 1954 and was available in roadster, fixed-head and drophead forms. Provided by Alan Holdaway.*

The XK140

Jaguar's engineers then devoted their energies to developing the legendary D type sports-racing car for Le Mans (see page 114) before revising the XK120 in the light of comments from sales forces, particularly in the export markets, which took most of the production. The result was the XK140, which used the same body pressings as the XK120 and was available in roadster, fixed-head and drophead forms, but was considerably different under the skin. The chassis was almost exactly the same as that of the XK120 except that the engine was moved forward 76 mm (3 in) to make more room in the cockpit and improve weight distribution from 48 per cent front and 52 per cent rear to nearer 50/50. The central crossmember was modified to allow an overdrive made by Laycock to be fitted as an option, the battery and bulkhead positions were changed, and rack and pinion steering was fitted. The rack, which had been developed for the C type, transformed the car in conjunction with the revised weight distribution and more up-to-date shock absorbers.

On the roadster and drophead cars the bulkhead was moved forward 76 mm (3 in) to give more room in the cockpit; on the fixed-head coupé the bulkhead was reshaped to

designations given to export XK120s. A close-ratio gearbox, which had been available as an option on XK120s since 1953, was now standardized, and more cars left the factory with wire wheels.

This range continued virtually unchanged until October 1956 as the factory concentrated on introducing the Mark 1 saloon (see later) and revising the Mark VII. It was at this point that automatic transmission like that offered on the Mark VII became available as an option on the drophead and fixed-head coupés.

The XK150

Soon after, in May 1957, the XK was revised dramatically for the last time, as the XK150. The XK150, introduced at first in drophead and fixed-head forms, was as near as you could get to an XK saloon. It was bigger and heavier, but a good deal faster in the middle range of its performance because it was fitted with a new B type cylinder head. This developed only 190 bhp but gave the engine a lot more torque in mid-range. The C type head was still available for ultimate top-end performance and the original head became known as the A type. Almost as soon as the XK150 went into production,

following considerable difficulties with a factory fire, it was fitted with disc brakes all round which – like the C type on which they had been pioneered – made the new car far faster from point to point.

The chassis and running gear of the XK150 were substantially the same as on the XK140, but the coachwork looked very different. The body was given a raised waistline with bulbous doors and wings to allow the interior to be widened by 102 mm (4 in). This gave the passengers more room; and they also benefited from a further raising of the scuttle line. A wrap-around windscreen was also fitted now that glass of the right quality was available and the fixed-head coupé was given a large saloon-style rear window to make it feel more spacious and airy. Other body changes included wrapping the rear bumper around the flanks for greater protection and fitting a wider radiator grille to improve cooling further. The fixed-head and drophead coupés shared a similar interior, but the XK150 roadster was far more spartan. This variant was not introduced until March 1958 because the factory was still recovering from the fire, and to have launched it earlier would have added complications to already stretched resources.

Then, in October 1959, an enlarged engine was offered to provide even more power and torque. This was the 3.8-litre unit, which became available on all XK models; it had been under development by the factory since it was first used on a D type in 1956. The factory's version of the 3.8-litre XK unit was considerably different to what had been achieved by people such as Phil Hill. Jaguar stepped up the capacity of the factory engine to 3781 cc by increasing the bore to 87 mm in a new block with dry liners, rather than by boring out the existing 3.4-litre block as practised by Hill and his contemporaries, which had proved risky.

THE BIG SALOON

The Mark VII saloon introduced in 1950 laid the foundations of continuing prosperity for the Jaguar Car Company. It was the culmination of years of development and designed to sell in larger quantities than the XK sports car: although the XK achieved far greater popularity than anticipated, the saloon was still produced at the rate of about 100 per week against the XK's 60 or so. The reasons for its success were threefold: it was extremely good looking, it could carry up to six passengers in great comfort, and it was very fast. In fact, the advertising men who launched the Mark VII had no trouble in backing up their claim that it had unparalleled 'Grace, Space and Pace'.

The chassis was the same as the Mark V saloon except that the 3.4-litre XK engine, which replaced the pushrod unit, was mounted 127 mm (5 in) further forward, to give more room in the passenger compartment. Three of these additional inches were used to increase the legroom at the back, and

the other two inches were taken up by moving the rear seat forward. This meant that the rear wheel arches hardly intruded into the rear-seat space and the luggage boot (trunk) became very large. The rear-seat passengers also benefited enormously from an extra 127 mm (5 in) of interior space achieved by adopting full-width coachwork. This extra space contributed to the additional boot capacity, of course – an important factor in the American market. The Mark VII's 3048 mm (10 ft) wheelbase was no longer than that of most American cars, but its width – 1854 mm (6 ft 1 in) – was greater and there was far less overhanging weight, ensuring better handling. This was vital because of the exceptional performance: with a maximum speed of 166 km/h (103 mph) and a 0–60 mph acceleration time of 13.4 seconds (acceleration standards were conventionally expressed in mph), it was in a class of its own.

Those customers who were more interested in labour-saving devices than outright sporting performance were not neglected either. By 1953, most Americans expected luxury cars to be available with automatic transmission. Rolls-Royce and Bentley were already offering this as an option, so Jaguar could not stand aloof. It would have cost the company much time and money to develop its own automatic gearbox, so Jaguar simply adapted a Borg-Warner, which had originated in America. The Borg-Warner box was modified slightly to suit the XK engine and fitted as an option on export Mark VIIs from mid-1953. Then overdrive was offered as an extra on

manual-gearbox cars from January 1954. This immediately became popular as a fuel-saving device in Europe, where pump prices were high, whereas the automatic gearbox was favoured in North America.

The Mark VII's performance was further improved with the introduction of the Mark VIIM in September 1954, which used a 190 bhp version of the 3.4-litre XK engine with a closer-ratio gearbox. Various styling changes were also made in keeping with those on the new XK140 sports car. It was during this year that the automatic transmission option was finally made available in Britain, before most of the large saloons were fitted with automatic gearboxes from 1956. This was because, by then, Jaguar had introduced a 2.4-litre compact saloon for the more sporting driver.

The VIIM was constantly being improved in production, as the compact Jaguar saloons took over in competition. The B type cylinder head was fitted, the automatic gearbox further improved, and there was a certain amount of restyling, such as two-tone paint and cutaway spats for the Mark VIII's introduction in October 1956. It was also easily distinguished from the Mark VII in that it had a one-piece windscreen rather than one split in the middle. Towards the end of the Mark VIII's relatively short production run, in April 1958, some left-hand-drive versions were fitted with power-assisted steering. This feature, which was popular in America, made the cars much easier to park. It was fitted as standard when the Mark VIII was further developed as the Mark IX in October 1958. The Mark IX was virtually the same as the Mark VIII except that it had the new 3.8-litre XK engine that was to be fitted to the XK150S a year later, and disc brakes all round like the XK150s. The new engine had much more torque than the 3.4-litre unit and greatly improved flexibility, with a good deal of extra performance as well –

184 km/h (114.4 mph) maximum speed against 171 km/h (106.5 mph). This was becoming necessary to keep Jaguar's flagship ahead of its American rivals.

The Mark VIII, in 3.4-litre form, continued in production in small numbers alongside the Mark IX until December 1959. However, the Mark IX went on until late in 1961, when it was replaced by the sophisticated new Mark X (see page 130).

The big saloon range, which had begun with the Mark VII in 1950, had lasted 11 years, during which time over 47,000 had been produced. The Mark VII had also been the most popular model with sales of around 31,000. These were impressive figures for a large, luxury saloon.

THE GLORY YEARS

Such was the performance of the XK120 sports car at Le Mans in 1950 that Lyons authorized a special competition version aimed at winning the race in 1951; and because of the pressure of work on developing the Mark VII saloon for production, Heynes and his team found themselves with only six months in which to prepare the competition XK120 – the C type – before the great race in June. The extent of their work was incredible in view of the time available. The engine's

power was increased by more than 30 per cent to 210 bhp, by means of a new high-compression cylinder head with bigger carburettors and a better exhaust. In addition, a new chassis was designed with torsion-bar rear suspension and the whole car was clothed in a brand-new body! The chassis was very different from the XK120's, being made mainly from tubes to save weight without sacrificing rigidity. The rear suspension was designed with trailing links for better traction than was possible with the standard leaf-spring arrangement.

Le Mans was a glorious début for the C type with Moss, Biondetti and Walker occupying the first three places before Biondetti's car came into the pits with the oil-pressure gauge on zero. An oil pipe in the modified sump had fractured in such a way that it was obvious the same fate might befall the other two cars, and this is exactly what happened to Moss. But Walker and Peter Whitehead drove on with great smoothness and precision, avoiding a critical vibration period which endangered the engine, to win by some 11 km (7 miles) from the Talbot of Meyrat and Mairesse, with Macklin and Thompson third in an Aston Martin.

Numerous other victories followed all over the world. There was John Heath and his star driver George Abbecassis who did well in their all-enveloping H.W.M.-Jaguars. The Edinburgh-based Ecurie Ecosse team also frequently picked up places where the works cars failed or did not enter. Also worthy of mention are the Cambridge-built Lister-Jaguars which first appeared in 1957 and continued to make an impact on the sports racing scene until 1960.

There seemed to be little mechanically that could be improved on the C type for its chief objective, Le Mans, apart from odd points like dry-sump lubrication, which eliminated the oil surge that had ruined the engine's bearings previously. But the body could certainly be improved for a higher top speed.

The D type

The result of this redesign was one of the most beautiful and charismatic racing sports cars ever made, the D type Jaguar produced for 1954. Its aerodynamic lines, with distinctive tailfin, were largely the work of Malcolm Sayer, who had joined Jaguar from the Bristol Aircraft Company. Although the car retained some kind of tubular chassis, particularly on the first ones built in 1954, the centre section was really a monocoque, like an aircraft fuselage. And in the 1954 Le Mans race it showed itself to be capable of 274 km/h (170 mph) – 32 km/h (20 mph) faster than a C type – as it battled for the lead with a team of massive 4.9-litre Ferraris.

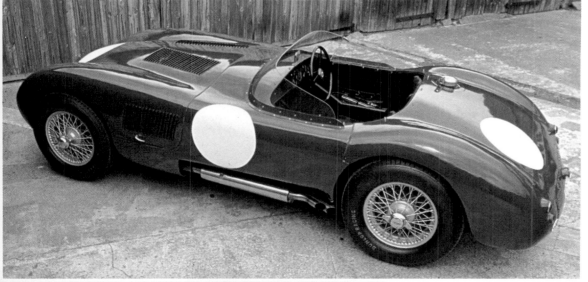

LEFT **1951 C type**. *This car was originally run by the Edinburgh-based Ecurie Ecosse racing team, when it was driven by Jimmy Stewart, brother of Jackie, later to be world champion in 1969, '71 and '73. Top speed is 230 km/h (143 mph). Provided by the Nigel Dawes Collection.*

JAGUAR D TYPE (1955–6)
Number built 62

ENGINE

No. of cylinders	Six
Bore/stroke mm	83 × 106
Displacement cc	3442
Valve operation	Twin overhead camshaft
Compression ratio	9:1
Induction	Triple Weber carburettors
BHP	250 at 5750 rpm
Transmission	Four-speed

CHASSIS

Construction	Monocoque with front subframe
Wheelbase mm	2302
Track – front mm	1270
Track – rear mm	1219
Suspension – front	Independent wishbone/torsion bar
Suspension – rear	Live rear axle, trailing links/torsion bar
Brakes	Hydraulic disc

PERFORMANCE

Maximum speed	274 km/h (170 mph)

Once again Moss, partnered by Ken Wharton, was the pacemaker until the car was eliminated by various ailments. The Ferraris were suffering, too, and eventually the race developed into a thrilling battle between the Ferrari of Gonzalez and Trintignant, and the D type of Rolt and Hamilton. Towards the end, Gonzalez, the Buenos Aires taxi driver known as the Pampas Bull, had to call on his last reserves of strength to win with the ferocious Ferrari by only a minute from the Jaguar in a glorious second place. After that, D types won everywhere, especially when they were put into

LEFT **1955 D type**. *Cockpit of Jaguar's most famous sports racer. The 3.4-litre XK engine, with triple Weber carburettors, develops 250 bhp. The torsion bar front suspension and Dunlop disc brakes are readily apparent. Provided by the Nigel Dawes Collection.*

ABOVE **D types in production** *at Jaguar's Browns Lane factory in 1955. A total of 45 production D types was built in 1955–6.*

BELOW **1966 XJ13**. *The mid-engined 4.9-litre twin cam V12-powered car was built for Le Mans but never raced there. Provided by Jaguar Cars Ltd.*

production for 1955. Cooper, the British racing car builders, also made a special with a Jaguar engine for Walker to compete in the same races as the H.W.M.-Jaguars, but it never achieved the same success.

Meanwhile the works cars were further improved with longer-nosed bodywork for better air penetration. In addition some D types appeared without tailfins to save weight and drag on short circuits where the top speed could not be attained, and the straight-line stability imparted by the fin was not needed.

Le Mans was the big race in 1955 for the works Jaguars, with Hawthorn racing neck and neck with Fangio in a Mercedes. But disaster struck when Levegh's Mercedes collided with Macklin's Austin Healey in a mix-up involving Hawthorn. The Mercedes disintegrated and pieces fell into the crowd, killing Levegh and 81 other people. Moss took over the leading Mercedes as Ivor Bueb replaced the shocked Hawthorn. Eventually all close rivals were eliminated before Mercedes withdrew its cars in sympathy for the dead. The D type soldiered on to win an event marred by motor racing's worst accident.

Jaguar then announced its withdrawal from racing, though in 1956 the Scottish Ecurie Ecosse team entered a D type at Le Mans, and Sanderson and Flockhart took the chequered flag for Jaguar. Thereafter the company maintained a low key interest in the event but in 1960 an experimental car, coded E2A, foreshadowing the E type (see page 116), ran there but retired with engine trouble.

Far more specialized mid-engined cars with wider wheels which could not be used on the road were taking over sports car racing by 1964, and the basically production E types were being rendered uncompetitive. The Jaguar factory, however, had been experimenting with a V12-cylinder engine since 1955, and began thinking again in 1964 about Le Mans. The engine they had in mind was a four overhead camshaft unit with two banks of cylinders at an angle of 60 degrees to each other. The bore and stroke of 70 mm by 87 mm gave a capacity of 4994 cc, producing more than 500 bhp at 7600 rpm. This alloy unit was fitted into an advanced mid-engined monocoque body that strongly resembled a D type's in construction and detail appearance. The suspension was similar in many ways to that of an E type and a ZF five-speed gearbox, which had been used in some of the lightweight E types, was employed. This car, called the XJ13, was completed in 1966 and could have been used at Le Mans that year. But by then, Jaguar was deeply involved in amalgamation with the British Motor Corporation, and any plans for Le Mans were disrupted. Testing showed that the XJ13 could have remained competitive until the late 1960s, but development was curtailed when it became apparent that many changes would have had to be made to accommodate new tyre technology. XJ13 was never raced and the only example is now in Jaguar's own collection.

SENSATIONAL E TYPE

The E type Jaguar that replaced the XK150 in 1961 caused a similar sensation to the original XK120 in 1948. It was quite simply the fastest and most spectacular sports car available to the general public. It was also far ahead of its competitors in that it was based on well-tried components that gave it a rugged reliability. The steel monocoque, which closely resembled that of the alloy D type in its roadster form, was also made with a sleek fixed head; the bonnet was similar to the one on the long-nosed D type with small bumpers reminiscent of those on the XK120, and later ones fitted to a few road-going versions of the D type called the XKSS. The XKSS was exactly the same as the production D type except that it was equipped with tiny slim-line bumpers, a full-width windscreen, silencers and lighting suitable for road use. Some of the very few XKSSs were even fitted with a luggage rack for touring! The object of producing this very fast model in 1957 was to use a surplus of D type parts rather than to launch a car to be produced in quantity.

The E type was the production reality. Its interior was lighter and simpler than the XK150's but the engine and gearbox were the same as in the 3.8-litre XK150S, except that there was insufficient room for the optional overdrive or an automatic transmission. Roadster versions of the E type were available with an optional hard top that followed established Jaguar lines. The front suspension was mounted on a subframe bolted to the scuttle in the same way as the later D types, and was traditional Jaguar in its torsion-bar layout. But the rear suspension was now independent, and based on the system used on the E2A prototype. Wire wheels and disc brakes all round were fitted as standard on this rakish and astonishing machine. Apart from its extraordinarily low

ABOVE **XKSS**. *This car started life as a 1955 production D type, but was converted to roadgoing XKSS specifications by the Jaguar factory for its then owner Phil Scragg. The idea of the XKSS was to utilise surplus D type parts, rather than to launch a new car. Provided by Bryan Corser.*

RIGHT **1962 E type coupé**. *As it was in the beginning, with 3.8-litre engine and covered headlamps. This car is standard, with the exception of D type camshafts and lightened flywheel/clutch. Provided by Derek and Graham Bovet-White.*

basic price of £1600, what stuck in most people's minds was the fantastic performance – 240 km/h (150 mph) on road test with a 0–60 mph acceleration time of only 6.8 seconds, and a fuel consumption of 16.6 litres/100 km (17 mpg). Not only did the E type perform well and sell at an amazingly modest price, but it also looked far more attractive than any of its rivals: a true Jaguar. As could only be expected, the E type, in both fixed-head and open forms, was an immediate sales success, particularly in Jaguar's main export market, the United States.

When the big saloons described subsequently needed more torque, the 3.8-litre engine's capacity was increased to 4.2 litres by using a bigger bore of 92.07 mm, with the existing 106 mm stroke. In this form the 4235 cc engine gave the same 265 bhp but had seven per cent more torque. Performance was slightly down because the XK engine in its 4.2-litre form could not rev quite as fast with reliability as the earlier 3.8-litre. But that change cost only about 8 km/h (5 mph) on top speed. This development of the E type engine, which went into production on all models from October 1964, was allied to a much-improved new all-synchromesh gearbox, in common with Jaguar's contemporary saloons.

In March 1966, the wheelbase of the fixed-head car was stretched from 2438 mm (8 ft) to 2667 mm (8 ft 9 in) and the roof raised to make way for XK150-style rear seats. The original fixed-head body shape continued in production with two seats only as did the roadster, the new model being known as the 2 plus 2. The increase in wheelbase also allowed sufficient room for automatic transmission to be offered as an option. The extra weight and bulk of this variant of the E type brought its top speed down towards the 210 km/h (130 mph) mark, but it soon became popular with customers requiring more room, particularly in the United States.

Safety and emission regulations began to dictate the shape of cars bought by Americans during the mid-1960s – and not always for the better. Jaguar had to cater for these changes,

some of which were so extensive that they would not have been economical had they been introduced purely on North American export models. As a result, the E type's enclosed headlights had to be elevated slightly and exposed in 1967. This, together with other less obvious alterations, and the addition of power-sapping anti-emission devices on North American-specification cars, changed the model's appearance. These were the cars with the original E type slim radiator air intake and exposed headlights that were to become known by enthusiasts everywhere as the 'series 1½'; the original pre-1967 cars became the 'series one'; and later models with a much larger air intake and similar exposed headlights were called, officially this time, the series two.

These series two cars, introduced in October 1968, be-

ABOVE **Series 3 E type** *was the first Jaguar to instal the V12 engine; it also featured the long-wheelbase bodyshell as standard. This example, fitted with a detachable hard top, has won many concours awards. Provided by Alan Hames.*

BELOW **Racing E type**. *This Series 3 V12 E type, modified to Group 44 specifications, was successful in Sports Car Club of America Group B events. Provided by Jaguar Cars Ltd.*

THE BUSINESSMAN'S EXPRESS

The success of the sports cars and the extraordinary performance of the Mark VII saloon established Jaguar's world-wide reputation for highly desirable cars that offered exceptional value for money. Of course, not everyone wanted a two-seater, nor indeed a six-seater. Most customers wanted something in between: a compact saloon with four or five seats and the same Jaguar performance, opulence and value for money. Happily, Jaguar was able to give them just what they wanted in 1955: the Mark 1 saloon. This delightful 2.4-litre car was designed from the start with an eye to economy, but such was its potential that it was soon given the larger 3.4-litre engine to make it one of the fastest saloon cars in the world. It was then developed into what many people considered the greatest Jaguar of them all: the Mark 2 saloon of 1959. To discerning enthusiasts this certainly became the definitive Jaguar and it formed the basis for the more sophisticated saloons to follow: the large Mark X, and the smaller S types, and the Daimler variants when that long-established Coventry car maker was taken over by Jaguar.

The Mark 1 and the classic Mark 2

In the 1950s the Mark 1 saloon's unitary method of construction was a new venture for Jaguar. This type of body – in which the basic shell doubled as the chassis – had an advantage in that it saved weight and was inherently more rigid.

Naturally, this new bodyshell did not abandon all resemblance to the older separate-chassis system. It still had two channel sections running from the front to the rear wheel arches. The steel floor and transverse members were welded to this to form a rigid platform. The scuttle and rear seat pan were welded to this structure with well-reinforced roof supports, and the roof itself formed the top of the box. The outer body was then welded on to the structure for even greater rigidity.

TOP **1957 Mark 1 2.4-litre saloon**. *With the introduction of classic saloon car racing in 1976, this ex-works car won Group B in the series in 1976 and 1977. Provided by Graig Hinton.*

RIGHT **1955 Mark 1 saloon**. *Jaguar's first monocoque, it also heralded the introduction of a 2.4-litre version of the famous XK engine. This example has the popular late-style rear-wheel spats. Provided by Graig Hinton.*

With such a stiff basis to the car, relatively soft suspension could be used, which paid dividends in ride and roadholding. The front suspension was similar to that of the Mark VII saloon, except that it used coil springs rather than torsion bars. This was because Jaguar was not confident that the bodyshell would be strong enough to take the stress of the rear anchorage of the torsion bars. The tops of the coil springs were mounted in turrets on the engine bay sides, with the rest of the suspension on a subframe, which also carried the steering gear. The rear suspension used normal half-elliptic springs turned upside down with one end attached to the live rear axle and the front half clamped to the bodyshell so that they acted, in effect, as quarter-elliptic springs.

All the basic dimensions on the Mark 1 were smaller than those of the Mark VII, especially the engine, which was a 2.4-litre version of the XK unit. This reduction in capacity, aimed at economy, was achieved by reducing the stroke to 76.5 mm, which enabled the engine to rev faster and helped to make up for some of the power lost by the capacity reduction. The original XK cylinder head – retrospectively called the A type – was used with twin Solex carburettors, rather than SU, to save petrol at the expense of all-out performance. Nevertheless, the 2.4-litre Mark 1 was still capable of 154 km/h (96 mph), so its Jaguar pedigree remained intact.

Although the Mark 1 was a great success, selling four times as many as the larger Jaguar saloons, Lyons was not content. He knew it could be improved. Happily, virtually every aspect that had been criticized received attention in the new Mark 2 Jaguar saloon range introduced in October 1959. These cars were to rank among the best-loved Jaguars ever made, and they are still regarded as ultimate classics. The changes that were most readily apparent were in appearance. The windows were made larger, mainly by using slender roof supports now that it had become evident that those on the Mark 1 were thicker than necessary. The rear axle was also made much wider to remove the crab-tracked appearance, with the result that the new car's stability margin was greater. There were other detail changes including a redesigned interior that was not only more modern, but retained the traditional Jaguar image.

The Mark 2's performance was also made even more impressive by three new engine options, all using the B type cylinder head. The power of the 2.4-litre was increased to 120 bhp; that of the 3.4-litre to 210 bhp, and the Mark IX saloon's 3.8-litre engine was fitted to a new top-of-the-range model. This 220 bhp unit gave the Mark 2 a maximum speed of 201 km/h (125 mph) with a 0–60 mph acceleration figure of 8.5 seconds. The ultimate 265 bhp triple-carburettor straight-port cylinder head version of the 3.8-litre unit, as

LEFT **The 3.8-litre Mark 2** *showed its mettle in saloon car racing in the 1960s. The wire, rather than disc, wheels also helped cool the hard-pressed disc brakes.*

BELOW **1962 Mark 2 3.8 saloon.** *Introduced for 1960 the style remained until 1969. Improvements, compared with the Mark 1, included slimmer window pillars, built-in spotlamps and more substantial bumpers. This example is fitted with a full-length Webasto roof. Provided by Graig Hinton.*

fitted to the XK150S sports car, was not used in the 3.8-litre Mark 2 because extensive changes would have been necessary to the engine bay to accommodate the extra carburettor. One of the reasons for using the 3.8-litre unit was that it produced far more torque than the smaller engines, which worked better with the automatic transmission now available as an option throughout the range. The limited-slip differential was fitted as standard to the 3.8-litre Mark 2 because the extra power and torque made it easy to wag the tail of the car when using full throttle from a standstill. Power-assisted steering, as used on the Mark IX saloon, was also offered as an option on the Mark 2.

JAGUAR MARK 2 (1959–67)	
Number built 92,560	
ENGINE	
No. of cylinders	Six
Bore/stroke mm	87 × 76, 83 × 106, 87 × 106
Displacement cc	2483, 3442, 3781
Valve operation	Twin overhead camshaft
Compression ratio	8.1:1 (2.4); 8:1
Induction	Twin Solex, twin SU, triple SU carburettors
BHP	120 at 5750, 210 at 5500, 220 at 5500 rpm
Transmission	Four-speed, optional three-speed automatic
CHASSIS	
Construction	Monocoque
Wheelbase mm	2677
Track – front mm	1397
Track – rear mm	1356
Suspension – front	Independent coil and wishbone
Suspension – rear	Cantilever
Brakes	Hydraulic disc
PERFORMANCE	
Maximum speed	160 km/h (100 mph), 193 km/h (120 mph), 201 km/h (125 mph)

The Mark X saloon

Lyons had kept abreast of technical trends by introducing a new large saloon to replace the ageing Mark IX. This was the Mark X of 1961, the first of a new generation of Jaguar saloons. In some respects it was technically similar to the E type sports car in that it used a wider version of the new independent rear suspension, with front suspension along the lines established by the smaller saloons. The rear suspension not only improved the car's handling but gave the rear-seat passengers a much better ride. The Mark X, which used the same 265 bhp engine as the E type, with the Mark IX's transmission options, was one of the widest cars ever made in Britain. It was also long and low, but the significant dimension was its width of 1930 mm (6 ft 4 in). Not only was the Mark X's body very large, but it was also exceptionally strong, being based on two massive sills – like the E type – with the steel floor to connect them.

At the same time as the Mark X was being introduced in October 1961, the other end of the saloon car range was under consideration. Jaguar had bought Daimler in 1960 primarily to expand production facilities, but in the process the company had found itself with two excellent V8 engines. The larger of these, a 4½-litre, powered Daimler Majestic saloons and could have been used in the Mark X Jaguar, but it seemed likely to endow that car with such a high performance that the other Jaguar saloons would have suffered in comparison. In addition, one of the ways in which Jaguar kept down costs was by virtual standardization of items such as power units. So the 4½-litre V8 did not find its way into the Mark X. But the smaller, 2½-litre Daimler V8 gave such an improvement in the performance of the 2.4-litre Mark 2 saloon that it was put into production, because that was one

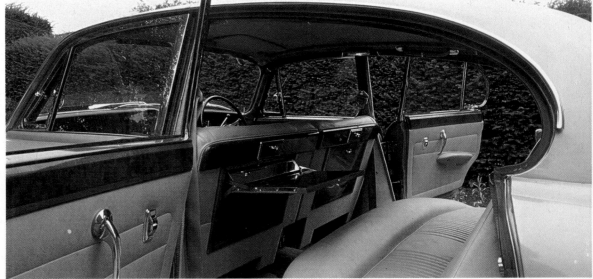

ABOVE RIGHT AND RIGHT **420G**. *The Mark X saloon of 1961–6 was renamed the 420G in 1966 and remained in production until 1970. The engine was a 4.2-litre version of the XK unit, reflected in the model's title, and suspension was all independent. It differed only externally from its predecessor by the addition of a chrome waistline strip and repeater lights on the front wings. Inside, the cars were up to the usual Jaguar traditions of leather and walnut veneer. Occasional tables were a pleasant feature. Provided by Graig Hinton.*

car which could do with some extra urge. A new radiator grille, fluted in the traditional Daimler style, was fitted with different badges, and automatic transmission was standard, when the new car was introduced as an up-market version of the 2.4-litre Mark 2 in November 1962.

There was a considerable demand for a more luxurious version of the compact saloon, and Lyons decided to combine the major improvements of the Mark X with the established features of the Mark 2, once the Daimler had been launched. The result was the Jaguar S type saloon introduced in 3.4- and 3.8-litre forms in September 1963. These cars were similar to the Mark 2 in most dimensions and running gear, except that they had the new independent rear suspension – in narrower form than on the Mark X – and extended rear bodywork, along the same lines as the big saloon, to give more room for luggage.

Lyons's next step was to ring the changes once again by

fitting the 4.2-litre XK engine in twin-carburettor form into the S type saloon to produce the Jaguar 420 – which was an immediate success as a truly luxurious compact saloon. This model, introduced in August 1966, also had its frontal aspect redesigned along the lines of the Mark X with a four-headlamp lighting system, but retained the original Mark 2 narrow bonnet opening to save extensive retooling. A Daimler version with the same engine and running gear, but with a fluted radiator grille and different badges, was introduced at the same time with the model name Sovereign. The Mark X also received a new radiator grille and a little extra chrome – and a new name, the 420G (for Grand) – to please its American distributors.

Next in line for revisions were the Mark 2 saloons and the small Daimler V8. Items such as leather upholstery were made optional extras to keep the price down and the 3.8-litre version was discontinued now that the 420 was in production

LEFT **S type**. *This saloon was introduced in 3.4- and 3.8-litre form in September 1963. It was similar to the Mark 2, but had new independent rear suspension, and extended rear bodywork to give a larger boot. The roofline was also changed to provide better headroom, and new Mark X-type slim bumpers were fitted. After introduction, an improved gearbox was installed. This example has optional wire wheels and Sundym glass. Provided by Phil Docker.*

(although the 3.8-litre S type was still listed). The expensive old Mark VII-style bumpers were replaced with slim-line versions like those on the other Jaguar and Daimler saloons. The new models, introduced in September 1967, were called the Jaguar 240 (with the 2.4-litre engine); the 340 (with the 3.4-litre engine); and the Daimler V8 250 (with the Daimler V8 engine), thus tidying up the nomenclature.

All these cars were to be replaced from October 1968 by a brilliant new saloon, the Jaguar XJ6. But there was one final combination of their floorpans, bodywork, engines and transmission that is still in production today: the Daimler Limousine, introduced in June 1967 to replace British Leyland's Austin Princess, the 4½-litre Daimler Majestic Major limousine, and the occasional Jaguar Mark X or 420G with limousine fittings that had been produced in the 1960s. This enormous car, which used an extended version of the 420G floorpan with the 420G's running gear, was no less than

5740 mm (18 ft 10 in) long and a full seven-seater. As such, with bodywork designed by the British Leyland subsidiary, Vanden Plas, it sells for less than a quarter of the price of a Rolls-Royce.

EVERGREEN XJ SERIES

The XJ6, which was to take over from Jaguar's rather confusing range of saloons in 1968, was one of the most significant cars made. It set new standards in handling, comfort and silence without losing any of the company's established attributes, such as performance and value for money. No wonder a *CAR* magazine panel voted it 'Car of the Year' in 1968 and later, in 12-cylinder form with Daimler livery, the 'Best Car in the World'. Although it was a big car, slightly longer (32 mm; 1¼ in), wider (76 mm; 3 in) and lower in overall height (38 mm; 1½ in) than the 420 from which it inherited most of its running gear, it was in fact based on the 420G. Its proportions were midway between those of the 420 and 420G and, as such, it was one of the best-looking Jaguars. The body followed the 420G's massive form of construction with a wide engine bay and bonnet opening to accommodate the V12 engine, which was still under development during the 1960s.

The new XJ6 (6 for six cylinders) was therefore introduced in October 1968 with either the 4.2-litre engine and transmission options previously available on the 420, or a new economy 2.8-litre version of the XK unit. This was based on the earlier 2.4-litre engine with a bore of 83.1 mm and stroke of 86.1 mm, giving a capacity of 2790 cc. This unit could be revved faster than the earlier XK engines because of its nearly square dimensions and, for a maximum power of 180 bhp, was fitted with the same straight-port cylinder head and SU carburettors as the 4.2-litre. This was enough to propel this relatively heavy new car to 190 km/h (118 mph) with a 0–60 mph acceleration time of around 11 seconds. Capable of 204 km/h (127 mph), the 4.2-litre XJ6 was slightly faster than the 420 because of its superior aerodynamics and could achieve 0–60 mph in 9 seconds.

The old team from Browns Lane showed that it had lost none of its touch with the XJ6. The lines were unmistakably those of Lyons, so much so that the name Jaguar appeared nowhere on the body because everyone knew it was the best of the 'Big Cats'! The engineering was the responsibility of Heynes. It was superb, particularly in the suspension, which varied in detail from that of the 420 and made the XJ6 one of the quietest saloons in the world, and probably the best-handling. The V12 engine that was to transform its performance from 1972 was developed by a team that included

sophisticated combination of rubber mountings – that they were able to use specially designed, very wide, radial-ply tyres from the start. These tyres, made by Dunlop, contributed enormously to the roadholding, but like all radial-ply tyres were inherently more noisy than the earlier cross-plies. The design was so successfully adapted that Jaguar led Rolls-Royce by four years, as the Crewe firm was not able to fit radial-ply tyres until 1972, when it had redeveloped its suspension. As a result, in terms of roadholding and handling, the Rolls-Royce Silver Shadow, which cost four times as much as an XJ6, was simply not in the same league as the Jaguar for this period. No wonder the XJ6 was an immediate success and had long waiting lists from the moment it was introduced.

The Daimler Sovereign continued in production for a year until a Daimler version of the XJ6, also called the Sovereign, was launched; it was distinguished from the Jaguar by a different radiator grille and badges. Daimler Sovereigns, however, sold for a higher price than the equivalent Jaguars and usually had more options fitted, such as electric windows. Production of the earlier Jaguar saloons was eventually terminated when the 420G ended in July 1970, so that as much space as possible could be devoted to XJ6 lines. Around 650 XJ6s were built every week; of these 100 went to the United States – only in Jaguar form as it was not considered worth the expense and complication of qualifying the Daimler version to be sold there. In fact 56 per cent of the total production was exported. During this period, from 1968 to 1972, extensive work was needed to meet US emission regulations and the introduction of the V12 engine had to be delayed several times until it was eventually fitted to the XJ in July 1972.

Hassan, who had returned to the fold when Jaguar took over the engine-builders Coventry Climax in 1963, and Harry Mundy, who rejoined Chief Engine Designer Claude Baily as Chief Engine Development Engineer following a spell as technical editor of *Autocar* magazine. The team was further reinforced by Bob Knight who, as Chief Chassis Development Engineer, had been responsible for the refinement of every post-war Jaguar.

The designers were so successful in their efforts to keep down the road noise on the XJ6 – mainly by the use of a

ABOVE **An American specification Series Two XJ6,** *as available in California. William Lyons exported his cars to America from pre-Second World War days, and today the current XJ6 is still selling strongly in the United States. Provided by Ed Harrell.*

RIGHT **1968 XJ6.** *This model became a best-seller from the moment of its introduction in 1968 and is still being produced at the time of writing. This 4.2-litre example was used by Sir William Lyons until his 1972 retirement. Provided by Jaguar Cars Ltd.*

The arrival of the XJ12

The XJ12 was an astounding car: a full five-seater saloon capable of 233 km/h (145 mph) and 0–60 mph time of only 7.4 seconds; faster than the majority of Grand Touring cars offering inferior accommodation and handling, and often costing three times as much. The only disadvantage was that the XJ12 used fuel at around 23.54 litres/100 km (12 mpg), which was not considered excessive for such a car at that time. There was an immediate demand for the XJ12 everywhere, even in countries where taxation and insurance were based on engine size. It proved the theory that if such potential customers could afford to tax an XJ12 they could manage to pay for the fuel; a view that was reinforced by the relatively small demand for the 2.8-litre, whose capacity had been aimed at taking maximum advantage of European tax laws. Lyons had always considered it wise to market an economical Jaguar, but at that time the majority went for those with the higher performance.

The XJ12 was available only with automatic transmission because there was no suitable overdrive that could cope with the engine's massive torque; but there was so much power and torque available in any case that the extra acceleration that manual transmission would have given was not needed. Apart from the engine, transmission and cooling system, there was little difference between the XJ6 and the XJ12: just more efficient ventilated front brake discs, higher speed rated tyres, and stiffer front springs to cope with the extra weight of the engine (308 kg; 680 lb against 272 kg; 600 lb). The engine bay was packed full, however, and the battery had to be fitted with its own fan to keep it cool! A Daimler Double Six version of the XJ12 was also introduced in 1972, along the lines of the Daimler Sovereign. Both the Daimler and Jaguar models had slightly different trim to their six-cylinder equivalents.

The 12-cylinder engine was not the only variant of the XJ theme that was introduced in 1972. A hurried decision was taken to 'stretch' the bodyshell by 102 mm (4 in) when Jaguar's chief rival, Mercedes-Benz, launched a new longer-wheelbase series. The idea, which was particularly successful on both marques, was to give back-seat passengers more legroom. Jaguar did it by inserting the extra length entirely in the rear compartment, behind the front door line. The weight penalty was only an extra 77 kg (170 lb) on an already hefty 1588 kg (3500 lb). Performance was hardly altered, with an acceleration time to 60 mph of only half a second more. These new models carried an L suffix to denote the long wheelbase.

XJ12 saloon. *The 12-cylinder version of the XJ was introduced in 1972, and in 1981 the model benefited from new, high-efficiency cylinder heads which greatly improved the fuel consumption of its 5.3-litre engine. Other improvements, aimed at better economy, included a higher rear axle ratio and limited slip differential. Note the wash/wipe headlamp cleaners.*

OHP 680 X

By that time, demand for the 2.8-litre XJs had fallen off to such an extent that this model was terminated in April 1973. A relatively ill-fated car, it was beset by piston problems during its early life and, in terms of performance, it paled in comparison with the larger-engined XJs. Only its superior fuel consumption (about 12.84 litres/100 km or 22 mpg against 17.66 litres/100 km or 16 mpg for the 4.2-litre XJ) and slightly lower price could be offered as advantages.

American crash regulations were becoming more demanding every year, and these led to the introduction of a Series Two version of the XJ range in September 1973 that was carried over to the Daimlers in the interests of standardization. The main differences between the earlier cars and the Series Two models were in the outward appearance and in the interior. A new front bumper was fitted 406 mm (16 in) from the ground to comply with laws that decreed that fender heights should be standardized.

The Series Two models were introduced at the 1973 Frankfurt Motor Show alongside yet another variant on the XJ theme: a two-door coupé. This model, which carried the suffix C (for coupé), was especially significant in that it represented Sir William Lyons's last project before his retirement from active design in 1972. The XJC used the short-wheelbase floorpan with larger front doors and a slightly different roofline, but was otherwise substantially the same as the four-door saloons. However, there were considerable problems with sealing and raising and lowering the small rear windows, so the coupés did not go into production until early in 1975. Lyons had insisted that the front and rear windows met in a pillarless construction, which was very elegant, but posed many problems for the development engineers who had to keep down the wind noise on these fast cars! When they were eventually introduced, the option became available throughout the range, except on a Vanden Plas version of the Daimler, which was made in small quantities from 1973 to a higher standard of finish and trim than the Double Six. The coupés also remained in relatively restricted production because, by the time they had been introduced, the short-wheelbase floorpan had been dropped – everybody wanted a long-wheelbase XJ!

Production of XJ6s carried on at the established high level as the world energy crisis during the winter of 1973 and 1974 hit sales of the XJ12. The effects of this crisis on cars such as the Jaguars and Daimlers with their high fuel consumptions led to a considerable number of changes in the range from April 1975. A 3.4-litre economy version of the XJ was introduced, using another version of the XK unit with the 'old' 3.4-litre bore and stroke measurements of 83 mm x 106 mm, in a new cylinder block designed to use the same tooling as the 4.2-litre. Fitting this engine improved fuel consumption to around 14.12 litres/100 km (20 mpg) on manual versions.

The XJ-S

The range was also extended further by the introduction in April 1975 of a new Grand Touring version of the XJ, the XJ-S which had been under development since 1968. This two-

ABOVE **1977 Tourist Trophy**. *Tim Schenken leads team-mate Andy Rouse's racing XJ coupé at Silverstone. Schenken crashed after his front hub sheared, while Rouse later hit an oil patch and also crashed.*

BELOW **1976 4.2-litre XJ6 Coupé**. *This handsome pillarless model was produced between 1973 and 1977, a mere 6505 being built. Provided by Roy Harris.*

plus-two seater fixed-head coupé was also meant to replace the E type sports car, which became defunct at the same time. When the design was under way in the late 1960s, it appeared that the Americans would legislate against open-topped cars in the interests of safety in roll-over accidents. However, such dramatic dictates were seen to be an infringement of the liberty of the people who wanted to buy these cars, but not before most manufacturers had stopped making open-top models. Unfortunately, this decision also came too late for Jaguar, who had decided that the XJ-S would have to be a fixed-head coupé and had designed the superstructure accordingly. This new body structure was mounted on an XJ floorpan, with its wheelbase shortened to 2590 mm (102 in), against the earlier 2764 mm (108¾ in), by moving the rear suspension forward and reducing the size of the rear-seat pan. The front bulkhead and engine-bay sides were modified to take the outer body and the screen pillars were made as strong as possible. Massive 8 km/h (5 mph) impact-absorbing bumpers were built in front and rear in a similar manner to those on the Porsches, the chief competitors in the GT field. The XJ-S's fuel tank was also moved forward to the front of the luggage compartment to protect it from possible impact (the extreme rear mounting of the E type sports car's

tank was one of the reasons why it would not have met the 1975 American impact regulations).

Jaguar's four-speed manual gearbox was offered as an option without overdrive for ultimate performance. With a weight of just over 100 kg (225 lb) less than an XJ12, the XJ-S was endowed with a formidable performance of around 240 km/h (150 mph) with a 0–60 mph figure of 6.7 seconds. Despite some criticism that its lines lacked the flair associated with Lyons, the XJ-S sold well.

Jaguar's return to competition

Jaguar sales, however, could not be compared with the glory years of the late 1960s and early 1970s, although it must be said they were not so badly hit as those of many competitors in the luxury car field. Consequently it was decided by Jaguar's parent firm, British Leyland, to return to international competition with a works team. The decision was taken in 1976, when the XJC was still in production, to use the coupé for an assault on the European Touring Car Championship, which had given one of Jaguar's rivals, the German BMW firm, a large amount of publicity. This made sense at the time because the XJC more closely resembled the standard XJ saloons than the lighter XJ-S. With the relatively untapped

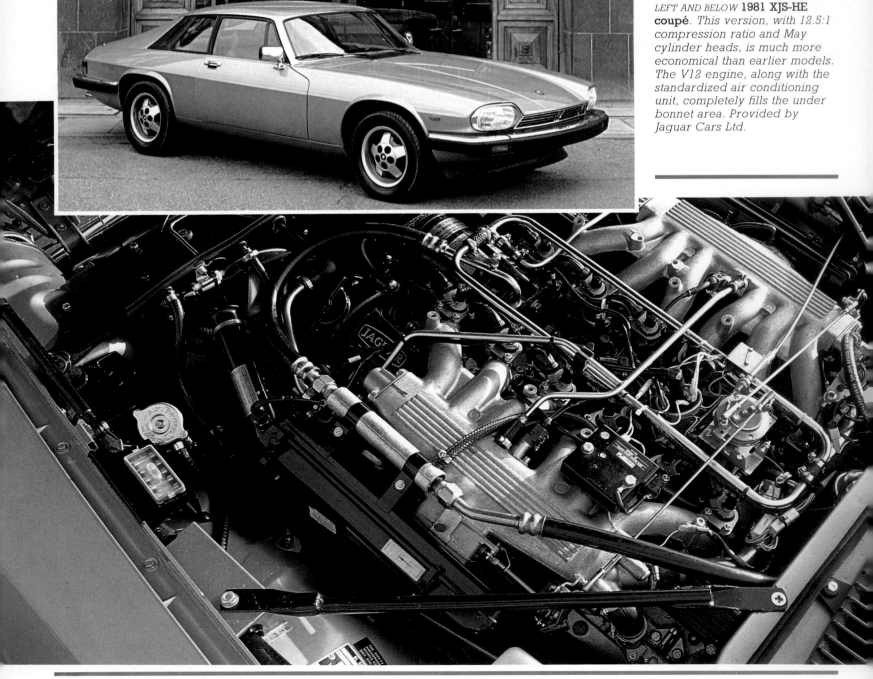

LEFT AND BELOW **1981 XJS-HE coupé**. *This version, with 12.5:1 compression ratio and May cylinder heads, is much more economical than earlier models. The V12 engine, along with the standardized air conditioning unit, completely fills the under bonnet area. Provided by Jaguar Cars Ltd.*

power of the 12-cylinder engine, British Leyland realized that it had a potential world-beater. The British tuning firm of Broadspeed was therefore commissioned to prepare a team of XJCs for long-distance racing, following a great deal of success with smaller Broadspeed Triumph Dolomites in saloon car racing.

It took Broadspeed most of 1976 to prepare the XJCs, however, because of the complex problems associated with making such a heavy car raceworthy. Power was the least of the tuners' problems – they extracted the best part of 600 bhp from their bored-out 5.4-litre engines. The British motor industry supported the effort magnificently, producing special wheels, brakes and tyres. The Jaguars became the great British national team whose début was eagerly awaited in the Tourist Trophy race late in 1976.

Derek Bell and David Hobbs duelled for the lead with a BMW 3.2CSL, driven by Jean Xhenceval and Pierre Dieudonné, before they were sidelined with a broken half-shaft, which was blamed on a flat tyre. Sadly, repeated trouble with items that included half-shafts, and a long delay before regulations allowed dry-sump lubrication, continuously defeated the Jaguars. They hardly finished a race in 1977 despite thrilling the crowds with amazingly fast practice lap times that frequently gave them pole position.

Lyons had envisaged a production run of seven years when the XJ was introduced. But such was its reception and continuing popularity (a Daimler Double Six Vanden Plas was acclaimed in 1977 as the 'Best Car in the World' by *CAR* magazine as a result of comparison with Rolls-Royce, Mercedes and Cadillac) that it remained substantially unaltered when a Series Three version was introduced in March 1979. The Series Three changes applied to the entire range except the XJ-S and the XJC (which had been dropped because it had become uneconomic to produce it in small volume). The main changes in the Series Three were a raised roofline to give more headroom, and bumpers along the lines of those on the XJ-S to meet US safety regulations. An

electrically operated sunroof was fitted – the first as standard on a Jaguar since the Mark IX – and the trim improved. Fuel injection was standardized on the 4.2-litre engine as work continued on their cylinder heads to reduce fuel consumption. This work, instigated by Mundy, was based on revolutionary 'Fireball' principles discovered by the Swiss engineer, Michael May.

The Fireball design was essentially a split-level combustion chamber which ensured rapid and complete burning of a very lean fuel mixture. Jaguar redeveloped the XJ12's cylinder heads under licence from Michael May for a dramatic improvement in fuel consumption and a slight increase in performance when used in conjunction with a higher rear axle ratio. The additional torque and power generated by the May heads enabled the Jaguars to overcome higher axle ratios without a drop in performance and take advantage of them for improved fuel consumption when cruising. After much experimentation, the new cylinder heads were introduced in July 1981 with a 2.8:1 rear axle ratio in place of a 3.07 on the 12-cylinder cars. The top speed was increased by about 8 km/h (5 mph) and the fuel consumption out of town improved to around 13 litres/100 km (22 mpg).

In addition, the XJ-S was revised in detail, in keeping with the Series Three saloons, with new bumpers, wheels and a much plushier interior. This new model was called the XJ-S HE (for high efficiency). The new cylinder heads, with attendant detail modifications to the engine, cost only £500,000 – a very small investment by the standards of 1981.

Jaguar vs BMW

At the same time British Leyland was rationalizing its existing range of sporting cars by dropping the disappointing Triumph TR7 and TR8, which had been made in open form, and concentrating on design studies for a new open Jaguar. Meanwhile former BMW driver Tom Walkinshaw decided that the XJ-S had strong potential against the German marque in the European Touring Car Championship. With finance from the French Motul concern, his XJ-S became more and more competitive in 1982, winning four rounds despite a weight penalty Jaguar returned to the fold officially in 1983, resulting in a season-long duel between two XJ-Ss and dozens of BMWs. In the end, the British cars were narrowly beaten six-five, but triumphed in the championship in 1984. Consequently Jaguar capitalized on the publicity, introducing the Cabriolet, a two-seater, soft-topped version of the XJ-S, in 1983, using a new twin-cam in-line six-cylinder 3.6-litre engine that would power the XJ6's successor, the XJ40, planned for the 1985 model year.

The chief aim of these products is to produce more economical cars without losing any of Jaguar's long-established attributes of outstanding performance, quality and value for money. With so much at stake for such a great and established marque, the only object is to continue producing the 'Best Car in the World'.

JAGUAR XJ-S (1975 to date)	
Number built **Still in production**	
ENGINE	
No. of cylinders	V12
Bore/stroke mm	90 × 70
Displacement cc	5343
Valve operation	Overhead camshaft
Compression ratio	9:1
Induction	Lucus fuel injection
BHP	285 at 3500 rpm
Transmission	Four-speed
CHASSIS	
Construction	Monocoque
Wheelbase mm	2590
Track – front mm	1488
Track – rear mm	1473
Suspension – front	Independent wishbone and coil
Suspension – rear	Independent wishbone/drive shaft, coil
Brakes	Hydraulic disc
PERFORMANCE	
Maximum speed	250 km/h (155 mph)

ABOVE RIGHT **Jaguar XJ-S in action**. *Walkinshaw at Spa in the 1983 European Touring Car event.*

LOTUS

Derived from a glass-fibre special of the 1950s, Colin Chapman's cars are distinctive and mechanically sophisticated. The racing Lotuses brought Britain to the very forefront of Grand Prix competition.

The Lotus marque is very much a child of the post-war world and owes its existence to the outstanding engineering abilities, grit and hard-headed commercial realism of its founder, Anthony Colin Bruce Chapman.

Chapman was born in Richmond, Surrey in 1928 and two years later his parents moved to London's Hornsey, where his father took over the Railway Hotel. Immediately after the end of the Second World War, in 1945, the 17-year-old Chapman entered University College, London to study for a degree in engineering. He was already committed to the internal combustion engine but of the air-cooled single-cylinder variety, for he rode a 350 cc Panther motorcycle though it was destined for a relatively short existence after Colin attempted to enter a taxi cab while astride it! This meant he was without transport but Chapman was lucky when his parents presented him with a maroon 1937 Morris Eight tourer. It was his first car.

ABOVE **1980 Esprit Turbo**, *about to be dispatched from Lotus's factory at Hethel, Norfolk. Its 2.2-litre twin overhead camshaft engine develops 210 bhp, compared with the standard Esprit's 160 bhp.*

LEFT **Lotus's racing workshop**, *pictured in 1981. Although originally based at Hethel, it was subsequently moved to Ketteringham Hall, Norfolk, which also houses Lotus's research and development department.*

Colin used the Eight to commute from his home at 44 Beech Drive, East Finchley to university, though he was soon travelling via Alexandra Park Road to pick up his girl friend Hazel Williams whom he had met at a dance earlier that summer. Another regular passenger in the maroon Morris was fellow student Colin Dare and he and Chapman soon went into the part-time business of buying and selling cars, as anything on four wheels was in demand during those early post-war years. Messrs Chapman and Dare were soon well into the wheeling and dealing world of the second-hand car trade and its switchback economics.

Unfortunately their activities came to an abrupt halt in the autumn of 1947 when the basic petrol ration was cancelled and the pair was left with £900 worth of cars on their hands, some of decidedly questionable value. This was no mean sum in those days. The luckless vehicles were finally off-loaded for £400 and, as the Chapman/Dare balance sheet stood at around £500 at the time, the duo had little to show for their trading activities.

But there was one car that was not sold, a 1930 fabric-bodied Austin Seven, registered PK 3493, which had belonged to an old lady and had been residing, on bricks, in her front garden when young Chapman spotted it. A deal was effectively struck and the Seven had been duly towed away behind the faithful Morris Eight to a lock-up garage behind girl friend Hazel's house. Having been left with the Seven, Chapman decided to turn it into a special. The car was completely dismantled and the body, no doubt in poor condition, discarded. Meanwhile Colin stiffened up the whippy A-frame chassis by adding a further reinforcement to the channel section. But it was the bodywork that Chapman constructed that showed the signs of things to come. It was an open doorless structure and Colin designed it at university, his lectures no doubt suffering in the process. Applying aircraft principles to its construction, Chapman used alloy bonded plywood mounted on a stressed framework along with triple bulkheads, all intended to re-inforce the Seven's flexible frame. The radiator, of beaten copper, was angular and rather distinctive echoing that of a Rolls-Royce.

A Lotus blossoms

The conversion was not completed until 1948 when the Seven was re-registered OX 9292 as a Lotus after Hazel, whom Colin called 'my little Lotus Blossom'. The car was soon in action, for Colin Chapman had intended to use it in trials and the Lotus was entered in two events in the spring of 1948. Shortly afterwards some modifications were carried out; to permit the fitment of wider section tyres, Ford disc wheels replaced the wire ones on the car's rear, while the beam front axle was divided at its centre providing a rather crude independent front suspension layout. Unfortunately Chapman's studies rather interfered with further competitive activities but, at the end of the year, Colin obtained his bachelor of science engineering degree.

This was followed by National Service in the Royal Air Force but Chapman still found time to produce a second Lotus, the original vehicle being retrospectively titled Mark One. This was built in the same lock-up garage and was also Austin Seven based. Its body was smaller and less angular than the original rendering and the Seven engine proved inadequate for trials, so Colin fitted a side-valve Ford Ten unit while the transverse leaf front suspension also hailed from Dagenham. The Mark Two was completed in 1949 and first used by Chapman in trials events the following year.

The car also had to serve as Colin's regular transport but the fact that it was open meant it was not an ideal all-weather vehicle and so an Austin Seven saloon was purchased for everyday motoring. Nineteen fifty-one saw a shift away from trials cars, which were becoming continually more specialized, towards 750 cc Formula racing, and Chapman was al-

ready a member of the 750 Motor Club. He therefore became intent on producing a car that could effectively take on and trounce the opposition on the race track. So the Ford-engined Mark Two was disposed of, though it later attained immortality by featuring in the Boulting Brothers' 1957 British comedy *Brothers in Law*. Chapman had also parted with the Mark One Lotus by this time.

So yet another 1930 Austin Seven saloon was purchased, for £15 on this occasion, and at this time Colin had the good fortune to meet up with two brothers, Michael and Nigel Allen, who were also 750 racing enthusiasts. The latest Seven was to form the basis of the Mark Three Lotus and the Allens decided to build two identical cars. But, even more significantly, they had a well-equipped workshop at the bottom of their garden, so work on three Mark Three Lotuses began in January 1951 at the brothers' Wood Green premises. It was the first of Chapman's cars to be built purely for racing and the chassis was reinforced in the established manner, with two stronger cross members replacing the original ones. In the first instance the two main bearing engine was retained but soon after the car was completed it was replaced by a stronger three-bearing unit. Chapman was already acutely conscious of the weight-saving demands of car design and produced a neat two-seater aluminium body which weighed only 29.5 kg (65 lb), complete with its hoops and, very professionally, an undershield was also fitted. A radiator cowl similar to the Mark Two car was employed and it also embodied the car's headlamps.

The Mark Three made its competition début at the 750 Motor Club's Castle Combe race meeting in May 1951 with Chapman taking first place in a ten-lap race, lapping everyone except for the second man home. This reflected the fact that Colin had made his own unique modification to the engine by dividing the inlet manifolding and ports, thus improving engine breathing and gas flow. By the end of the season and with a string of successes to his name Chapman became known as the driver and constructor of by far and away the fastest 750 racer in the country. Before long other enthusiasts began asking him for replica Mark Threes and Colin realised that he had outgrown the Allen brothers' facilities and would have to look around for larger premises of his own, no doubt to the relief of the neighbours.

A new home for Lotus

He found the answer on his own doorstep because his father allowed him to use part of the stable block at the rear of the Railway Hotel in Hornsey. He decided to go into partnership with Michael Allen, who was to devote himself full time to the special building business while Colin, who had recently got a

job as an engineer with British Aluminium, was the part time half of the enterprise. Fortunately the Lotus Engineering Company, as it became on 1 January 1952, already had an order for a car from the owner of Chapman's old Mark Two trials car which was beginning to show its age. Therefore Chapman began work on a design that was to become the Mark Four Lotus. The resulting car was again Austin Seven based and Ford Ten powered and was also equipped as a road car. In theory the next Lotus should have been the Mark Five but this was purely a paper project. It would have been a 160 km/h (100 mph) Austin Seven-based sports racer but it was never built; for Chapman was pushing ahead with the idea of offering a car in kit form that the customer could then assemble himself.

The result was the Mark Six Lotus. It was effectively Chapman's first production sports car and is especially significant because it was the first Lotus model that dispensed with the Austin Seven frame. This was a far more sophisticated offering with a multi-tubular chassis, while the front suspension was a crude swing axle independent layout with coil springs. Coils were again used at the rear in conjunction with the live axle. Although the prototype was powered by a Ford Consul four-cylinder engine, the car was so designed that it could be fitted with almost any power unit of up to 1500 cc. It achieved a second place on its first Silverstone outing in 1952, though it was later written off in an accident while being driven by Michael Allen's brother Nigel. It was at the end of 1952 that Michael Allen decided to leave the partnership, taking the remains of the Mark Six prototype as his share in the company.

However, Chapman was convinced that a living could be made producing cars for club racing. His enthusiasm won over his girl friend Hazel and she loaned him £25 which bought new stationery and office equipment and in February 1953 the firm became the Lotus Engineering Company

Limited. Colin's optimism was justified and by the time the Mark Six ceased production in 1955 around a 100 had been built, fitted with a variety of engines ranging from the 1172 cc Ford side-valver, an old Chapman favourite, to a rather more sophisticated 2-litre BMW unit.

Chapman and the Costins

In these early days Colin was assisted in the design and draughting by Peter Ross and 'Mac' Mackintosh, who were both employed by the De Havilland Aircraft Company at Hatfield, Hertfordshire. It was through them that Chapman met another De Havilland employee, Mike Costin, who later joined the small Hornsey team and proved a tireless and inspired worker. Meanwhile Chapman was pressing ahead with yet another sports racer, the Mark Eight, with a triangulated spaceframe intended to produce the maximum of rigidity with the minimum of weight. The only trouble was that when the prototype was completed in 1954 it took 12 hours to remove the M.G. engine from the network of tubing and double that to replace it! Front suspension followed Mark Six practice though a de Dion axle featured at the rear. But the really significant aspect of the Mark Eight was its aerodynamic bodywork which was the work of Mike Costin's brother Frank, an aerodynamicist with De Havilland. It was a distinctive and impressive offering and reflected the importance Chapman gave to good aerodynamics that featured on practically every Lotus afterwards.

The Mark Eight had a low nose for good air penetration while two large fins to provide directional stability dominated the car's rear. Even the headlamps were made fully retractable in the interests of air flow. After an unfortunate crash, Chapman's prototype, memorably registered SAR 5, became the fastest M.G.-engined sports racer in the country. As in the case of the Mark Six, customers were soon demanding similar cars which were powered by a range of engines of which the most notable were 1100 cc Coventry Climax units and a 1½-litre Connaught four. However, 1954 was not all work for, in October, Colin and Hazel were married and moved to a small cottage at Monken Hadley, near Barnet, Hertfordshire. It was to be the venue of many a Lotus 'board' meeting.

It was soon after his marriage that Chapman decided to devote himself completely to Lotus activities and on 1 January 1955 he and Mike Costin became full-time Lotus Engineering employees. The designs continued to spew forth from the tiny Hornsey workshop. The Mark Nine was a smaller-engined version of the Mark Eight, while the Ten was intended to take larger power units. In addition, Chap-

man's reputation was growing; the first two Mark Nines, for instance, went to American owners to race at the Sebring circuit. Also Lotus cars were giving a good account of themselves in sports car racing on both British and European tracks either campaigned by Lotus themselves or privately entered by a growing band of enthusiastic owners. Nineteen fifty-five marked the make's first Le Mans sortie, when Chapman drove a Mark Nine though it was disqualified, much to his disgust. It was during the year that the firm applied and was accepted for membership of the Society of Motor Manufacturers and Traders and was consequently able to exhibit at the annual Earls Court Motor Show. So Lotus Engineering took a stand at the 1955 event displaying its front and rear suspension systems and chassis frames rather than complete vehicles. They would have to wait until 1956.

The following year Chapman and Costin decided to bring some sense of order to the somewhat haphazard nature of

Lotus operations by producing just one chassis which nevertheless permitted a number of variations. The Lotus 11 was derived from the Mark Nine and was mostly Coventry Climax engined, the unit having first appeared in the earlier model. In its most expensive Le Mans form it was fitted with a de Dion rear axle while the Club version had a live unit with the bottom of the range Sports model having the cheap but reliable Ford 100E engine under its bonnet. The 11 proved to be the most successful Lotus produced so far, with nearly half of the 150 built going to American owners. Le Mans proved altogether more successful for Lotus in 1956 for, although Chapman's 11 retired with big-end failure, another driven by Peter Jopp and Reg Nicknell won the 1100 cc class and was placed seventh overall. Chapman's disqualification of the previous year was thus avenged!

But Chapman was not a man to rest on his laurels and he and his small design team were pushing ahead with a single-seater racing car aimed at Formula Two events, with a 1½-litre engine capacity limit. The Lotus 12 drew on the 11 for some of its inspiration but many of its features were new. The swing axle layout that featured on all Lotus models since the Mark Six of 1953 was dispensed with and replaced by a more conventional wishbone layout, and initially a de Dion rear axle with coil spring featured. However, this was soon discarded and replaced with what became known as a Chapman strut, after its inventor, which was an independent strut-type suspension which greatly improved the car's handling. The 12's chassis was a tubular structure while the engine was a twin overhead camshaft 1½-litre Coventry Climax unit. To permit the lowest possible seating Chapman very ambitiously decided that the car should have a combined rear axle and gearbox unit, no small undertaking for a firm with somewhat limited resources. In this design Chapman was assisted by Harry Mundy, formerly of Coventry Climax and at the time technical editor of *The Autocar* and Richard Ansdale. The layout meant that gear ratios could be quickly changed, a great advantage as racing circuits varied considerably in concept and gradient. During their first season the cars performed with sporadic success but there were the inevitable teething troubles with the complex rear axle/gearbox unit. Seven cars were made during 1957; all but three were team cars run by the Lotus factory.

TOP LEFT **Mark 8 Lotus.** *John Coombs' Lotus 8 in action. Beneath Frank Costin's aerodynamic bodywork is a spaceframe chassis and de Dion rear axle.*

ABOVE **Mark 10,** *and a larger engined version of the Mark 8. A 2-litre Bristol engine was a popular fitment.*

LEFT **Lotus Mark 11.** *Built between 1956 and 1958, the 11 was a replacement for the Mark 9 car, a smaller-engined version of the Mark 8.*

Success at Le Mans

Le Mans in 1957 proved a considerable success for Lotus when five cars were accepted for the event with four lasting for the 24 hours and the marque being placed first and second in the prestigious Index of Performance rating. In addition, a Lotus driven by McKay Frazer and Chamberlain set a new record in the 751 to 1100 cc class.

The observant reader will have no doubt noticed that seven had so far not appeared in the Lotus model nomenclature, and this is because the Mark Six's replacement did not appear until the 1957 Motor Show. The rapid strides that Chapman had made in design were reflected in the model having wishbone independent front suspension, as pioneered on the Formula Two car, in place of its predecessor's swing axle, and a coil-sprung live rear unit was employed. A Ford 100E side-valve engine featured in this exceptionally low car which measured just over 69 cm (27 in) from the ground to the top of the scuttle. The car was also very light, in the best Lotus traditions, and turned the scales at only 324 kg (714 lb). In addition to the Ford-powered version, a Coventry Climax-engined Super Seven was offered, while the good mannered BMC A Series unit also became a factory option. A Series Two version followed in 1960, though the multi-tubular chassis was simplified to some extent and there were improvements to the steering and suspension, and rather better weather protection. Later cars had longer flowing wings in place of the original cycle-type ones.

Although ostensibly outdated, the Seven soldiered on with a Series Three version appearing in 1968. It was still Ford powered (Escort or Cortina) while the Super version had a twin cam unit. In 1970 there came a Series Four car which dispensed with the tubular chassis and replaced it with a steel ladder chassis, and glass fibre took over completely as the body material. But, although it sold fairly well during its first couple of years, sales soon dwindled as many enthusiasts looked upon the car as a positive step away from the original concept. The model therefore faced the axe in 1973 but Caterham Cars of Caterham, Surrey decided it would be worth taking the model over and Lotus granted them a licence to manufacture it. Re-named the Caterham Seven, the Series Four car was manufactured for a year but then the Series Three model, in improved form, took its place and this Super Seven continues in production at the time of writing, 27 years after it was first announced.

BELOW LEFT **1969 Lotus Seven Series Three**. *The Brand Lotus aluminium wheels were an optional extra.*

LEFT **1958 Lotus Elite**, *the world's first glass-fibre monocoque, Coventry Climax-engined and magnificently styled by Peter Kirwan-Taylor.*

LOTUS ELITE (1958–63)
Number built 998

ENGINE	
No. of cylinders	Four
Bore/stroke mm	76 × 66
Displacement cc	1216
Valve operation	Overhead camshaft
Compression ratio	10:1
Induction	Single SU, twin SU carburettors
BHP	71 at 6100, 83 at 6250 rpm
Transmission	Four-speed

CHASSIS	
Construction	Glass-fibre monocoque
Wheelbase mm	2235
Track – front mm	1143
Track – rear mm	1143
Suspension – front	Independent transverse wishbone and coil
Suspension – rear	Independent Chapman strut
Brakes	Hydraulic disc

PERFORMANCE	
Maximum speed	180 km/h (112 mph)

The sensational Elite

But back to the 1950s when the Lotus marque was still finding its feet! A major landmark in the company's fortunes appeared at the 1957 Motor Show for the Lotus stand featured the firm's really significant road car, the Elite, which was the world's first glass-fibre monocoque car. Chapman had long nursed the ambition of producing a lightweight coupé for the general motorist to be marketed alongside the cars he provided for the out-and-out sports enthusiast. He shared these thoughts with Peter Kirwan-Taylor, who had become a close friend since the latter had purchased his own Mark Six in 1953. It was to prove to be a far-reaching purchase.

Although on the point of becoming a fully qualified chartered accountant, Kirwan-Taylor had a great interest in body styling and he had already produced a design for his own Mark Six. He agreed to style the new car which carried the 14 mark number and there was much midnight oil burnt at the Chapman home as the design evolved. For not content with it being the first closed Lotus, Colin had decided that the car should have no chassis, the glass-fibre bodywork doing duty as such, something which had never previously been attempted by a car manufacturer. Invaluable help came from John Frayling, then working for Ford, and Frank Costin, who contributed aerodynamic advice. The result was a visual sensation, arguably one of the best-looking closed British cars of the 1950s. It was, inevitably, Coventry Climax-powered and the suspension echoed that of Lotus Formula Junior Mark 12. However, it was not until December 1958 that the first production Elite was handed over to its owner Chris Barber, the bandleader. But it was after Lotus had moved to new premises in Delamare Road, Cheshunt, Hertfordshire in June 1959 that production really got under way, with an improved Series Two version appearing in 1961. With the coming of the Elite, Lotus established itself as a quantity car manufacturer even though fewer than 1000 Elites were made before production ceased in 1963. Although the car's performance echoed its good looks it proved unbearably noisy, a legacy of its unique construction, and Chapman calculated that the company was losing £100 on every one sold. Nevertheless invaluable design and production lessons were learnt with the Elite which paved the way for the profitable Elan in 1963.

While the Elite was going into production Lotus was pressing ahead with its latest sports racer, the 15, intended to take engines in the 1½- to 2½-litre range and again of Coventry Climax manufacture. But the really big event of 1958 was Lotus's first Formula One car, the 16, with Chapman following in Cooper's wheel tracks by mounting the 2½-litre Coventry Climax engine *behind* the driver. Front suspension followed the proven wishbone layout, though at the rear the familiar

Chapman strut was dispensed with, as there was insufficient height for it to be employed effectively, and a double transverse link featured. The cars suffered from some mechanical shortcomings but by the conclusion of 1960, when the 2½-litre formula came to an end, Lotus had won two grands prix and Stirling Moss, who had driven the winning car on both occasions, was third in the drivers' world championship. These successes were attained in the Lotus 18, the 16's successor; its 1961 derivative, the 21, with body-hugging front suspension units to improve air penetration, paved the way for even greater things.

A REVOLUTION IN MOTOR RACING

Innes Ireland had taken the chequered flag in a Lotus 21 at the 1961 American Grand Prix and the little car harried the Ferrari opposition to effect in other events. When fitted with the new Coventry Climax V8 in place of the four-cylinder unit it was redesignated the 24 and looked all set for an impressive 1962 season. But Lotus astounded the opposition by producing the 25, the first monocoque racing car in the world and destined to revolutionize single-seater design. The car's body was 5.5 kg (12 lb) lighter than its spaceframe predecessor and the use of rubber fuel bags in place of aluminium tanks saved a further 22.5 kg (50 lb), while engine and suspension were carried over from the 24. The car made its first sensational appearance at the Dutch Grand Prix at Zandvoort in May 1962 and, at a stroke, it rendered the multitube spaceframe design obsolete. Unfortunately the car went out with clutch trouble and Monaco proved unsuccessful, but Jim Clark won the Belgian Grand Prix at Spa and went on to win four more championship events, just being beaten to the world championship by Graham Hill in a BRM.

However, 1963 proved to be a golden year for Lotus, with the marque winning its first manufacturers' cup and Clark becoming the world championship driver. Although the following year was less successful the Clark/Lotus combination repeated the double in 1965; this time the Flying Scotsman was at the wheel of the 25-derived Lotus 33. Significantly by then every other Formula One competitor, bar two, had followed Chapman's example and adopted monocoque construction for their racing cars.

Chapman caused a trans-Atlantic flurry in 1963 when Jim Clark was placed second in the famous Indianapolis 500 race in a car that Lotus had built specially for the event. It had been in 1962 that American racing driver Dan Gurney acted as an intermediary between Colin Chapman and the Ford Motor Company, with the result that the latter supplied a 4.2-litre version of its Fairlane V8 engine. This was fitted in a specially lengthened Formula One Lotus 25, and the resulting 29 was both larger and wider than its predecessor. Two cars were built with Gurney being placed seventh in the 1963 event though Clark's second place indicated that Lotus was in earnest.

The cars were revamped for 1964 with improvements to the suspension and transmission, more powerful engines were fitted and, although both Lotuses were undoubtedly the fastest cars in the field, tyre troubles put Gurney and Clark out of the race. In 1965 the cars, by then full monocoques and redesignated Lotus 38s, tried again and this time there were no mistakes when Jim Clark took the chequered flag at a record average of 242.49 km/h (150.68 mph). It was the first win at Indianapolis by a European car for 49 years, the first time a British marque had won the event, and the first occasion on which a rear-engined car had been victorious there. Clark gained a second place at the 1966 event when, significantly, practically every other car was rear engined. The age of the archaic front-engined roadsters was over and it had taken the superlative driving of Jim Clark and Colin Chapman's design expertise to show the Americans the error of their ways.

LEFT **1964 Dutch Grand Prix**. *Jim Clark in his Coventry Climax-engined Lotus 25 in which he won the event.*

BELOW **1965 Indianapolis 500 Mile Race**. *The first win at the American circuit by a European car for 49 years, Jim Clark in his victorious Lotus 38.*

ABOVE **1962 Lotus 25 and 1964 Lotus 33**. *The 25 (in background) was the world's first monocoque racing car and in 1963 gave Lotus its first Manufacturers' Cup and Jim Clark the World Drivers' Championship. The 33 derivative of 1964 saw both Lotus and Clark repeat the feat in 1965. In both instances a 1½ litre Coventry Climax V8 engine was fitted.*

LEFT **Jim Clark**, *victorious at the Brands Hatch-staged British Grand Prix in 1964 which he won at a speed of 151.5 km/h (94.14 mph) in a Lotus 25. Colin Chapman can be seen on Clark's left. BRM (Graham Hill) and Ferrari (John Surtees) were in second and third places respectively.*

The Elan takes over

Lotus's first sortie into production cars had, it will be recalled, been the Elite. This had been offered in kit form from 1962, a favourite Chapman ploy to speed up sales of a slow-moving model and for 1963 it was replaced by the Elan. The Elite with its revolutionary monocoque construction did have a major shortcoming because it could only be offered in closed form as the roof provided essential reinforcement, though many Lotus enthusiasts delighted in the joys of open air motoring. As a result the Elan was an open car so this meant that Chapman would have to revert to the use of a chassis frame. Carrying the 26 factory designation, the Elan was built up around a fabricated backbone but it was predictably ingenious being splayed at either end to receive respectively the independent rear suspension and twin overhead camshaft engine which appeared with the model.

Chapman had long wished to develop his own engine and initially work began on a 1600 cc Ford Consul unit. But then, in 1959, Ford announced its new Anglia model and its power unit looked a far more acceptable proposition from a technical standpoint. Harry Munday and Richard Ansdale, who had been involved with the Formula Junior Mark 12 Lotus, were called in and Munday designed an aluminium twin overhead camshaft cylinder head that could be mated with the Anglia block which was of 997 cc. However, in 1961 Ford launched its 1340 cc Classic and Lotus immediately recognized that the engine would provide a far better basis for its new power plant. The experimental unit ran for the first time in October 1961 but Ford developments again outstripped the Cheshunt engineers when the Classic was offered in 1962

with a new 1498 cc engine with a robust five-bearing crankshaft. However, work continued on the original unit until Chapman was able to obtain one of the new blocks and an experimental engine was fitted in a sports racing Lotus 23 which Jim Clark drove in the 1962 Nürburgring 1000-Kilometre race. Although he had to retire after an exhaust flange broke, Clark managed to lead the race for a time and also put in a record-breaking lap. Initially the 1498 cc unit was fitted in the Elan but, after about 50 cars were built, the engine capacity was upped to 1588 cc and the earlier cars recalled.

This potent engine gave the Elan a 160 km/h (100 mph) plus top speed and, although the car perhaps lacked the sensational good looks of the Elite, the model and its derivatives were to continue selling for ten years. The open two-seater glass-fibre body contributed to an overall weight of 584 kg (1290 lb) while its vacuum-operated headlamps which swung into position when in use, thus permitting a more aerodynamically efficient forward profile, were a notable feature. The car sold for £1499.

A programme of continual refinement began with a Series Two Elan, featuring improved brakes and better interior with veneer dashboard, which appeared for 1965. That September the Series Three Elan arrived in fixed-head coupé form with electric windows, while November saw the introduction of a close ratio gearbox option. A Special Equipment version of the Elan became available at the beginning of 1966 with engine output increased from 105 to 115 bhp and close ratio gearbox, centre lock wheels and servo-assisted brakes as standard equipment. In June 1966 a Series Three convertible Elan was introduced.

LOTUS ELAN (1962–73)
Number built 12,224

ENGINE

No. of cylinders	Four
Bore/stroke mm	82 × 72
Displacement cc	1558
Valve operation	Twin ohc
Compression ratio	9.5:1, 10.3:1
Induction	Two twin-choke Weber, or Dellortos, or Zenith Stromberg carburettors
BHP	105 at 5500, 115 at 6000 rpm
Transmission	Four-speed

CHASSIS

Frame	Backbone
Wheelbase mm	2438
Track – front mm	1143
Track – rear mm	1143
Suspension – front	Independent wishbone and coil
Suspension – rear	Independent strut, single wishbone and coil
Brakes	Hydraulic, front disc

PERFORMANCE

Maximum speed	182 km/h (113 mph)

BELOW **1971 Elan + 2 S130**. *The +2 Elan was introduced in 1967; this version is distinguished by its silver roof and is powered by the 126 bhp Sprint engine. A five-speed gearbox followed in 1973.*

ABOVE **1972 Elan Sprint**. *The Sprint arrived in 1971 and was powered by a big-valve version of the versatile twin cam engine. Strengthened drive shafts also featured to cope with the extra power.*

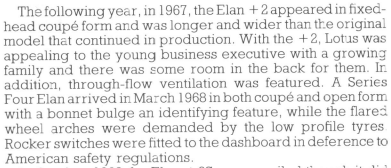

The following year, in 1967, the Elan +2 appeared in fixed-head coupé form and was longer and wider than the original model that continued in production. With the +2, Lotus was appealing to the young business executive with a growing family and there was some room in the back for them. In addition, through-flow ventilation was featured. A Series Four Elan arrived in March 1968 in both coupé and open form with a bonnet bulge an identifying feature, while the flared wheel arches were demanded by the low profile tyres. Rocker switches were fitted to the dashboard in deference to American safety regulations.

In October 1968 the Elan +2S was unveiled though it did not go into production until March of the following year and was the first Elan not to be offered in kit form. Improvements were mainly confined to the interior but fog lamps were also standardized. The Elan +2 was dropped at the end of 1969 though the +2S continued in production alongside the original model, which was re-named the Sprint in February 1971. The latter was easily identifiable by its duo-tone paintwork and there was a 126 bhp engine under the bonnet. Simultaneously the Elan +2S 130 made its début powered by the Sprint engine and distinguishable by its silver roof. For 1973 the +2S benefited from a five-speed gearbox and all models ceased production that August.

The Ford Cortina Lotus

The Lotus Elan engine was also used in Ford's new Cortina saloon from 1963, the resulting Mark 28 Cortina Lotus proving a potent 160 km/h (100 mph) model. Although closely resembling the production car, there were some subtle differences in its construction. The door, bonnet and boot lid were aluminium while the clutch housing, gearbox extension and differential casing were also made from the material. In a bid to improve roadholding, Lotus dispensed with the Cortina's leaf-sprung rear and replaced it with an A bracket layout. But the arrangement proved troublesome and the model reverted to its traditional layout from mid-1965. Other departures from standard were an improved interior with special seats and aluminium finished instrument panel.

The Cortina Lotus was only produced in two-door form with white paintwork and distinctive green side stripes. The cars were completed at Lotus's Cheshunt factory where the twin cam engines and suspension changes were introduced. A team of special Cortina Lotuses was also prepared by the factory for use in Group Two racing events where they proved very successful. Ford themselves ran an equally successful team of cars in rallies both at home and abroad. In 1966 Ford replaced its best-selling Cortina with a Mark Two car and there were no more Lotus-assembled models. Nevertheless the Cortina Lotus name continued on the Dagenham-built successor. In any event, at the end of 1966 Lotus was on the move again to new premises at Hethel, near Norwich. The new factory was built on a pleasant 16-hectare (40-acre) site so there was plenty of room for expansion and the 2.4 km (1½-mile) test track was a further bonus.

Lotus, like other British racing car constructors, was thrown into confusion in 1965 when Coventry Climax, who had produced high performance engines for ten years, announced that they could no longer do so. Lotus was therefore forced to adopt a BRM engine of dubious dependability for 1966. Fortunately help was at hand in the shape of the Ford Motor Company, who were building up a formidable performance image in the 1960s of which the Cortina Lotus was a part. It was Ford's director of public affairs, Walter Hayes,

1964 Oulton Park Gold Cup Saloon Car Race. *Mike Spence at the wheel of one of the works Cortina Lotuses in an event that was dominated by these fast Fords (Jim Clark first and Bob Olthoff second), ahead of Jack Brabham in a Ford Galaxy.*

who in the first instance agreed that the company would contribute £17,500 to Cosworth Engineering, because he wanted to develop a new Formula Two engine based on the Cortina block. The Cosworth firm had been established by two former Lotus employees, Mike Costin and Keith Duckworth (hence the company name), and had made its mark by producing Formula Junior engines based on the Ford Anglia unit in the early 1960s. The contribution that Hayes arranged ensured that the resulting power unit would carry the Ford as well as Cosworth names on its valve cover but, significantly, it was the first occasion that the company had made a financial contribution to an independent.

The world's most successful Formula One engine

With this precedent established, Colin Chapman invited Walter Hayes to dinner and then vigorously expounded on the need for a new British Formula One engine in the wake of Coventry Climax's decision to withdraw from the market. Hayes, who knew Chapman of old – he had once employed Lotus's founder as a motoring correspondent when he had edited the *Sunday Dispatch* – was impressed by the force and cogency of Chapman's arguments, succeeded in obtaining corporate backing for a new engine and it was agreed that £100,000 be paid to Cosworth to develop two engines, the aforementioned Formula Two unit and a completely new Formula One 3-litre. The contract specified that the latter should be completed by May 1967 and Keith Duckworth was soon at work on the design of a V8 engine characterized by its four overhead camshafts and four valves per cylinder. It was designated the Ford Cosworth DFV, the initials standing for double four-valve, which were destined to become famous the world over.

most successful Formula One engine ever built. As every power unit carried the Ford name on its cam covers, the £100,000 that Walter Hayes succeeded in securing for the project could not have been better spent.

The Lotus 49 was replaced in 1970 by the 72, again Ford Cosworth engined and sporting a distinctive 'wedge' profile, chisel nose, side-mounted radiators and three-tier rear spoiler. Below the sleek bodywork, compact torsion bars replaced coil springs as a suspension medium while the inboard *front* brakes were a notable feature. The cars took a little time to find their form but Jochen Rindt won the 1970 Dutch Grand Prix and went on to win the French, British and Belgian events. Tragically he was killed during the Italian Grand Prix and was posthumously awarded the world championship title in 1970, Lotus again winning the manufacturers' cup. Nineteen seventy-one, by contrast, was dis-

ABOVE **A winning partnership**, *Colin Chapman (left) with Keith Duckworth, designer of the Ford Cosworth DFV Formula One engine, on the occasion of the production of the 200th unit.*

LEFT **1967 Dutch Grand Prix**. *A victory first time out for the new Ford Cosworth-engined Lotus 49, driven by Jim Clark.*

ABOVE RIGHT **1969 Lotus 49B**. *A derivative of the 49 with longer wheelbase, revised suspension and complete with aerofoil.*

RIGHT **1970 Dutch Grand Prix**. *Jochen Rindt drives to victory in a 72, the World Drivers' Championship, and Lotus's fourth Manufacturers' Cup.*

In the meantime Lotus was pushing ahead with the design of a new car specifically conceived for the new engine, of which the most notable feature was that the Cosworth unit played a stress-bearing role and was bolted directly to the rear end of the car's monocoque hull. The resulting Lotus 49 made its competition début right on time at the Dutch Grand Prix at Zandvoort in May 1967, with Jim Clark taking the chequered flag. It was a sensational start for the new engine but there were the inevitable teething troubles experienced through the ensuing season though Clark succeeded in winning the British, US and Mexican GPs.

Tragically the following year Clark was driving an uncompetitive Lotus 48 in an unimportant Formula Two event at Hockenheim, Germany when he slid off the track and hit a tree at high speed and died from the injuries he received. Chapman, a close friend of Clark, was stunned by the news, as was the motor racing world, so it was Graham Hill, driving the Ford Cosworth-engined 49, who gave Lotus its fourth manufacturers' cup and his second world drivers' championship. It was also in 1968 that the Ford Cosworth DFV became available to other British manufacturers and Lotus lost its monopoly. The engine – its reliability and performance became legendary – went from strength to strength and in 1977, ten years after its introduction, it chalked up 100 world championship grand prix wins and at the time of writing (1984) the figure stands at 155, making the DFV the

appointing from a competitive standpoint but the following year the 72 appeared resplendent in distinctive black and gold John Player Special livery, Chapman having obtained sponsorship from the cigarette manufacturer in 1968. There had been some modest refinement of the design with the three-tier wing giving way to a single unit. Twenty-five-year-old Emerson Fittipaldi had a sensational season with five grand prix wins, giving Lotus its fifth constructors' championship and the Brazilian became the youngest ever world champion racing driver. It was to be another six years, in 1978, before Lotus attained the championship accolade again, on that occasion Mario Andretti emerging as the top driver, ahead of his team mate Ronnie Peterson.

All these successes on the race track should not overshadow the development of the Lotus road cars. In 1966 there had been the Europa, a mid-engined two-seater, powered by a modified Renault R16 engine and initially intended for export only. There was a Cosworth twin cam-engined model for racing and a detuned version was fitted to the road cars from 1971, superseding the Renault unit. A Europa Special with big valve engine followed later in 1972, with five-speed gearbox as an optional extra, and the model continued in production until 1975.

LOTUS EUROPA (1966–75)
Number built 9230

ENGINE		CHASSIS	
No. of cylinders	Four	Frame	Backbone
Bore/stroke mm	76 × 81; from 1971 82 × 72	Wheelbase mm	2311
Displacement cc	1470, 1558	Track – front mm	1143
Valve operation	Overhead pushrod, twin overhead camshaft	Track – rear mm	1143
		Suspension – front	Independent wishbone and coil
Compression ratio	10.25:1, 9.5:1, 10.3:1	Suspension – rear	Independent trailing radius arm, lower links, and coil
Induction	Single Solex carburettor, twin cam, as Elan		
		Brakes	Hydraulic, front disc
BHP	80 at 6000, 105 at 5500, 126 at 6500 rpm	**PERFORMANCE**	
		Maximum speed	174 km/h (108 mph), 185 km/h (115 mph), 193 km/h (120 mph)
Transmission	Four-speed, five-speed		

Europa Special, *introduced in 1972 and also available in black and gold John Player livery in recognition of its sponsorship of Lotus's racing programme since 1968. The mid-engined power unit was the 126 bhp twin cam Elan Sprint version.*

SAH 759M

The Elite revived

The Elite name was revived for a new Lotus that appeared in the spring of 1974, an utterly distinctive wedge-shaped closed car, echoing the theme of the grand prix models, with two-door four-seater glass-fibre bodywork. A backbone chassis with all-independent suspension was by then a Lotus trademark and the new Elite represented a deliberate attempt by the firm to move progressively up market though the economic climate was far from receptive. The new model, with air conditioning and a radio/stereo tape deck as standard, had the doubtful distinction of being the most expensive four-cylinder car in the world, selling for £5749 at the time of its announcement.

The Elite was powered by Lotus's Type 907 engine which represented a major landmark for the firm as it had been designed and produced at Hethel. The idea had germinated back in 1964 when Lotus design staff began a series of studies for what was to be a 100 per cent Lotus engine and by the end of 1966 the layout had gelled as a 2-litre slant four with a twin overhead camshaft 16-valve layout. But when members of the Lotus team visited the 1967 Motor Show, there on the Vauxhall stand was that company's new Victor which boasted a new 2-litre four-cylinder engine with its overhead camshaft driven by a tooth rubber belt, the first British production car to offer this cheap and effective drive system. Its dimensions almost exactly coincided with the ideas Lotus had already formulated, so what better basis for the new unit? Former Coventry Climax engineers Steve Sanville and Ron Burr then began work on the aluminium cylinder head while

Chapman began negotiations with Vauxhall for the use of its cylinder block. Eventually this idea was dropped and a special Lotus block was cast for the engine. But, ironically, the engine did not make its public début in a Lotus, but in the Jensen-Healey sports car, announced early in 1972.

The West Bromwich based Jensen company had assembled much of the Austin Healey 3000 sports car for BMC up until the model ceased production in 1967. Thereafter Jensen had to rely on sales of its low production, high cost Interceptor, and the Jensen-Healey was intended to take over in America where the Big Healey had left off. Unfortunately a hoped for 10,000-a-year output failed to materialize and only 10,912 sports cars were built by 1976 when output ceased and Jensen closed down its manufacturing operations. Unfortunately the car had gained a questionable reputation with some of the complaints aimed at the Lotus engine. These shortcomings had been resolved when the Type 907 was used in the 1974 Lotus Elite, giving the car a top speed in the region of 200 km/h (125 mph), but the following year, 1975, represented a low point in Lotus fortunes when only 655 cars were produced; back in 1969 output had stood at 4506.

BELOW **Lotus Eclat**. *Announced in 1975, and similar to but cheaper than the concurrent Elite, it lacked that model's opening tailgate. A derivative is still in production.*

RIGHT **1977 Lotus 78**. *What Colin Chapman described as 'my something for nothing' car. It achieved five Grand Prix wins in 1977 and in 1978 gave Lotus its seventh Manufacturers' Cup.*

Financial ups and downs

Like any other small company Lotus was vulnerable to the fluctuations of the economic barometer. The 1960s had represented a period of growth for the firm and, with a world-wide reputation assured, in October 1968 Group Lotus Car Companies had offered its shares for public subscription on the stock exchange, though Team Lotus, established by Chapman in 1954 to handle the firm's racing programme, was excluded. The flotation made Chapman a millionaire at the age of 40 but the shares later plummeted from a 250p high, while the economic crisis of 1973, triggered by the Arab/Israeli war and the escalating price of fuel, wrought havoc with the world's economies.

Nevertheless the firm pressed ahead with yet another new model; the Esprit, which continued the Europa mid-engined layout, was announced in 1975, and perpetuated the Elite's 'wedge' theme. Simultaneously the front-engined Eclat was unveiled with the same 907 engine which was similar to but £1700 cheaper than the Elite. It was during this period that Lotus's financial problems were to some extent alleviated by American Express, well known for their universal charge card, who took a £2 million stake in the firm. Nineteen eighty saw the arrival of the Essex Turbo, a turbocharged version of the Esprit and later in the year all models benefited from a larger capacity 2.2-litre engine.

But 1980 was to prove a crucial year for the firm because it was then that Lotus decided to develop a new, cheap sports car in the Elan mould especially as the current model range represented a considerable departure from previous themes. But such was the nature of the development costs that Lotus decided to approach a Japanese manufacturer with a view to using its engine and drive train in the new model. It was also in 1980 that Lotus offered research and development services to other manufacturers which followed on from an agreement the firm made in 1978 for a major redesign of the DeLorean sports car, intended for production in Belfast, Northern Ireland by former General Motors vice president John DeLorean.

It was Toyota, the Japanese car manufacturer, who not only took advantage of Lotus's research facilities but also agreed to supply engine and gearboxes for the new car. Meanwhile Lotus was pressing ahead with refinements to its existing car range, a Series Three Esprit arriving in 1981 with new wrap-around bumpers and improvements to the braking and seats. A new turbocharged version was announced at the same time. In 1982 the Eclat was revised, the resulting Excel having increased headroom, new interior and somewhat softer body lines, though the Elite was discontinued during the year. But in December Lotus received a bodyblow with the unexpected death, at the age of 54, of Colin Chapman, the firm's founder and its driving force.

The following month Lotus again talked with Toyota suggesting that the firm might like to build on their existing relationship and the Japanese company responded positively by sending a team of experts to Britain to evaluate the company's prospects. But Lotus was facing a cash crisis and in March 1983 realized that it would be running out of funds by the end of the month, needing around half a million pounds to keep going. Within the required fortnight Toyota forwarded the necessary amount as an advance payment for engineering contracts and Lotus was pulled back from the brink. It had been a close call.

Then, in April, came a dialogue with the buoyant British Car Auctions, who had a world-wide expertise in vehicle marketing, always something of a Lotus weak point, and an agreement was concluded by the firm's annual general meeting held in August 1983. This gave BCA a 25-per-cent holding in Lotus with its chairman David Wickins also taking over the Lotus chair, while Toyota's commitment was reflected by its 16 per cent of Lotus equity.

So, after many vicissitudes Lotus's future prospects look brighter than they have for many years. At the time of writing, production is running at about 65 cars a month and the firm's new Toyota-engined sports car, code-named M90, is scheduled for announcement in 1985/6. What's more, it will cost under £10,000 and will be more in the spirit of the cars that Colin Chapman began building in that Hornsey stable block back in 1952.

Lotus Esprit S2. *Flagship of the current range is the Giugiaro-styled mid-engined model, turbocharged from 1980, and with luxurious 1982 interior.*

LOTUS ESPRIT (1976 to date)	
Number built **Still in production**	
ENGINE	
No. of cylinders	**Four**
Bore/stroke mm	**95 × 69; 1980: 95 × 76**
Displacement cc	**1973, 2174**
Valve operation	**Overhead camshaft**
Compression ratio	**9.5:1, 9.4:1**
Induction	**Twin carburettors**
BHP	**160 at 6200, 6500 rpm**
Transmission	**Five-speed**
CHASSIS	
Frame	**Backbone**
Wheelbase mm	**2438**
Track – front mm	**1155**
Track – rear mm	**1155**
Suspension – front	**Independent**
Suspension – rear	**Independent**
Brakes	**Hydraulic disc**
PERFORMANCE	
Maximum speed	**219 km/h (136 mph)**

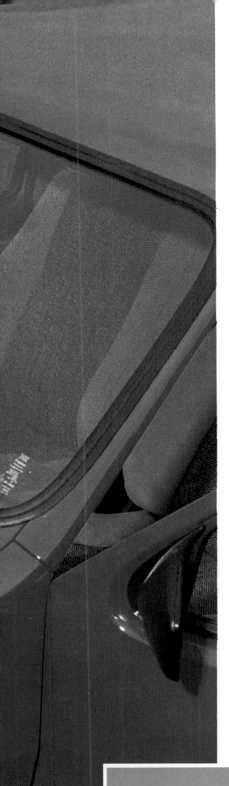

M.G.

Conceived by Cecil Kimber in the 1920s, M.G. became Britain's most famous sporting marque and, although eclipsed during the Leyland years, it has been popularly revived on the new Metro, Maestro and Montego models.

Seldom has any make of car aroused more emotion than M.G., emotion that has, above all, been fired by love. This is because M.G.s have always been cheap and cheerful sporting cars, dream machines that the ordinary man and woman could afford. These were cars you could depend on because they were built from rugged, well-tried components that started life in stolid saloons.

The first M.G.s grew from the frustration felt by Cecil Kimber, manager of Morris Garages in Oxford, at having to sell the products of Morris Motors. These sturdy, but rather staid cars, distinguished by their 'bull-nosed' radiators, became very popular as their maker, William Morris, cut his prices dramatically during a period of great depression. Kimber, a man of diverse talents, ranging from cost accountancy to writing and drawing, knew that he could sell Bullnose Morris cars for a higher price, and as a result make more profit on each vehicle, if he tuned them to go faster and fitted a more sporting body.

LEFT **1983 MG Metro Turbo.** *Fastest version of the best-selling Austin Metro, its engine develops 93 bhp, while the wheels are special and there are ventilated front disc brakes. Provided by BL Cars Ltd.*

BELOW **1925 M.G. Super Sports.** *Its Morris origins all too obvious, the famous Bullnose radiator lasted until 1927, after its Morris parent had changed to a flat-fronted one. The engine is an 1806 cc four, similar to that used in the Morris Oxford.*

The first cars that could be attributed to Kimber and Morris Garages were built in 1922. They used the chassis and running gear from the cheaper of the Bullnose cars, called the Cowley, and with special bodywork they sold for around the same price as the more fully equipped Oxford. Kimber's system was to order a standard Cowley chassis, lower the suspension, and have it fitted with a 'Chummy' body to his own design. At first they were produced in Oxford at the Longwall Street depot of Morris Garages, and were known as the Morris Garages Chummies. Early in 1923, production was transferred to a mews workshop to allow the Morris Garage fitters to carry on unhindered with their normal work of servicing Morris cars and preparing new vehicles for sale.

Kimber, an enthusiastic sportsman with a flair for publicity, was keen to indulge in competition with one of his cars, so he had it tuned at Longwall Street, and in March 1923 won a gold medal in the classic London-to-Land's End Trial. Kimber exploited this success by ordering six two-seater bodies from Raworth of Oxford to be fitted to slightly modified Cowley chassis. These featured a raked windscreen, with scuttle ventilators like those on a yacht: it was no coincidence that boating was another of Kimber's interests. However, these were priced at twice the cost of a Morris Cowley, so sales were slow. But they were the first cars to be known as M.G.s, the full name of Morris Garages being thought rather cumbersome by Kimber.

At the same time, Morris Motors – stung into action by Kimber's success – introduced its own version of the Chummy at a lower price. With his base whipped from under him, Kimber first tried the Chummy body on a Morris Oxford chassis, and then a more powerful 14 hp engine as standard. As neither venture repeated the success of the Chummy, he therefore tried a better-finished saloon body on the Oxford chassis, called the 14/28 because of its new engine. But again, the price was too high at 15 per cent more than a standard Oxford saloon. It was, however, the first M.G. advertised as such. Various other models followed before Kimber started building 14/28 four-seaters, known as M.G. Specials.

Octagons everywhere
It was also during this period, in the summer of 1924, that the M.G. motif appeared inside an octagon, the eight-sided symbol that was to become a trademark of M.G. Many devoted enthusiasts still make a point of signing letters to like-minded friends, 'Yours octagonally'.

The relentless march of William Morris swallowed up his suppliers, including Hotchkiss, the engine makers. This company's powerful overhead valve unit really interested Kimber: during 1924 he had one fitted to a modified Cowley chassis and, early in 1925, it acquired a skimpy two-seater body. It was a pure competition special, and took him to another gold medal in the Land's End Trial that year, before being sold to a friend. That was the last the M.G. works saw of it – until it was rescued from a scrapyard by an M.G. employee in 1932 and returned to Abingdon in 1933. It was then restored to be used for demonstrations, before being heralded, by Morris Motors as 'The first M.G., built in 1923!' Not only was the date incorrect, but also it was not actually the first M.G.; nevertheless, it has been known ever since as Old Number One.

This car coincided, however, with the start of serious production, so perhaps the corporate publicists, who have since come in for considerable criticism for treating the sacred octagon's history in such a cavalier manner, were not committing such a serious crime. It is very difficult to pick an exact point when M.G.s stopped being simply modified Morris cars and became a great marque. Production expanded at such a rate in 1925, however, that the M.G. works was moved in September that year to the Morris Radiators factory in Bainton Road, Oxford, where there was more room. The

M.G. range stabilized with sporting models (the open two-seater, open tourer and Salonette) on modified Oxford chassis, and special models (a landaulette, Weymann fabric-bodied sedan, and V-front saloon) on standard Oxford chassis; all were smart, stylish offerings.

Meanwhile, William Morris's empire had continued to expand, greatly to the benefit of M.G., when he took over the bankrupt Wolseley concern in 1927. This company had developed a brilliant little 8 hp overhead camshaft four-

cylinder engine for a baby car that appealed to Morris because he wanted to produce a rival for the Austin Seven. However, this 847 cc Wolseley engine endowed a prototype Morris Minor with such a good performance that Morris decided to have it detuned for everyday use. Kimber got hold of one of the prototype cars, and quickly saw how it could be modified and rebodied in a similar way to the old Bullnose to produce a nippy little sports car.

At the same time, Hotchkiss – whose manager, Frank Wool-lard, was a good friend of Kimber's – produced an 18 hp overhead camshaft six-cylinder engine, ostensibly for a new Morris car. The resultant Isis turned out to be heavy and uninspiring, but Kimber saw it was a vehicle for his ambition to make a big sports car to match the best, namely Bentley. He designed a new chassis, and a cylinder block to take twin carburettors, and built what amounted to a completely new car, the 18/80 M.G. Six. This magnificent beast also bore a proud new radiator, which was so elegant that its essential

shape survived on M.G.s for more than 25 years. The new small M.G., the Midget, was fitted with a scaled-down version of the radiator and, together with the 14/28-derived 14/40, the two new models made their début at the 1928 London Motor Show. The larger model used the Morris Oxford engine.

The Midget, with a performance as good as the 14/40 at half the price, was an immediate success. The 18/80, at around half as much again as a 14/40, enjoyed more modest sales.

The move to Abingdon

During the year that followed, M.G. production figures tripled, with the M-type Midget, as the new small car was known, accounting for more than 50 per cent of the firm's total sales. The 18/80 was also quite popular, making up one third of the M.G. turnover; the 14/40 was about to be discontinued. Such was the volume of cars – around 1000 – that the emergent M.G. Car Company had to move again at the end of 1929, to Abingdon, 10 km (6 miles) from Oxford, but at least on the same side of the city as Cowley. This site, next to the Pavlova Leather Works, was to become the world's biggest sports car factory, distinguished by its brown-and-cream colour scheme (and octagonal embellishments!). It was also at this time that the enduring M.G. slogan 'Safety Fast' was coined. It was to serve M.G. well for many years.

During this period, the nucleus of Abingdon's formidable workforce was formed; it included Hubert Charles as Kimber's right-hand man on design, with Cecil Cousins and engine expert Reg Jackson, and was reinforced by relative newcomers such as Gordon Phillips and Syd Enever, who provided outstanding talent on development. It was in 1930, too, that a young accountant, John Thornley, helped to start the M.G. Car Club, which was to become the world's biggest single-marque club. It was only natural that Thornley should join the M.G. staff in 1931, and it was a good job, too; eventually he was to take over Kimber's role as defender of the M.G. faith in the face of big business interests.

By this time, M.G.'s competition experiences were beginning to pay off, not only in sales, but in development. A new, longer-wheelbase chassis (2134 mm; 7 ft) was developed from a special record-breaking Midget. In competition guise, it gave a better ride and, as a result, improved roadholding. In production form, there was enough space at the back for extra seats to be fitted. This new chassis was adopted for the D-type Midget production car introduced in 1931, which remained available until 1932.

The prototype competition machines made at that time were known by EX-for-experimental numbers, so it seemed quite natural to designate M.G.'s next model, which was introduced in late 1931, the F-type. And because it was a six- rather than four-cylinder version of the D-type it was called the Magna. The engine was not a new design, however, although M.G. tried to give the impression that it was. The 'new' 1271 cc power unit was basically that of a Wolseley Hornet with a lot of sheet metal surrounding the cylinder

FAR LEFT **1932 F-type Magna.**
Introduced in 1931, it was M.G.'s first small six and similar to the unit used in the Wolseley Hornet, its first cousin. Provided by Elwin S. Sapcote.

BELOW **Abingdon 1931.** *The C-type, or Montlhéry Midget, under construction. The assembly line was not power-driven and was never mechanized in this way even in MGB days!*

block to disguise its origin. The F-type was given a wheelbase of 2388 mm (7 ft 10 in) to accommodate both the longer engine and the rear-seat passengers. It was also offered with bodywork like that of the D-type.

The J2: a classic M.G.

These new cars sold well alongside the evergreen M-type, as competition M.G.s went from success to success. However, they were underpowered, a fault that was made all too apparent by the extra weight brought about by their longer wheelbases and the extra passengers they could carry. This applied particularly to the Midget, which still had an engine of only 847 cc. Therefore Kimber started work immediately on a sensational new Midget with an engine uprated along racing lines and a body using all the competition styling, such as cutaway doors, fold-flat windscreen, double-humped scuttle, cycle-type wings, and a large external slablike fuel tank at the back. This new Midget, called the J2 (what happened to the other letters of the alphabet is a mystery) was to set the style for sports cars for years and form the distinctive shape that took M.G. into the 1950s. It had the fashionable stiff suspension of that era, and an engine that developed its maximum power (some 36 bhp) at no less than 5500 rpm, despite having only a two-bearing crankshaft. Its wheelbase of 2184 mm (7 ft 2 in) was the same as later versions of the D-type and was to remain available until 1934.

The J2 was introduced in August 1932, alongside a J1 open four-seat tourer on the same wheelbase. This latter car had the option of Salonette bodywork, but the J2 was the undoubted star, particularly as it cost little more than the M-type. Kimber was not slow to cash in on this success, fitting the J2's distinctive body to the Magna chassis, with a suitably lengthened bonnet, soon after the J2 had been introduced. The new Magna then adopted the F2 designation, and a four-seater Magna was designated the F3.

And just to keep the ball rolling, Kimber announced in late 1932 yet another line – now that the 18/80 was on its last knockings – named the Magnette. This new six-cylinder car with a 1087 cc engine cost more than the Magna, but was intended at first as the basis of a new racing machine for the 1100 cc class. More Midgets, the P, Q and R types, followed and there were the low-production Magnettes of which the most famous was the 1932 racing K3. The great Tazio Nuvolari won the 1933 TT in one of these cars while two of them were placed first and second in class in the famous Italian Mille Miglia event the same year.

However, by 1935 M.G. sales had fallen to around half those of the 2500 produced in the peak year, 1932, and the company was making a loss. The main reason for the decline was the rising price of the cars, supplemented by increasing insurance premiums that accompanied their high-performance image.

It was also a time of great upheaval for M.G. as Morris's new managing director, a ruthless production engineering

RIGHT **1933 L-type Magna**. There were only 486 of this L1 car, power coming from a 1087 cc six. This example was fitted with L2 cycle-type wings in 1944. Provided by Nicholas A. Dean.

BELOW RIGHT **1935 KN Magnette**. The body is a University Motors Speed Model, an unusual fitment as most KNs were saloons. Provided by Martin Warner.

BELOW **1933 J2 Midget**. Announced in 1932 when it was fitted with cycle wings, the following year they were replaced by these handsome full length ones, representing a model style that was to figure on two-seater M.G.s until the TF was discontinued in 1955. Provided by Paradise Garage.

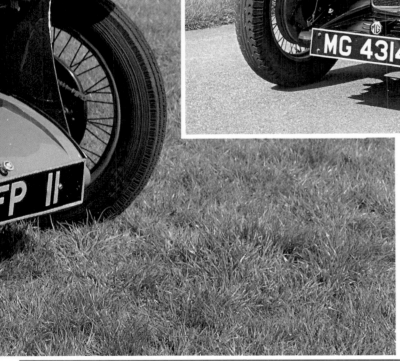

expert named Leonard Lord, began welding the group together and disposing of parts that did not quite fit in – such as the M.G. design office. The first victim of this streamlining process was M.G.'s racing programme; to the horror of all the staff at Abingdon it was axed in the middle of the 1935 season. The M.G. and Wolseley concerns were transferred from their previously favoured position under Lord Nuffield's personal ownership to Morris corporate responsibility. (Morris became Lord Nuffield in 1934.) Leonard Lord decided that this meant that the Wolseley-based overhead cam engines had to go, and would be replaced with the far cheaper Morris pushrod units.

Nevertheless, the five years or so of factory-sponsored racing were to reap benefits for M.G. in the future.

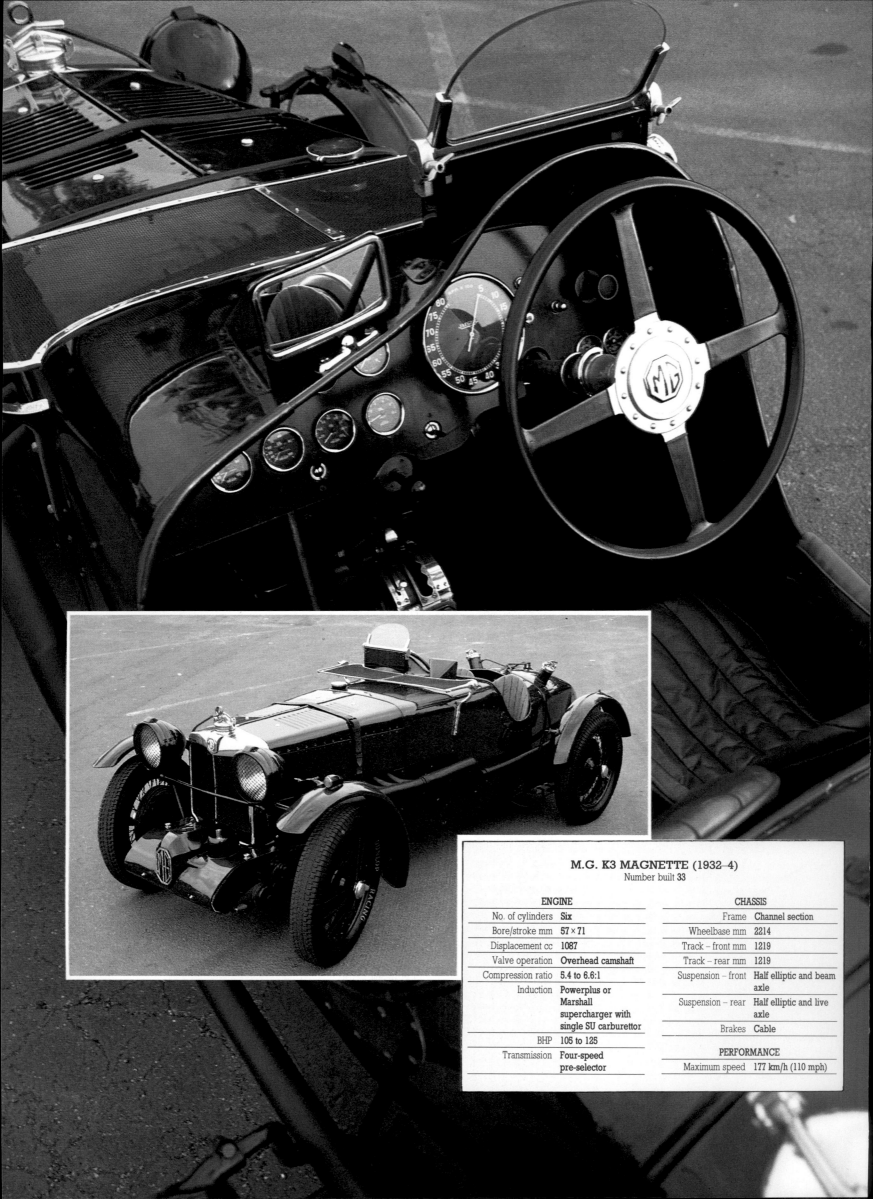

M.G. K3 MAGNETTE (1932–4)
Number built 33

ENGINE		CHASSIS	
No. of cylinders	**Six**	Frame	**Channel section**
Bore/stroke mm	**57 × 71**	Wheelbase mm	**2214**
Displacement cc	**1087**	Track – front mm	**1219**
Valve operation	**Overhead camshaft**	Track – rear mm	**1219**
Compression ratio	**5.4 to 6.6:1**	Suspension – front	**Half elliptic and beam axle**
Induction	**Powerplus or Marshall supercharger with single SU carburettor**	Suspension – rear	**Half elliptic and live axle**
		Brakes	**Cable**
BHP	**105 to 125**		
Transmission	**Four-speed pre-selector**	PERFORMANCE	
		Maximum speed	**177 km/h (110 mph)**

HARD REALITY

The revolution that swept through Abingdon in the summer of 1935 involved not only the end of the works racing cars, but also the amalgamation of M.G. with the Morris and Wolseley concerns at Cowley. This took place in July 1935 as the projected V8 sports car was cancelled and Hubert Charles was transferred to Cowley. Kimber remained at Abingdon for much of the time, although there was little that he could do without the approval of Leonard Lord.

To begin with, Lord said he did not want any more M.G. sports cars. They were more trouble than they were worth to his plans for streamlining Morris Motors. But Kimber still had a lot of influence and rallied enough support to change Lord's mind. The results of Lord's initial edict and Kimber's fight to keep M.G. as a separate marque were seen in the new model introduced in 1936.

Everything except the body was relatively run-of-the-mill: it had an ordinary swept-up chassis, rather than M.G.'s established underslung one, and a pushrod engine instead of the glorious overhead cam; but it cruised happily at 129 km/h (80 mph), although it took rather a long time to reach this speed. The Two-Litre, or SA saloon as it was known, was a heavy car and benefited from the use of hydraulic brakes, which Kimber, in a rather blinkered attitude, had refused to fit to previous M.G.s, maintaining that the old-style cable brakes were more dependable.

The T-series Midgets

It was back to basics for the new Midget (designated the TA) introduced at the London Motor Show in 1936, with no choice of transmission other than the existing Morris/Wolseley units. But Charles was allowed to design a new chassis – using the Q-type for inspiration – with a 2388 mm (7 ft 10 in) wheelbase, and a 1143 mm (3 ft 9 in) track. This made it much bigger than the P-type, more of a Magnette, in fact: therefore, with Kimber's far roomier body, it did effectively replace both models. Its suspension was softer, in keeping with saloon car trends; it had the new hydraulic brakes; and the engine

produced 50 bhp in tuned form, so it was just as fast as the old Midget and Magnette.

Meanwhile, the Nuffield men were occupied on completely different lines. They were anxious to propagate their new family of M.G.s with a larger and a smaller version of the SA. The smaller car, the VA, came first, halfway through 1937. It was based on the contemporary Wolseley Twelve, with a 1548 cc four-cylinder engine, a wheelbase of 2743 mm (9 ft) and a track of 1270 mm (4 ft 2 in). It was offered with similar four-seater body styles to those of the SA, in open tourer, saloon or drophead coupé forms. It took just as long to put into production as the SA, and it was not until the summer of 1938 that the larger WA made is appearance.

It was in August 1938, however, that the T-series was extended to include a drophead coupé. This was a two-seater that fitted in well with the larger S, V and W ranges because it was built by the same specialist firm, Tickford, that was responsible for the other dropheads. It was also especially significant in that it was 102 mm (4 in) wider across the seats, making it feel much roomier inside. Naturally, it cost more, but it was considerably more comfortable, although the extra weight reduced its performance a little.

The performance, however, was soon to be improved, in April 1939, by fitting a better engine – a modified version of the new Morris Ten unit – with the VA gearbox's closer ratios. The new four-cylinder 1250 cc engine, code-named XPAG, was a much more modern design, and was used in the new TB Midget, also introduced that year.

By this time war was already on the way and the Abingdon workers were just as patriotic as everyone else in Britain: all they wanted to do was to join the military services or make fighting machines. But the slow-moving Nuffield Organization – as the Morris Group was renamed in 1940 – starved them of work and Kimber, with factory manager George 'Pop' Propert, obtained contracts independently from various government departments.

Activity of this nature was not really appreciated by the Nuffield Organization, which had always treated Abingdon as the Cinderella of its family of factories. Oliver Boden, who had taken over from Lord as managing director of Nuffield,

manufacturers had survived in good enough fettle to meet the demand. Sports cars were even rarer, so the M.G. Midget sold extremely well. The first post-war machine, called the TC, was virtually the same as the TB, except that the rear suspension had been simplified and the width of the body increased to that of the Tickford coupé – which was discontinued – to give more elbow room inside.

Among the most affluent groups of people in Britain at that time were the American servicemen, paid at their home-country rates. With the thrills of war behind them, they turned to sports cars, and, in reality, there was only one new car available in any quantity: the M.G. TC. The craze spread

M.G. TC (1945–9)	
Number built 10,000	
ENGINE	
No. of cylinders	Four
Bore/stroke mm	66 × 90
Displacement cc	1250
Valve operation	Overhead pushrod
Compression ratio	7.5:1
Induction	Twin SU carburettors
BHP	54 at 5200 rpm
Transmission	Four-speed
CHASSIS	
Frame	Channel, partially box
Wheelbase mm	2388
Track – front mm	1143
Track – rear mm	1143
Suspension – front	Half elliptic
Suspension – rear	Half elliptic
Brakes	Hydraulic
PERFORMANCE	
Maximum speed	126 km/h (78 mph)

died suddenly and was replaced by Miles Thomas. He was adamant that the group should be considered as one unit for producing armaments, with centralized control under one person: himself. Therefore Thomas dismissed Kimber in November 1941.

Nevertheless, an earlier aircraft contract proved to be a great success for M.G. and Abingdon went on to produce more bomber and tank equipment. Kimber, in the meantime, went to Charlesworth, the coachbuilders who had produced touring bodies for the SA. He spent 1942 reorganizing the factory for war work before moving on in 1943 to Specialloid Pistons in a similar capacity. In 1944, he was 56 years old and considering retirement when the war was over, or possibly even taking over as head of Triumph, to continue his policy of producing highly saleable sports cars from humble family saloon components. But, tragically, Kimber died in a London train crash in February 1945.

Sports cars again

One of the men who came back from the war was Lieutenant-Colonel John Thornley, who was service manager at Abingdon from 1934 to 1939. He got back his old job, with Propert continuing as general manager; but the old independence enjoyed under Kimber had been lost. Harold Ryder, who was in charge of M.G. for Nuffield and rigidly opposed to all forms of motor sport, kept a firm control of Abingdon on behalf of Cowley.

However, Nuffield could not kill the spirit that flowed through Abingdon. Within weeks of the war ending this incredibly happy little factory was producing sports cars again. There was not time to design a new model and, in any case, the market was starved of new cars, because few

BELOW **1953 YB**. *The Y-type saloon was the first M.G. to go into production with independent front suspension – and was in demand in the immediate post-war years in a world starved of sporting cars. Provided by Jonathan Oglesby.*

quickly, not only in America, but all over the world, so that when in 1947 Sir Stafford Cripps, President of the Board of Trade, cut steel supplies to any manufacturer who did not export enough, M.G. was in a good position.

With an eye to the future, Abingdon resurrected a project that Enever had been working on with Cowley suspension designer Alec Issigonis in 1937. This was an M.G. version of the Morris Eight saloon, planned for introduction in 1941. The main advantage of its specification, apart from the fact that it had a single-carburettor version of the XPAG engine, was that it had an excellent new chassis with independent front suspension, a rarity at that time. Enever used Issigonis's wishbone and coil system, which was to become so popular in later years, rather than the torsion bars of the R-type. This new Y-type M.G., introduced in April 1947, was extraordinarily attractive and at first it sold well. Although Y-series production meant that Abingdon could turn out only 3500

FAR LEFT **1938 SA saloon**. *After 1935 M.G.'s trend was towards closed cars. Introduced in 1936, the roomy SA reflected Morris's demand for cheaper pushrod engines. Provided by Michael Turvill.*

BELOW **1946 TC**. *Unashamedly pre-war in concept, the TC spearheaded M.G.'s export drive in the early post-war years. Provided by Alastair Naylor, owner Derek Farley.*

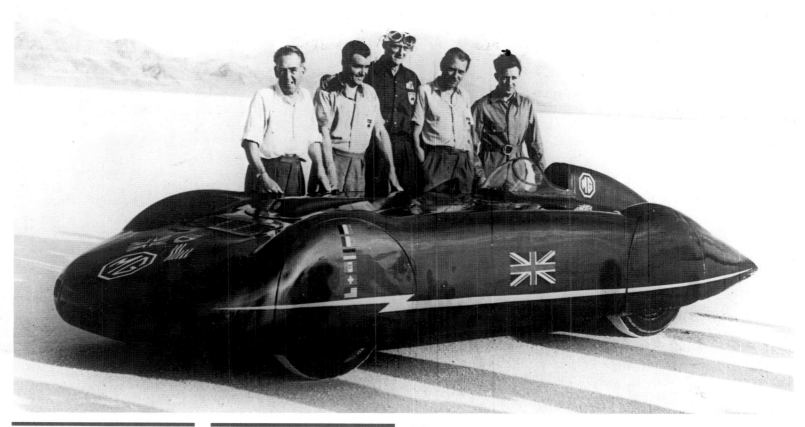

LEFT **EX135 record-breaker**.
Based on a 1934 K3 chassis, its streamlined body was the work of Reid Railton. The perspex panels on the top are for display purposes only. Provided by BL Heritage Ltd.

ABOVE **EX135** *pictured at Bonneville, USA, in August 1951. Left to right: Gardner supporter Dick Benn, M.G. designer Syd Enever, driver Goldie Gardner, tuning specialist Reg Jackson, and electrical expert George Perry.*

TCs in 1949, the factory was happy because it meant that it was no longer dependent on one very aged model.

The Y-type, with its track of 1270 mm (4 ft 2 in) and substantial body, was rather heavy, but made up for this deficiency by having a very good ride, and by the ability of its engine to accept all the tuning gear that was being produced to make the TC go faster. An open touring version of the YA, as the new saloon was called, was designated the YT: it was introduced in October 1948, but looked bulky against the rakish TC and sold only in small numbers. Most of the production was for export, with Australia as the main market.

M.G. sales were going so well, at nearly 1700 in 1946, and rising fast to 5000 in 1949, that Ryder could see little reason for relaxing the ban on competition. However, EX135, an M.G. record-breaker built for Goldie Gardner in the 1930s, was privately owned and had survived the war, although its 1100 cc engine had not; there was little that Ryder could do to stop Gardner fitting it with a 750 cc engine – built at Abingdon before the war for an attack on Bobby Kohlrausch's record – and trying again.

The Jabbeke motorway between Ostend and Brussels proved ideal and Gardner smashed the record at 256.13 km/h (159.15 mph) in October 1946. In July the following year, with two of the six cylinders put out of action, he took the 500 cc record at 190 km/h (118.06 mph), also at Jabbeke.

Meanwhile, there had been a revolution at Cowley in 1947: Miles Thomas departed after a row with Lord Nuffield, and S.V. Smith took over from Ryder as the director in charge of Abingdon. Once more, with M.G. maintaining healthy profits, the ban on competition was relaxed a little.

Riley moves in

The new Nuffield board had transferred production of one of M.G.'s erstwhile rivals, Riley, from Coventry to Abingdon in 1948 in the interests of rationalization. The little town in Berkshire (county changes have since placed it in Oxfordshire) was well on its way to having the world's biggest factory for the exclusive production of sporting cars. Two months after the arrival of the Rileys, Propert retired and was replaced by Riley general manager Jack Tatlow who, as luck would have it, got on extremely well with the Abingdon men.

The relatively cool reception of the YT, and the demands of the American dealers for something a little more sophisticated than the TC, convinced Tatlow and his new colleagues that another project should be designed. As ever, Abingdon was starved of investment – the available money all went into new head office models from Cowley – but it proved equal to the occasion. With Cecil Cousins and Syd Enever to the fore, the development men removed 127 mm (5 in) from the Y-type chassis centre section to give it a wheelbase of 2388 mm (7 ft 10 in) and fitted it with a hacked-about TC body. It was only then that the rough and ready prototype, duly approved by the Nuffield Organization, was sent to the drawing office at Cowley for plans to be prepared from which to produce it.

Although it had been decided that the new sports car's chassis would be basically the same as the Y-type saloon's, it had to be redesigned to a certain extent. The main problem was that there was not enough room at the back for adequate axle movement with the traditional underslung chassis members. Cowley got around this by sweeping up the side members over the rear axle so that the suspension could be made sufficiently supple to give an even ride with the shorter wheelbase and lighter two-seater body. The independent front suspension also made it necessary to fit new, smaller steel disc wheels in place of the delightful old wire ones used on the TC. Cowley really could not understand why people should be so in favour of the old-fashioned wire wheels, and, for once, they had the support of Thornley and Enever.

The new car's body was also widened by a further 102 mm (4 in) because of American demands, and looked considerably different once new wings had been designed to cover the wider track, new wheels and tyres. Bumpers (fenders) were also fitted at front and rear in deference to the American customers' wishes. The new model, designated the TD, was introduced in November 1949 and was to take Midget production to even greater heights. In 1950, Abingdon's total production exceeded 10,000 for the first time.

The relaxation of control at Abingdon had also enabled some competition support to be given to private entrants using its products. Photographer George Phillips drove a modified TC with a low-drag body shaped rather like a cigar at Le Mans in 1949 and 1950, finishing runner-up in his class at the second attempt. In other events, a works team of three practically standard TDs was successful – it took the first three places in class and the team prize in the Tourist Trophy race in 1950.

The battle for a new car

It seemed incongruous that Phillips should race on with an outdated car, and therefore a new special was built for him, based on a tuned TD, for Le Mans in 1951. Apart from a higher-output engine, the main difference was that it was fitted with an open low-drag body to take advantage of the fast French circuit's long straight. The all-enveloping shape was similar to Gardner's car, and was so successful that the tuned TD showed itself to be capable of 190 km/h (120 mph) – nearly 80 km/h (50 mph) faster than the normal vehicle. The engine blew up in the race, but Enever, and Thornley, who had been appointed general manager in 1952 on Tatlow's retirement, were convinced that this should be the new M.G. to replace the TD.

Enever was not satisfied, however, because the driver and the passenger sat too high in the old-fashioned chassis, which had been intended for a narrow body with separate wings. His answer was to design a new chassis, with the side members spaced further apart so that the occupants could sit in between them, rather than on top of them. This was made possible by the use of a modern, all-enveloping body that cut down on the frontal area, which, in turn, reduced drag.

All looked well until the new car, called EX175, was presented for approval halfway though 1952, with a view to exhibiting it at the London Motor Show. Earlier that year, the Nuffield Organization had merged with Austin, Britain's other top motor manufacturer, to form the British Motor Corporation. In theory, Lord Nuffield was in charge, but in effect the chief executive was his former right-hand man, Lord, who had joined Austin after leaving the Nuffield Organization. To Lord's credit, he was not prejudiced against M.G.s in particular; he just did not like sports cars. Nevertheless, he realized that BMC would have to produce them to make profits out of that sector of the market, but he did not see why there had to be more than one model. And only three days before he was shown EX175, Lord had been presented with a new model by Donald Healey. Healey, an independent manufacturer who had worked for Triumph before the war, had built a similar car to EX175, the Healey 100, using Austin components made redundant by the failure of Lord's Austin Atlantic sports coupé.

Lord had promptly concluded an agreement to produce Healey's car as the Austin Healey 100 at Austin's works in Longbridge, Birmingham, on a royalty basis and so use up

LEFT **1951 TD**. *Based on the TC Midget but updated with independent front suspension, the TD was the best selling of the T Series cars. Provided by Alastair Naylor, owner Jack Tordoff.*

ABOVE **EX179 record-breaker**. *Successor to EX175, this car used the MGA prototype's spare chassis and was powered by a variety of engines. Provided by BL Heritage Ltd.*

his embarrassing stockpile of Austin Atlantic engines and gearboxes. These plans were made public at the Motor Show in October 1952 and Lord told Thornley that he could shelve his car and carry on producing the TD.

Abingdon was dismayed. The TD, and the YB – a revised version of the Y-type saloon introduced late in 1951 with improved running gear – were selling well, but they were vulnerable because they were dated designs. The factory could see demand dropping off with the advent of the new Austin Healey and the TR2, Triumph's similar new sports car, which had both appeared at the 1952 Motor Show.

As a result of protests about changes in specification made to works racing TDs, a modified model had been offered from mid-1950. This was the Mark 2 fitted with a variety of works-approved tuning aids to make it go faster, although it was produced in only very small quantities. Thornley's worst fears were realized towards the end of 1952 when the demand for the TD started to fall away in America, its largest market. But still Lord would not lift his ban on EX175 because he was concerned that a modern M.G. would have taken sales away from the Austin Healey 100.

Consequently Cousins and Enever went to work again to facelift the TD, doing it in an even simpler manner than they had achieved with the TC. No capital was available for development, or even the special tools needed for production, so they modified the TD's body to make it lower and sleeker along the lines of a new saloon which was to be introduced at Abingdon to replace the antique YB. The more powerful TD Mark 2 engine was fitted and the new model called the TF (to avoid having people say 'Tee-Hee', which was likely if it had

been called a TE). Wire wheels were also offered as an optional extra because the Austin Healey 100 was equipped with them, and because enthusiasts never stopped clamouring for them. Just a few customers had managed to persuade the factory to fit wire wheels to the TD. Although it has since been accepted that the TF was one of the prettiest of the traditional 'square-rigged' M.G.s when it was launched in October 1953, it needed all the help it could get in competing against the more up-to-date Austin Healey, Triumph and Volkswagen-based Porsches on the American market.

The TF had a 1250 cc engine, but late in 1954 the capacity was increased to 1466 cc. With the new unit installed, the car became the TF1500, but it was a short-lived model. It stayed in production only until May 1955 before it was replaced by a new M.G., the MGA, but the TF1500 has since become the ultimate attraction for T-series enthusiasts as the fastest and most appealing of the line

A great M.G. record-breaker

It was at this time that the former driver of EX135, Captain George Eyston, managed to persuade BMC to build him another record car – and for old time's sake, and because Abingdon knew more about the business than anybody else, to make it a fully fledged M.G. Eyston's ideas also carried considerable weight with Lord because he was a director of the oil firm, Castrol, which would sponsor such a car. Eyston could not use the Gardner-M.G., even in revamped form, because it was the personal property of Gardner and, in any case, had been sponsored by a rival oil company, Duckham. At first, it was thought that Eyston could use EX175, duly modified with an undershield and tiny 'bubble' cockpit cover. But it proved unsuitable for use as a record car because its body was too closely related to a production vehicle and therefore produced too much drag. Fortunately, Enever had ordered a left-hand drive version of EX175's right-hand drive chassis at the time he was building the prototype, and this second frame was used for the new project, code-named EX179 in M.G. nomenclature.

Gardner's M.G. had been fitted with highly supercharged

versions of the XPAG engine, but for EX179 it was decided to go for a different set of records and take full advantage of the 1500 cc class limit by using a new enlarged engine, called the XPEG, without a supercharger. The 1466 cc capacity of this four-cylinder unit had been achieved by relocating the cylinders in joined or 'Siamese' (after the original Siamese twins) form so that the bores could be enlarged within the same overall external dimensions. Although this process has since become commonplace, it was considered quite revolutionary at the time. With the new engine installed in the spare chassis, and fitted with running gear and a body similar to the Gardner-M.G., EX179 took eight endurance records on the Utah salt flats in the United States in August 1954 at speeds of up to 247.34 km/h (153.69 mph).

BOOM-TIME AT ABINGDON

When the Nuffield Organization and the Austin Motor Company came together in 1952 to form the British Motor Corporation it was not so much a merger but rather, for practical purposes, a take-over by Austin. Lord Nuffield was 73 years old and, although he remained as president of BMC until his death in 1963, it was an honorary position. Leonard Lord, Austin's chairman and managing director, became the first to occupy this position at BMC, and he was in total charge. There is little doubt that he would have liked to have swept aside the Nuffield marques – Morris, Wolseley, Riley and M.G. – and produced only Austins in his new-found empire.

One of Lord's first moves in this programme of rationalization was to axe Nuffield's engines. The Morris Minor's unit was replaced by an A-series engine from the Austin A30 and, in 1954, the Morris Oxford received an enlarged, 1489 cc version of the Austin A40's B-series four-cylinder engine. Later, the big cars – the Austin Westminster and the Morris Isis – were powered by the same 2.6-litre six-cylinder Austin C-series engine.

At the same time, Lord started standardizing the bodyshells. The Wolseley 4/44, which had been launched in 1952 with the XPAG 1250 cc engine, was modified to take the B-series unit and M.G. grille and badges. For this new Z-series M.G. introduced in October 1953, M.G. resurrected

the name Magnette, which had not been used since 1936. Despite its close relationship to the 4/44 – Wolseley models had for so long formed the basis of M.G.s – it was completely unlike any previous M.G. It was a pleasing Italian-style saloon of unitary construction – i.e. it had no separate chassis, the bodyshell providing mountings for the engine, gearbox and suspension.

Its introduction was the start of a revolution at Abingdon, in which the little factory changed from being a works where cars were built from hundreds of small components to one where they were simply assembled, in much greater quantities, from a few large parts (such as the ready-trimmed bodyshells) which were made by outside suppliers.

The MGA prototypes

Once the new Magnette was well under way, Abingdon was given the go-ahead to produce EX175, the prototype for the new sports car to be known as the MGA. This went against the grain with Lord because he had given virtually all design authority to Austin's office at Longbridge, but there was sound commercial sense in letting M.G. produce its own car now that the Midget was on the way out. The new M.G. would use the Austin B-series running gear and needed only a body and chassis that were already developed and could be produced within BMC or by its established suppliers; and the American sports car market had expanded so much that there was room for a 1.5-litre Austin Healey, and Jaguar's 3.4-litre XK. BMC had also been persuaded to set up a competitions department following the success (and sales) enjoyed by Jaguar as a result of racing, and by Triumph in rallying. Abingdon was the obvious place to establish the department, because Lord had plans to turn the works into his sports car centre – and, in any case, it was where all the enthusiasm, skill and specialized knowledge were located. Donald Healey's company at Warwick was closer to Longbridge, but it had never been on a par with Abingdon.

With this welcome change of attitude at BMC in 1955, Thornley very shrewdly planned to announce the new sports car, the MGA, at the beginning of June and then run three of them at Le Mans a few days later. Unfortunately the body tooling took longer than expected and the Le Mans entries were taken up by three prototypes bearing the designation EX182. These cars were almost exactly the same as the actual

LEFT **1955 TF 1500.** *Although it was introduced as a stopgap between the TD and MGA, the TF is one of the prettiest, most sought-after post-war M.G. cars. Provided by Alastair Naylor; owner Vicki Fell.*

RIGHT **1956 ZA Magnette.** *With bodywork derived from the contemporary Wolseley 4/44 the ZA was the first M.G. to use the BMC B Series engine of Austin ancestry. It also witnessed the revival of the pre-war Magnette name, even though the ZA was a four rather than a six. This particular model incorporates later ZB components. Production began in 1953 and lasted until 1958. The ZB of 1957 had a more powerful engine, 68 rather than 60 bhp. Provided by Warren Marsh.*

MGA (1955–62)
Number built 98,970

ENGINE
No. of cylinders	Four
Bore/stroke mm	73 × 89; 1959: 75 × 89; 1961: 76 × 88
Displacement cc	1489, 1588, 1622
Valve operation	Overhead pushrod
Compression ratio	8.3:1, 8.9:1
Induction	Twin SU carburettors
BHP	68 at 5500, 79 at 5600, 86 at 5500 rpm
Transmission	Four-speed

PERFORMANCE
Maximum speed	156 km/h (97 mph), 160 km/h (100 mph)

MGA, with the chassis used in Eyston's 240 km/h (150 mph) record car the year before, and a body based on the 1951 Le Mans car, which could trace its ancestry to the Gardner-M.G. The engine and running gear, which were basically similar to those used in the Magnette, had already been developed in saloon car racing.

The three new M.G.s were running well in the 1955 Le Mans until everything was overshadowed by motor racing's worst accident in which 81 people were killed as a

Mercedes-Benz collided with an Austin Healey and flew into the crowd. In the confusion following the disaster M.G. stalwart Dick Jacobs also crashed and nearly lost his life. But the remaining two M.G.s ran better than expected to finish 12th and 17th in the hands of Ken Miles and Johnny Lockett, and Ted Lund and Hans Waeffler.

The prototypes had been built with a view to running soon after in the Alpine Rally, but this event was one of the many cancelled in 1955 in the aftermath of Le Mans. Nevertheless, it was planned to enter the EX182 cars in the Tourist Trophy at Dundrod in September to coincide with the MGA's new launch date. Because the new car would then be a reality, two of the EX182 cars were fitted with twin-cam development engines and the third, the Le Mans spare, retained the original pushrod unit. In this way, Abingdon felt that it could demonstrate that not only did it have a fast new car, but even

1959 MGA 1600. *When first announced the MGA's 1489 cc engine was of similar specification to that used in the ZA Magnette, but its capacity was increased to 1588 cc in 1959, and front disc brakes were introduced at the same time. Provided by Simon Robinson, owner Harold Corkhill.*

greater performance could be achieved with the more powerful twin-cam engines.

One of the new twin-cam conversions on the B-series unit had been developed by Austin and the other by the Morris engine works, but when both gave trouble in practice it was decided to go ahead with only the Austin. A spare pushrod engine replaced the Morris unit. The car that retained its twin-cam engine, driven by Lockett and Ron Flockhart, was also fitted with experimental disc brakes and low-drag bodywork. It proved to be practically as fast as the class-winning Porsche before retiring with head gasket trouble. One of the pushrod cars also failed to finish because of a split fuel tank, but the other, driven by Jack Fairman and Peter Wilson, survived to finish 20th, a lap ahead of the Triumph TR2s. This race, too, was marred by tragedy as three drivers died in horrifying accidents.

The death toll was giving motor racing a bad name in Europe and BMC decided to concentrate on rallying, in which its near-standard cars would have a better chance of success in any case, and to develop the Morris version of the twin-cam engine as it was more closely related to the B-series unit and was cheaper to manufacture.

It was in this stern atmosphere that the MGA was launched as an open tourer, with spartan equipment, a very low price and a top speed of nearly 160 km/h (100 mph). Wire wheels were also offered as an option to the cheaper steel disc

variety, M.G. having learned its lesson in that area. The MGA, with its superbly safe handling, high top speed and good fuel consumption of around 9.4 litres/100 km (30 mpg), was an immediate sales success, the vast majority of cars going to America, as before. The tragedies of Le Mans and the TT had not had such an impact across the Atlantic, so BMC allowed its North American subsidiary to enter three MGAs in the Sebring 12-hour race. They won the team prize and helped start a tradition: BMC sent works teams of sports cars to the event for more than ten years.

Meanwhile, Abingdon was developing a fixed-head coupé version of the MGA along the lines of Jaguar's popular XK fixed-head. This poor man's Jaguar, with a more luxurious interior than previous M.G.s, glass side windows and a slightly higher top speed because of its superior aerodynamics, was introduced at the London Motor Show in October 1956. At the same time, the Magnette, which had progressed to a ZB with a higher-output engine when the original MGA was launched, appeared in its final form, as the Varitone with a two-tone colour scheme and a larger, more modern rear window.

1957 EX181 record-breaker. *M.G.'s earlier record cars were front-engined, but 181's power unit was placed amidships, thus permitting a low nose and improved aerodynamics. In 1959, Phil Hill (below) drove this car at 410.2 km/h (254.9 mph). Provided by BL Heritage Ltd.*

Transition and expansion

The mid-1950s were a time of great expansion for Abingdon as MGA production rose to 20,000 a year and the more traditional RM Rileys were phased out to be replaced by badge-engineered versions produced at Cowley. (Badge engineering means producing a basic model and then dressing it up with different badges and trim to give the impression that more than one type of car has been produced, and also to take advantage of brand loyalty.) The Riley's place at Abingdon was taken by M.G.'s rival, the Austin Healey, manufacture of which moved there in late 1956, to make this the world's most productive factory devoted entirely to sports cars.

Meanwhile, EX179 had been used as part of the development programme for the twin-cam engine during its record run in August 1956 before a new record car, EX181, was built to take the engine in 1957. Nevertheless, EX179 was retained to help develop the A-series engine for a new small Austin Healey sports car, the Sprite. EX181 was a tiny teardrop-shaped car based on a tubular frame designed by Enever. M.G. realized that this lighter and more rigid type of chassis would be needed if it was to keep in the forefront of sports car racing. In the event it was too expensive to make, but EX181 proved ideal for developing the new twin-cam engine, which was intended to give the MGA a good performance in production car racing. With Stirling Moss at the wheel, and a supercharged version of the twin-cam installed, EX181 broke five international records, achieving 395.32 km/h (245.64 mph) at Utah during the 1957 session with EX179.

MGA TWIN CAM (1958–60)
Number built 2111

ENGINE		CHASSIS	
No. of cylinders	**Four**	Frame	**Box**
Bore/stroke mm	**75 × 89**	Wheelbase mm	**2388**
Displacement cc	**1588**	Track – front mm	**1203**
Valve operation	**Twin overhead camshaft**	Track – rear mm	**1230**
Compression ratio	**9.9:1 or 8.3:1**	Suspension – front	**Independent wishbone and coil**
Induction	**Twin SU carburettors**	Suspension – rear	**Half elliptic**
BHP	**108**	Brakes	**Discs**
Transmission	**Four-speed, optional four-speed with close-ratio gears**		
		PERFORMANCE	
		Maximum speed	**182 km/h (113 mph)**

The Twin Cam MGA and the 1600 Mark II

This notable success gave Abingdon the boost it needed to introduce the twin-cam engine in a new MGA, alongside the existing models in July 1958. The Twin Cam cars, as they were called, available with open or closed bodywork, were also fitted with Dunlop disc brakes all round to cope with the extra performance of the engine, which had been bored cut to 1588 cc to take full advantage of the 1600 cc international competition classes. The power output of 108 bhp, against the normal engine's 72, gave the new car far better acceleration and a high top speed of 182 km/h (113 mph), although fuel consumption increased to 14.12 litres/100 km (20 mpg). The Twin Cam was not a great success, however, either in competition or in production. As a result, only just over 2000 Twin Cams were made before the model was discontinued in 1960; redundant chassis were used to produce a rare hybrid known as the De Luxe, in effect a Twin Cam with a pushrod engine of which only limited quantities were made.

Meanwhile, as Abingdon production soared to more than 40,000 cars a year with the introduction of the new small Austin Healey, the Sprite, the Magnette Varitone – selling

better than ever – was replaced in 1959 by a badge-engineered version of Austin's wallowing Cambridge 1½-litre saloon: the Magnette Mark III. This family four-seater M.G., with a massive body designed by the Italian firm of Farina, was not even built at Abingdon. It was entirely the brainchild of Longbridge.

Abingdon's disappointment at losing the Varitone was mollified by an improvement in the MGA's specification. The capacity of the engine was increased in July 1959 to that of the Twin Cam and disc brakes were fitted at the front. This was the MGA 1600, which was to be relatively short-lived. The engine's capacity was increased again in April 1961 to 1622 cc by means of a longer stroke. This was logical because it made it the same as the Farina-bodied BMC saloons, including the Magnette. The new MGA was designated the 1600 Mark II, and the older 1600 subsequently became known as the Mark I.

It was during this run that MGA production passed 100,000, a historic achievement for such a small factory. Meanwhile, EX181 was still active – Phil Hill used it to take six more international records at Utah with 408.77 km/h (254.91 mph) in September 1959 – alongside the revamped EX179, now designated EX219. Although factory involvement with the MGA in competition from 1957 was minimal, Abingdon supported a special version driven by Lund in the 1959 Le Mans race but he was eliminated by gearbox trouble. However, Lund and Colin Escott had better luck in 1960, when the car was fitted with a special hard top to complement new windscreen regulations, and took 12th place. Sebring continued to be a happy hunting ground for Abingdon: in 1960 Austin Healeys and MGAs did well, and a De Luxe coupé won its class. In fact, it performed so successfully that the BMC works team prepared one for rallying in 1961, and with it the Morley brothers, Don and Erle, won their class in the Monte Carlo Rally, before the Finn Rauno Aaltonen and the Swede Gunnar Palm repeated the trick in the Tulip Rally. It was a glorious swansong for a car that was to be replaced late in 1962 by the far more modern MGB, which was to become the best-selling M.G. of all.

LEFT **1960 MGA Twin Cam**. *The twin cam version of the MGA was introduced in 1958 and only remained in production for two years. Externally similar to the pushrod cars, with the exception of handsome Dunlop wheels, the model was not a great success, as it soon developed a reputation for unreliability. This is the last Twin Cam to be built and collected from Abingdon in June 1960 by its present owner. Provided by Mike Ellman-Brown.*

ABOVE **1960 Mark II MGA coupé**. *A coupé version of the A arrived in 1959 and the 1622 cc Mark II followed in 1961, identifiable by its recessed radiator grille. Provided by Mrs Jill Halfpenny.*

RIGHT **1961 Mark II de luxe coupé**. *This rare model employed the redundant Twin Cam chassis with the current pushrod engine. This was a successful rally car. Provided by Mike Harrison.*

CARS BY THE MILLION

The credit for M.G.'s greatest landmark, the day on which production passed a million, must fall to John Thornley, who re-established a design office at Abingdon in 1954 with Syd Enever in charge. As we know, one of Enever's first jobs was to put EX175 into production as the MGA. Various other projects followed, including the EX181 record-breaking car, which was to inspire the MGA's successor, and work on improving the Austin Healey Sprite, which went into production at Abingdon in May 1958. The tiny Austin Healey, with its running gear made from a combination of BMC A-series, Morris Minor and M.G. parts, was a spiritual successor to the M.G. Midget even if it did bear a rival marque's name. BMC managing director George Harriman, who had succeeded Lord on his retirement, saw no reason why the Sprite should not be badge-engineered as an M.G. Midget, so that it could be sold through the old Nuffield chain of dealers as well as the existing Austin outlets.

However, first the car needed a certain amount of development: it had a curious bonnet with high-mounted headlights resembling frog's eyes, no exterior bootlid, and quarter-elliptic rear springs that led to some instability. BMC's solution was to give the job of redesigning the front to Healey and the back to Enever! The exact reasons for this extraordinary decision have been lost in the mists of time, but in the event Enever and Healey's designers got together to produce the

LEFT AND ABOVE **1963 Mark I Midget**. *The Midget was introduced in 1961, an M.G. version of the Austin Healey Sprite which had appeared three years previously in 1958. The original 948 cc engine was replaced by a 1098 cc unit for 1963. Provided by J.A. Tassell.*

FAR RIGHT **1967 MGB**. *As the model should be remembered – in its original form before it was disfigured for the American market. Provided by E.F. Williams.*

Austin Healey Sprite Mark II in July 1961 with an M.G. Midget – known as the Mark I – version at a slightly higher price, but including a different grille and more chromium plating. Many enthusiasts ignored these minor differences and simply called the cars 'Spridgets'. It was decided that the boost to marketing offered by the new bodywork was more important than the rear suspension, so Enever's solution of half-elliptic springs was shelved.

The Sprite, with its economical 948 cc four-cylinder engine, top speed of 137 km/h (85 mph), short wheelbase of 2032 mm (6 ft 8 in), and very low price, had been selling at around 17,000 a year. With the introduction of the M.G. Midget version of the car, sales climbed to a total of 18,000 a year, with slightly more M.G.s sold than Austin Healeys: enough to justify the badge engineering for BMC. A Mark III Sprite (Mark II Midget), with wind-up windows and half-elliptic rear springs, followed in 1964.

The MGB

Happily, the appearance of the new M.G. Midget fitted in well with the shape of the MGA's replacement, the MGB, which Enever had been working on for more than four years. Although EX181 was mid-engined, he used the car's body as the inspiration for the new MGB. The tubular frame used in EX181 had to be abandoned on the grounds of cost, and therefore a way had to be found to make the car more rigid.

MGB (1962–80)	
Number built 512,880	
ENGINE	
No. of cylinders	**Four**
Bore/stroke mm	**80 × 89**
Displacement cc	**1798**
Valve operation	**Overhead pushrod**
Compression ratio	**8.8:1**
Induction	**Twin SU carburettors**
BHP	**95 at 5400 rpm**
Transmission	**Four-speed, overdrive, three-speed automatic**
CHASSIS	
Construction	**Monocoque**
Wheelbase mm	**2311**
Track – front mm	**1245**
Track – rear mm	**1250**
Suspension – front	**Independent coil spring/wishbone**
Suspension – rear	**Half elliptic**
Brakes	**Hydraulic, front disc**
PERFORMANCE	
Maximum speed	**171 km/h (106 mph)**

This was necessary so that it could use a modern soft suspension system to give it a better ride without deterioration in handling. Only in this way could the MGA be improved upon without drastic changes in the established mechanical components. BMC had other running gear on the drawing board, but it seemed unlikely that it would be much better than the old B-series parts.

Enever had little choice but to pursue the same line of approach to unitary construction as was taken on the Sprite. At first he tried to devise an independent rear suspension system, but it could not be made cheaply enough, so he tried coil springs and radius arms. The same fate befell that system, and he had to settle for half-elliptic leaf springs as intended for the Sprite and Midget. The rest of the MGB's monocoque was similar in principle to the new Midget in that it was based on a floorpan with substantial box section sills, but it was considerably stronger. Wonders had been achieved by paring down the wheelbase from 2388 mm (7 ft 10 in) to 2311 mm (7 ft 7 in), as the EX181-styled body was too bulbous in prototypes built around the MGA's frame. Because the MGB was turning out to be heavier than the MGA, it was decided to uprate the engine so that the performance did not suffer. This was achieved by increasing the capacity of the MGB's engine to 1798 cc with an enlarged bore and the 'Siamezing' techniques estabished on the XPEG (as described on page 164).

Sales bonanza

However, Enever and Thornley had done their arithmetic so well that the MGB was introduced in September 1962, in roadster form only, at a cheaper price than any rival, despite having comparable fittings such as wind-up windows in place of floppy sidescreens, locks and door handles. Sports cars were getting altogether more civilized and, with the MGB to the fore, sales went up and up, especially in America where the customers appreciated a little extra refinement.

The MGB might have been overweight for international competition, but it had the advantage of years of development on the B-series mechanical components. In 1963, three works MGBs were raced with moderate success in the long-distance events in which reliability was of paramount importance, and also in the *Autosport* championship. Alan Hutcheson was second in his class in the *Autosport* series behind Dickie Stoop's far more expensive Porsche Carrera, and, despite spending 85 minutes digging the car out of the sand at the end of the Mulsanne Straight, again finished second in class to a prototype Porsche 718/8 Spyder at Le Mans. This MGB was slightly modified from normal competition specificiation as it was fitted with a low-drag nose, taking it nearer to the shape of EX181.

It was also during 1963 that an overdrive was offered as an option on the road-going MGB. This immediately became popular as it allowed far more relaxed high-speed cruising

with greater economy, although it was withheld from the American market for a while because it was thought that the MGB in this form might further demolish the dwindling sales of the Austin Healey 3000. Following this, in September 1964, the MGB was given a more up-to-date B-series engine with five main bearings rather than three, but there were no significant changes to the best-selling range until October 1965. This was the date when the famous fixed-head MGB GT was introduced.

Thornley was very keen on the GT – which, with its hatchback rear door, he likened to an Aston Martin DB Mark III – because he felt that it would increase the MGB's sales potential dramatically. However, unlike the roadster that was styled in house, the GT conversion was the work of the Italian Pininfarina styling house. Its roof was slightly higher than the detachable hard top which had been introduced for the roadster in 1963, and the windows were larger. There was a good-sized platform for luggage behind two tiny rear seats that were just big enough for children of up to about 8 years old. In this way the range of potential customers for the MGB was increased considerably.

Meanwhile the development department at Abingdon had been busy with new models, the first of which, the Mark III Midget (and Mark IV Sprite), was introduced at the London Motor Show in October 1966. This was a more luxurious version of the Spridget with, among other fittings, a folding hood. The additional comfort was aimed mainly at the US market, but it was also important to make sure that the performance did not suffer because American cars were in the middle of a horsepower race at the time. So the heavier new Spridgets were fitted with a 1275 cc A-series engine based on that of the Mini Cooper S, raising their top speed slightly from 148 km/h (92 mph) to 150 km/h (93 mph) and improved acceleration marginally at the same time. These changes were particularly important because of improvements to Triumph's range of Spitfire-based sports cars, which now included the high-performance six-cylinder GT6.

The MGC

As sales of the larger and, it must be admitted, old-fashioned Austin Healey 3000 declined, BMC asked Abingdon to save money by revising the MGB to accept the Big Healey's six-cylinder engine rather than develop a completely new model. As plenty of room had been left under the bonnet of the MGB at the design stage, it was possible to fit the Austin

1966 MGB *Although the works MGBs are a thing of the past, enthusiasts continue to campaign their cars actively in club events. This MGB, outwardly unchanged with the exception of the front spoiler and modern slick tyres, echoes the colour scheme of the works cars of yore. Provided by Barry Sidery-Smith.*

BELOW **1968 MGC**. *Abingdon's most controversial car of the post-war years, its six-cylinder engine was similar to that used in the contemporary Austin Three Litre saloon. The bonnet bulge is to clear the larger radiator the new engine demanded. Restored by Derek and Pearl McGlen and provided by Richard Tasker.*

MGC (1967–9)
Number built **8999**

ENGINE

No. of cylinders	**Six**
Bore/stroke mm	**83 × 89**
Displacement cc	**2912**
Valve operation	**Overhead pushrod**
Compression ratio	**9:1**
Induction	**Twin SU carburettors**
BHP	**145 at 5250 rpm**
Transmission	**Four-speed, overdrive, three-speed automatic**

CHASSIS

Construction	**Monocoque**
Wheelbase mm	**2311**
Track – front mm	**1245**
Track – rear mm	**1257**
Suspension – front	**Independent wishbone and torsion bar**
Suspension – rear	**Half elliptic springs, live axle**
Brakes	**Hydraulic, front disc**

PERFORMANCE

Maximum speed	**193 km/h (120 mph)**

RCT 606

LEFT **MGC in competition**. *Abingdon produced a works competition version of the MGC, the GTS, in 1967, slightly ahead of the model's announcement. Extensive use was made of aluminium panels and the wheels are centre lock Minilite. Adjustable (a departure from standard) front torsion bars were fitted as were the four-wheel Girling disc brakes. A 109-litre (24 UK gallon) fuel tank also featured. The engines were slightly over bored, developed 200 bhp at 6000 rpm and had triple twin-choke Weber carburettors. Although the cast iron block/aluminium cylinder was used, an all-aluminium engine was also developed. Factory involvement with the GTS ceased in 1968 and the following year John Chatham of Bristol bought much of the competition stock and built up the racer shown on the left. It became an extremely potent circuit performer, though still identifiably an MGC.*

BELOW Chatham also campaigned a roadgoing version of the competition C, pictured here in the 1970 Sicilian Targa Florio.

Healey's C-series engine; the main problem was that it was too heavy.

However, Austin was reworking the engine in any case for a new saloon car, and said that the revised C-series engine would be far lighter, so Enever went ahead with adapting the MGB to take the new unit. It was then intended to badge-engineer the MGB as an Austin Healey 1800, with the new car being marketed as the MGC and the Austin Healey 3000 Mark IV. There were delays in completing the new C-series 3-litre engine and to Abingdon's dismay it turned out to be virtually the same weight as the old C-series unit because it incorporated seven main bearings instead of four. It also had a very conservative cylinder head design which limited power and revs: in fact, it was anything but a sports car engine. Enever had already redesigned the MGB's front suspension to use torsion bars rather than coil springs in a strengthened floorpan to accommodate the larger engine, but now he had to revise the settings hurriedly to cope with the extra weight. Inevitably the car could not be made to handle as well as an MGB, or an Austin Healey 3000, and Donald Healey flatly refused to lend his name to it. Nevertheless, BMC had to have a new 3-litre sports car to replace the existing Austin Healey 3000, because it could not be modified sufficiently economically to meet new American safety regulations. Therefore the new car was introduced in July 1967 only as an M.G., in roadster and GT form.

The unfortunate MGC was immediately criticized by the press because of its nose-heavy handling and inability to perform as vigorously as the old Austin Healey. In addition, it looked almost exactly the same as an MGB, except for odd protrusions such as a lump on the bonnet to clear the front carburettor. The result was that sales were far lower than expected. Nevertheless, because of its additional power and

high top speed (193 km/h, 120 mph), and relaxed high-speed cruising ability, the MGC has since become something of a cult car with M.G. enthusiasts.

At the same time, the MGB was revised to accept a more modern all-synchromesh gearbox and the option of an automatic gearchange, which was expected to be very popular in America (the MGC incorporated this from the start). The interior was also revised along the lines of the MGC to meet the American safety regulations and a US-specification engine was developed to meet emission regulations that were about to be introduced in 1968. The new model, which made its first appearance at the London Motor Show in October 1967, was subsequently known as the MGB Mark II.

BMC had merged with Jaguar to form British Motor Holdings in 1966, and then went on in 1968 to merge with Leyland (which also owned M.G.'s rival, Triumph). BMC, and subsequently BMH, had been having serious cash-flow problems with the popular family saloons, which meant that the heavy investment for a new projected MGD sports car (EX234) was not available. And when Leyland's Donald Stokes took over as chairman and managing director of the new group, called the British Leyland Motor Corporation (BLMC), his natural inclination was towards the Triumph management and its range of sports cars, which needed replacement far more urgently than M.G.'s.

As part of the rationalization that took place at the time of British Leyland's formation, the Magnette was dropped in 1968 and the smaller M.G. saloon – a 1962 variation on the Morris 1100 – received the 1275 cc A-series engine, now known as the M.G. 1300.

But there was one last attempt to produce a new M.G. and this was an exciting mid-engined project. The mid-engined configuration could endow a car with great traction and better handling in experienced hands, and potentially cost less to make with the elimination of the long drive line needed for a front-engined, rear-wheel-drive car. Against those advantages had to be set the difficulties in giving such a vehicle the popular two-plus-two seating plan (the engine and transmission would effectively have to be in the back seat!) and other problems, such as restricted rearward visibility. Nevertheless, a prototype mid-engined car to use a new Austin E-series overhead camshaft power unit was designed at Abingdon. This transverse engine and transmission, which had been introduced on the Austin Maxi, seemed ideal for the new car, designated AD021. This was an exciting new fixed-head coupé with a semi-wedge shape and de Dion rear suspension. The car was attractive because it represented the way in which sports car design trends were expected to go and it used a power unit which, although British Leyland recognized that it was far from perfect, had cost the organization a large amount of capital and needed using as much as possible to justify expenditure. In the event British Leyland's management decided to combine features of both AD021's advanced wedge fixed-head profile with a rival front-engined Triumph project which was to emerge as the controversial Triumph TR7!

In the meantime, the MGB was revised to meet increasingly stringent American emission regulations, with cosmetic changes only for the European cars in October 1969; these included a new black grille, chrome-plated wheels and Leyland badges on the wings, as the new group started a policy of promoting its corporate image rather than those of the individual marques.

It was during this period also that many of the old guard at Abingdon reached retirement age. The loss of Thornley in 1969 and Enever in 1971 was particularly deeply felt. However, the demise of the MGC in 1969 went virtually unlamented, although Abingdon still felt there was a market for a more potent sports car than the MGB. Some of Enever's last work included trying in the MGB the Daimler $2\frac{1}{2}$-litre V8 engine then being produced by the Jaguar division of British Leyland, but the unit Abingdon would really have liked, the all-alloy $3\frac{1}{2}$-litre Rover V8, was not available at that time because all supplies were needed for Rover saloons and Range-Rover production. The Healey contract with British Leyland also came to an end in 1971, and the Sprite variant of the small sports car was dropped soon after.

Triumph's new rival

Meanwhile, as British Leyland planned the new Triumph sports car, the MGB received further low-cost development to reach its Mark III form in May 1971. American export models had been fitted with progressively less powerful engines as emission regulations bit deeper, but, for the Mark

III, the European cars were given a new big-valve cylinder head which improved performance marginally.

Huge overriders were fitted to US export cars during the next year to meet tougher crash regulations, and the option of automatic transmission was withdrawn through lack of demand. The main problem was that the B-series engine was not sufficiently potent to cope with the power-sapping demands of an automatic gearbox during years in which straight-line performance was becoming more and more important for the people who bought sports cars. This was especially evident when the B-series engine was fitted with the emission equipment demanded in the USA.

Between 1970 and 1972, a freelance tuner, Ken Costello,

1973 MGB GT V8. *Only the GT was offered with the 3½-litre V8, as fitted to the Range Rover. Although the car performed well enough, its 1973 arrival coincided with that year's fuel crisis. V8-engined sporting cars became unfashionable, so sales never really took off. Provided by Barry Sidery-Smith.*

MGB GT V8 (1972–6) Number built 2591	
ENGINE	
No. of cylinders	Eight
Bore/stroke mm	89 × 71
Displacement cc	3528
Valve operation	Overhead, hydraulic tappets, pushrods
Induction	Twin SU carburettors
BHP	137
Transmission	4-speed, overdrive
CHASSIS	
Frame	Monocoque
Wheelbase mm	2311
Track – front mm	1245
Track – rear mm	1250
Suspension – front	Independent
Suspension – rear	Half elliptic
Brakes	Discs front, drums rear
PERFORMANCE	
Maximum speed	201 km/h (125 mph)

had been fitting Rover V8 engines to standard MGBs. It was a particularly successful conversion in that the 3528 cc Rover unit – which was by now readily available – weighed only about the same as the cast-iron B-series engine and fitted neatly under the bonnet to give a top speed of around 200 km/h (125 mph) with vastly improved acceleration.

This relatively cheap conversion received extensive publicity and British Leyland was stung into action to produce its own MGB V8, tooling for the stiffer and potentially more suitable MGC bodyshell having been scrapped in 1969. So they stopped supplies of new engines to Costello and authorized a hurried development programme at Abingdon. The main problems were that Abingdon considered the MGB

roadster bodyshell was not really stiff enough to cope with the tremendous torque of the Rover engine. In addition, the factory felt that the MGB's manual gearbox had only a marginal capacity to absorb the torque for a prolonged period. Rover had just introduced a manual gearbox for the V8, but the company needed all its supplies for its own cars first, so none could be supplied to M.G.

However, the MGB GT bodyshell was strong enough to take the V8 engine and, despite Triumph's objections, development went ahead on that basis. The Triumph men did not like the idea of an MGB GT V8 because it would be potentially faster than their TR6 sports car and Stag tourer, and they were afraid that their sales would suffer badly as a result. They wanted British Leyland to drop the MGB GT in any case because the new TR7 sports car was intended as a hard top. They were not too concerned about the four-cylinder MGB roadster because it was anticipated that American crash regulations would outlaw open cars by 1975, and it would not be worth manufacturing an open model for the European market alone.

But Stokes said that if Costello could make money from an MGB V8, despite paying the full price for the extra components and having to discard the existing engine, then Leyland should be able to do even better. So he gave Abingdon the go-ahead to produce the MGB GT V8 with an MGC gearbox on a short-term basis until Triumph could introduce a V8 version of the TR7. This new car, in four-cylinder, or in eight-cylinder form, could be badge-engineered as an M.G. in any case.

ABOVE **1978 Midget**. *Although the Austin Healey Sprite ceased production in 1970, the Midget continued and was re-engined with the Triumph Spitfire 1500 unit from 1975 in order to pep up its performance. Like its Big Brother B, it had rubber bumpers from 1975. Midget output continued until 1980, by which time 226,526 had been produced. Provided by Alan Baker.*

RIGHT **1983 Metro Turbo**. *Introduced in 1982, the M.G. name lives on . . .*

The tough new world

It was in this difficult political atmosphere that the MGB GT V8 was introduced in August 1973. Sadly, it ran into trouble straight away. Within two months Israel was at war with the Arabs and soon after the West experienced its first fuel crisis since 1956. An 80 km/h (50 mph) speed limit was imposed in Britain and everyone's attention turned from high performance to ultimate economy, and thirsty V8s became plain unfashionable.

By 1975, the American market was becoming really tough, as British Leyland and many other manufacturers had anticipated, although their worst fears that open cars would be banned were not realized. Some manufacturers, such as

Porsche, made an outstanding success of developing their range to pass the new crash regulations, which stipulated that the car must be capable of taking a blow from a massive concrete block at 8 km/h (5 mph) without damage to safety-related items such as the lighting. In addition, bumpers had to be of a standard height, which in the case of the low-slung M.G.s meant raising them level with those on an average lumbering American saloon. Jaguar had to drop its E-type as a result, but M.G. just scraped through by reworking the MGB and Midget with massive rubberized bumpers. Insufficient capital was available for a new floorpan because all the British Leyland cash available for sports cars was going into TR7 development. So the M.G.'s suspension had to be jacked up to increase the ride height and thus the bumper height. The Midget was not very badly affected by these changes, and even gained in performance. This was because it was given the 1491 cc four-cylinder engine used in the rival Triumph Spitfire, which could cope better with the strangulation of the American emission laws. But there was no such convenient unit for the MGB, and therefore its performance suffered from the extra weight of the new bumpers, and the handling deteriorated because of the increased ride height.

Sales did not suffer, however, because the M.G.s were among the few open sports cars that survived this traumatic year. The way that the MGB maintained its total sales also emphasized the regard in which the marque was held in America. The Triumph lobby within British Leyland had persuaded top management to drop the MGB GT from the American market to give a clear field for the TR7 when it was introduced for export only in January 1975. British Leyland felt, quite naturally, that having sunk so much money into the TR7 it should be promoted as much as possible. So the company's pricing policies were also heavily weighted in favour of the TR7 against the M.G. But the M.G. was a dependable open car and the TR7, with its controversial wedge shape and its teething troubles, fared badly against the MGB.

And so the MGB and Midget soldiered on until 1980 (the V8 was dropped in 1976), numerous detail changes being incorporated to improve handling and meet more stringent European regulations. But not even Abingdon could carry on selling an antique in numbers sufficient to keep one factory going as British Leyland floundered under increasingly severe cash problems. The TR7 was not a sales success and there was insufficient cash to design and develop a new sports car. Eventually Abingdon had to close altogether in 1980, as British Leyland drew in its horns. The tragedy was made even worse when it was realized that the superbly loyal workforce had hardly ever had a strike, whereas there had been serious problems in this area with TR7 production. What was more, because of the frugal way in which Abingdon was run, it cost less to make a car there than at any other British Leyland factory. Even so, BL claimed it was losing hundreds of pounds on every M.G. sold in the USA and eventually, after an unsuccessful attempt to rescue Abingdon by the small specialist car maker, Aston Martin, the famous M.G. factory was closed.

Latest Longbridge M.G.s

However, British Leyland refused to sell the legendary name of M.G., saving it for a high-performance version of the new car it saw as its salvation, the Metro. With a 1300cc engine based on the A-series unit, the light new four-seater MG Metro was launched in May 1982. It was capable of 142 km/h (88 mph) – making it one of the fastest-ever M.G. production saloons – and invited favourable comparison with the Mini Cooper of old. It was a product of Longbridge, but was welcomed by M.G. enthusiasts who recognized it as a modern sports car with excellent handling and economy. The days of the traditional open sports car might be over for a while, but an even faster turbocharged Metro was waiting in the wings. This exciting new car was introduced at the British Motor Show in October 1982 as a result of a joint development exercise with the British high-performance car maker, Lotus. This small specialist manufacturer already boasted one of the finest turbocharged engines available, installed in the very fast Esprit Turbo. With such a car, British Leyland could re-enter international competition in the top echelons of circuit racing and rallying.

During 1983 another M.G. joined the Metros, an up market 102 bhp Weber-carburettor version of BL's new medium-sized saloon, the Maestro. The Maestros were aimed at taking 25 per cent of the British family car market. With a 1½-litre version of the earlier Austin Maxi's overhead camshaft, four-cylinder engine, and a five-speed Volkswagen gearbox, this very fully equipped car even had a synthetic 'voice' to warn of malfunctions. This was followed in April 1984 by a 2-litre M.G. version of BL's large saloon, the Montego; to which was added, a year later, a turbocharged version developing 150 bhp, capable of getting from 0 to 60 mph in 7.3 seconds, and with a top speed of about 203 km/h (126 mph).

MORRIS

William Morris was an Oxford bicycle maker who went on to become Lord Nuffield. His vehicles were the most popular in Great Britain, but now, after 70 years, the Morris car is sadly no more.

ABOVE **William Morris,** *accompanied by his wife, at the wheel of a Continental-engined Morris Cowley at the Junior Car Club's rally at Burford Bridge, April 1919. Hollick and Pratt of Coventry was responsible for the handsome polished mahogany body.*

LEFT **Morris Minors in production** *at Morris Motors's Cowley factory in 1948. In the background is the Series E Eight, which shared its engine with the Minor, discontinued later that year. It remained available in original MM form until 1953.*

For most of the inter-war years Morris was Britain's top-selling make. However, after the Second World War its influence waned and it became the junior partner in the BMC alliance. Its position was further eroded by the creation of British Leyland, a decline that resulted in the last ever Morris car being built at the end of 1983 but the name will continue on commercial vehicles.

Though his parents were of Oxfordshire farming stock William Richard Morris (1877–1963) was born in Worcester but when he was three his parents returned to their native county. Morris's father became a farm bailiff to his blind father-in-law who had land at Headington Quarry, near Oxford. William left St James Church of England School, Cowley at the age of 15 and, although he signed on for evening classes in engineering, he only attended twice.

Had he had the opportunity for a better education Morris would have probably become a doctor but he had to pursue his natural engineering bent and in 1893 he went to work in an

Oxford bicycle shop. He soon left, however, after the proprietor had refused to increase his salary and he started to repair bicycles in his father's garden shed. This progressed to a modest manufacturing output, his first customer being the local vicar who required a massive frame to accommodate his lanky proportions. The trade of bicycle manufacturer is not quite as complicated as it sounds, for all Morris had to do was to buy his parts from specialist suppliers and then assemble the components himself.

Fortunately for Morris, bicycles were in regular demand in Victorian Oxford and in 1901 he even produced a motorcycle. The following year, in 1902, he went into partnership with a local cycle dealer but it proved a short-lived liaison. Nineteen hundred and three saw him as works manager of an undergraduate folly titled the Oxford Automobile and Cycle Agency but the enterprise was bankrupt within a year and Morris continued in business on his own account, producing bicycles and selling parts along with a few motor cars. The next few years were important ones for Morris for they gave him an opportunity to familiarize himself with the car market and he also gained a detailed knowledge of the various suppliers who catered for the motor trade. For he was intent, by 1910, on producing his own car. Morris decided to follow the approach he had successfully pursued with bicycle production of buying parts from specialist suppliers rather than manufacturing them himself. By adopting this system he could keep his costs to a minimum and would only require a modest outlay of funds.

W.R.M. Motors founded

What he really needed was a backer and in 1911 it came in the shape of the young Earl of Macclesfield, then an undergraduate at Oxford, who agreed to invest £4000 in the project. The following year Morris founded W.R.M. Motors. He was on his way. The Coventry firm of White and Poppe supplied the engine/gearbox unit for the new car, Sankey the artillery wheels, the Birmingham firm of E.G. Wrigley provided axles, while an Oxford coachbuilder named Raworth produced bodies for the new car. It was then a matter of having somewhere to assemble his cars and Morris took over a former military training college at Temple Cowley on the city's outskirts. It so happened that the building had once housed Hurst's Grammar School which his father used to attend.

As the engines were not completed by the 1912 Motor Show, where he had intended to launch his car, Morris went

armed with a set of drawings and these were sufficient for the London firm of Stewart and Ardern to place an order for 400. The car, appropriately named the Morris Oxford, finally appeared in the spring of 1913 and was well priced at £175. The 1018 cc four-cylinder engine was adequate for the car's two-seater bodywork but what Morris really wanted was to produce a cheap four-seater tourer on the lines of Henry Ford's famous Model T which was selling well in Britain. This spidery but deceptively tough car was destined to put the world on wheels and, incredibly, by 1919 every other car in the world was a Model T. In 1913, for example, Ford's British Manchester-based subsidiary produced 7310 cars and commercials and by that time was Europe's largest vehicle manufacturer.

Not only was the T relatively reliable it was also cheap and Morris was determined to discover just how the Americans

LEFT **1914 Morris Oxford.** *The price of this Standard model, when new, was £180. The 1017 cc engine was by White and Poppe of Coventry.*

ABOVE RIGHT **William Morris** *at the wheel of a Morris Oxford with Mr Varney, his accountant, outside Stewart and Ardern's original showrooms at 18 Woodstock Street, London. Gordon Stewart had ordered 400 Oxfords after Morris had shown him the blueprints of his car, prior to its manufacture.*

RIGHT **The Morris Oxford,** *as produced between 1913 and 1915. A total of 1475 was made; 495 Standard and 980 De Luxe models. Morris, however, believed that the two-seater bodywork was a limiting factor.*

achieved their low prices. He recognized that his projected four-seater Morris would be uncompetitively priced against cars imported from the United States and so he was determined to go there to study American production methods. Therefore, in 1913, Morris, accompanied by Hans Landstad, White and Poppe's Norwegian chief draughtsman, crossed the Atlantic and once in America headed for Detroit which was fast establishing itself as the capital of the US motor industry. While there the pair visited the Continental Engine Company and Morris told them his requirements, the firm responding with an $85 (then £17 9s 3d) quote for an engine and gearbox unit. Even after shipping costs had been added it was still substantially cheaper than the £50 White and Poppe had estimated. On his return to England Morris showed Continental's drawings to Peter Poppe, but there was no way that the Coventry firm could compete with the American price.

So, in August 1914, a mere ten days before the outbreak of the First World War, Morris and Landstad again set sail for America. On the first day at sea, on the *Mauretania* – it was a Sunday – Morris went down to the Norwegian's cabin; he had been directed to bring his drawing board with him, and there they planned the Morris Cowley which was destined to be the best-selling British car of the 1920s. Once more in Detroit, Landstad joined the Continental Engine Company's payroll and Morris ordered 3000 examples of the firm's U type 1½-litre Red Seal engine. The Detroit Gear and Machine Company provided gearboxes while axles and steering boxes were also ordered at the same time.

Having completed his task, Morris returned to Britain but Landstad remained behind to learn as much as possible about what was called the American System of Manufacture; in other words, mass production. He remained in Detroit until the end of 1914 and then, having left White and Poppe by this time, he joined Morris at Cowley. American parts had begun arriving there by the end of the year, so in April 1915 Morris was able to announce his Continental Cowley. The car's American origins were all too apparent as the gearbox, which was progressively mounted in unit with the engine, rather than being separate from it, had a central gear change while practically every other British car had its lever on the right-hand side.

Morris was unlucky, however, because in September 1915 the government introduced McKenna Duties (named after the Chancellor of the Exchequer Reginald McKenna) which levied a 33.3 per cent duty on imported cars and parts, so that shipping space might be reserved for vital commodities connected with the war effort. Clocks and watches were similarly sanctioned. Inevitably Morris's prices began to spiral and, in March 1916, the government banned all such imports but Morris had sufficient parts for around 1500 cars and a trickle of Continental Cowleys was made until 1920.

Hotchkiss to the rescue

With the coming of peace in 1918 W.R.M. Motors (re-named Morris Motors in 1919) was potentially in a strong position. The company had an up-to-date design with the Continental Cowley – the earlier White and Poppe-engined Oxford had been discontinued by this time – and there was a tremendous demand for cars, particularly in the medium-sized market. The only fly in the ointment was that Continental informed Morris that it could no longer supply him with the U type Red Seal engine as the company had decided to stop its manufacture since it was too small a capacity for the American market. All that Morris could do was to acquire the manufacturing rights and look around for a British firm to produce it for him. He tried his old pre-war supplier, White and Poppe, but it did not want the job. Then he heard that the Hotchkiss company, which had built a factory in Coventry during the war when they feared their French plant might suffer during hostilities, were looking for work. Morris told Hotchkiss what he wanted, the Coventry company took the job on and, above all, did not require a deposit.

Hotchkiss therefore copied the Continental engine though there were a few detail modifications. There was one, made at Morris's own suggestion, which was to introduce a cork-faced clutch running in engine oil. It was one of the few contributions he made to the detail of his cars and was prompted by the fact that the American engine leaked lubricant into the cluch housing anyway! With his engine production assured Morris could continue with his pre-war theme of assembling his cars from ready-made components. Before long 'Bullnose' Cowleys and the more expensive Oxford version were leaving Morris's factory.

However, in 1919 Model T Fords accounted for a staggering 41 per cent of British new car registrations, but it was a seller's market and Morris's output rose from a mere 360 cars that year to 1932 in 1920. Unfortunately the post-war boom evaporated at the end of 1920 and the following year saw a collapse in business confidence and widespread unemployment. Morris, like many of his contemporaries, had a factory full of unsold cars. In March 1921 he took the daring decision of slashing the price of his four-seater Cowley by £100 to £425 while the two-seater was reduced by £90 to £375. Demand picked up and Morris acted again at the 1921 Motor Show dropping the price of the four-seater to £341 and the two to £299. Output leapt to 6937 cars in 1922 which was more than double the previous year's total. In 1923 over 20,000 Bullnose Cowleys and Oxfords left Morris's works and the following year he overtook Ford as the country's largest car manufacturer. It should be said that Ford was beginning to suffer the effects of a horsepower tax that penalized big-bored American cars. The road fund licence for a Model T spiralled to £23 while a Bullnose Morris only cost a £12 annual fee.

One of the difficulties that Morris experienced was that his suppliers were unable to keep pace with his rapidly growing output so he was left with no alternative, in some instances, but to buy them and provide the necessary finance to expand their manufacturing facilities. It was in 1923 that he purchased Osberton Radiators of Oxford; the Coventry firm of Hollick and Pratt, which had taken over the production of Bullnose bodies in the post-war years; along with Hotchkiss in Coventry, his engine manufacturer since 1919, which was renamed Morris Engines. Nineteen twenty-four saw him

purchase axle specialists E.G. Wrigley and he used this Birmingham factory to expand into the commercial vehicle market. The SU carburettor company followed in 1926.

Morris triumphant

Bullnose Morris production peaked in 1925 when Morris sold 54,151 cars on the British market which amounted to an astounding 41 per cent of the country's total car production. The following year, 1926, Morris discontinued the top-selling Bullnose models and introduced the rather plainer flat radiatored Cowleys and Oxfords though the latter more expensive model was dropped in 1929. He also decided to enter the small car market, dominated throughout the 1920s by the Austin Seven, and in 1929 introduced the Minor, with an 847 cc overhead camshaft engine though this was not a great success (the engine did better in the M.G. M type), so a side-valve version was introduced in 1931 and continued in production until 1934. The original Minor engine had been a Wolseley design, Morris having taken over the old established firm in 1927, and with his M.G. marque beginning to find its feet Morris's empire was growing apace.

MORRIS COWLEY (1919–26)	
Number built 154,244 (also Oxford)	
ENGINE	
No. of cylinders	Four
Bore/stroke mm	69 × 102
Displacement cc	1548
Valve operation	Side
Induction	Single Zenith, SU, or Smiths carburettor
BHP	26 at 2800 rpm
Transmission	Three-speed
CHASSIS	
Frame	Channel
Wheelbase mm	2590
Track – front mm	1219
Track – rear mm	1219
Suspension – front	Half elliptic
Suspension – rear	Three-quarter elliptic
Brakes	Mechanical
PERFORMANCE	
Maximum speed	85 km/h (53 mph)

ABOVE RIGHT **'Flatnose' Morrises** *under construction at Cowley in 1927. The half elliptic rear springs, which replaced the 'Bullnose's' old-fashioned three-quarter elliptic ones, can be clearly seen. It never achieved the popularity of its famous predecessor.*

LEFT **1917 Morris Cowley** *with 1495 cc engine by Continental of Detroit, USA. Its central, rather than right-hand gear-change, gave away its trans-Atlantic origins.*

RIGHT **1927 Morris Oxford.** *The famous 'Bullnose' model was replaced by the 'Flatnose' for the 1927 season. For 1930 the Oxford became a six, though the Cowley version continued until 1934.*

Morris was, of course, no stranger to the United States and in 1925 he again visited America to study pressed steel body production techniques. A pioneer in this field was the Budd Manufacturing Company of Philadelphia and the American automobile industry was becoming increasingly committed to the process because it rendered obsolete the labour intensive traditional coachbuilding methods. As a result of this visit Morris and Budd established the Pressed Steel Company at Cowley, adjoining the Morris works, with the Americans having a controlling interest in the firm. These bodies began appearing on some Morris cars in 1927 but for the firm to operate efficiently it would have to take on outside business and Morris's rivals were reluctant to divulge their styling secrets to a firm that had two Morris directors on the board. Consequently Morris withdrew from the company in 1930, as did his representatives, and other British car makers began to avail themselves of Pressed Steel's facilities. In 1935 Budd withdrew his interest and the firm became completely British owned. It remained independent until 1965 when it was taken over by BMC, heirs to the Morris empire.

Meanwhile, back to the cars of the 1920s. In 1927 came the Morris Six with a 2½-litre overhead camshaft six-cylinder engine, designed by Morris Engines. The Six had a side-valve unit installed in 1930 and was re-named the Oxford, while its engine was used to power the new Isis of 1930. Morris reverted to the four-cylinder theme for his Ten of 1933 but this, along with many other models, was dropped by Leonard Lord, Morris Motors's new managing director.

The proliferation of models that had emerged from Cowley in the late 1920s and early '30s reflected a certain lack of direction in the company's affairs and in 1933 and 1934 Austin, Morris's arch rivals, had produced more cars. Lord soon had Morris back on top with a 918 cc Eight, inspired by Ford's

ABOVE **1930 Morris Isis.** *Produced between 1930 and 1935, the Isis was powered by a 2½-litre, six-cylinder overhead camshaft engine, also used in the M.G. 18/80. The American influence will be apparent.*

RIGHT **1937 Series III Morris Ten** *with a 1292 cc four-cylinder overhead valve engine under its bonnet. The painted radiator shell and Easiclene wheels identify the car.*

success with its Model Y. Unlike the Dagenham car which had Model T inspired transverse leaf suspension, Morris's Eight had half elliptics all round and also hydraulic brakes. The Eight coincided with Morris introducing Series versions of his cars intended to boost sales in the traditionally slack August months. Hitherto, like other manufacturers, he had introduced his new models, along with updates, at the annual Motor Show held during the month of October. A Series II version of the Eight was introduced in August 1937 and output continued for a further year by which time a total of 221,000 had been built, making the model the best-selling British car of the decade.

Leonard Lord also attempted to bring a great sense of order to Morris's rambling combine. The Morris Commercial, Wolseley and M.G. companies, which were the magnate's own property, were sold to the parent Morris Motors and an impressive modernization programme was instituted at Cowley. Unfortunately the abrasive Lord clashed with the testy tycoon, who had been made a baronet in 1928 and Lord Nuffield in 1934, and in 1936 he left Cowley, later to take over the running of the Austin Motor Company. Two years later, in 1938, Nuffield purchased the ailing Coventry-based Riley company.

Ten and Twelve horsepower Morrises followed in 1937, while the following year saw the arrival of the Series M Ten which represented Morris's first foray into unitary body construction. The same year saw the successful Eight replaced by the updated Series E version which featured a more modern look and faired-in headlights. During the Second World War the Nuffield Organization, as the Morris companies became collectively known in 1940, produced a variety of items, ranging from Crusader tanks to Tiger Moth aircraft. With the coming of peace the firm re-introduced two models from its pre-war range, the Series E Eight and Series M Ten, and these remained available until 1948. They were replaced by a new model range of three cars which all shared pleasing but distinctly trans-Atlantic inspired styling. These were the 1476 cc side valve-engined MO Oxford, the MS Six which used a 2.2-litre Wolseley overhead camshaft engine, and the 918 cc powered Minor, destined to become the best-loved British car of the post-war era.

The Minor is planned

This famous model was born, rather like the Jaguar XK engine, during wartime fire watching sessions. In the Minor's case the participants were Miles Thomas, the Nuffield Organization's managing director, Vic Oak, chief engineer, and Alec Issigonis, who had joined Morris in 1936 and whose earlier career is chronicled on page 49. Thomas encouraged Issigonis to create a small four-seater car for the post-war market, while Oak had the good sense to give him a free hand. The design was undertaken, not at the main drawing office at Cowley, but in a special development shop with a small body building facility nearby.

Issigonis not only styled the car and conceived its mechanical layout but was also responsible for such details as the dashboard and door handles. A small team was established and, by 1943, a prototype car, codenamed Mosquito, was well advanced. Like the Series M Ten it was of monocoque construction and Issigonis paid great attention to the car's

LEFT **The Morris Minor** *with overhead camshaft engine was offered in Semi-Sports two-seater form for the 1931 season.*

BELOW **1939 Morris Eight Series E tourer.** *The original Eight was replaced by the E for 1939, with faired-in headlamps and rear opening bonnet. This touring version was not continued after the war, though the saloon remained available until 1948. The engine was later used in the Morris Minor.*

LEFT **1936 Morris Eight.** *Produced in response to Ford's Model Y, the Eight became Britain's best-seller of the 1930s*

MORRIS EIGHT (1935–8)	
Number built 221,000 (approx)	
ENGINE	
No. of cylinders	Four
Bore/stroke mm	57 × 90
Displacement cc	918
Valve operation	Side
Compression ratio	5.8:1
Induction	Single SU carburettor
BHP	25 at 3900 rpm
Transmission	Three-speed
CHASSIS	
Frame	Channel
Wheelbase mm	2286
Track – front mm	1143
Track – rear mm	1143
Suspension – front	Half elliptic
Suspension – rear	Half elliptic
Brakes	Hydraulic
PERFORMANCE	
Maximum speed	93 km/h (58 mph)

independent front suspension which was a torsion bar system, while rack and pinion steering was another progressive feature. Torsion bars were also tried at the rear but convention, and cost, eventually dictated a straightforward leaf spring layout. Not only this but Issigonis had recognized the importance of making the car nose heavy to ensure good directional stability. Consequently, the power unit was mounted well forward and was unusual for a British car in that it was a flat four, of 800 and 1100 cc, coupled to a three-speed gearbox with column change. There was also a fearsome two-cylinder two-stroke engine employing no less than two crankshafts located on either side of the bores. Maybe fortunately it proved impracticable, fumed badly and suffered from lubrication problems.

LEFT **1966 Morris 1000 Traveller.** *The estate version of the Minor appeared for 1954 and remained in production until April 1971, five months after the last Minor saloon was built.*

BELOW **1949 Series MM Morris Minor,** *powered by the Series E 918 cc Eight engine until 1953. Note the spacer in the middle of the front bumper and accompanying bonnet ridge, a legacy of Issigonis's legendary widening operation.*

The flat four engine, with the smaller of the two capacities intended for the home market, powered the prototype Mosquito but, after the war, car tax was introduced on a flat rather than a horsepower rate so the 800 cc unit could be effectively dropped. Morris already had a sound but archaic 918 cc side-valve engine which was then doing service in the Series E Morris Eight. What was far better was that it fitted under the Mosquito's bonnet with ease and, with such overwhelming production advantages, there it stayed.

It was at a fairly late stage in the project's life, in 1947, that Issigonis decided that the car was too narrow. At 144 cm (57 inches) it was about the same width as the existing Eight but, with great courage, Issigonis instructed one evening that the prototype be sawn in half! The following morning the two halves were moved first 5 cm (2 inches) and then 15 cm (6 inches) apart and eventually he compromised on a 10 cm (4 inch) gap. Issigonis undertook this modification for purely aesthetic reasons but the car's already good handling also improved as a result. It was then a matter of making last-minute changes to the tooling, though by this time the front and rear bumpers had already been produced and were distinguished by 10 cm (4 inch) spacers on the production cars.

Then it was a matter of convincing the ageing Lord Nuffield of the car's potential. When he was first shown what was by then known as the Morris Minor, he took an instant dislike to it, said it looked like a poached egg and walked out. Neither would he sanction the model's production, maintaining that the already dated Series E Eight had plenty of orders. This was the culmination of some years of frustration for Sir Miles Thomas (knighted 1943), who had joined Morris back in 1924 and was the firm's most able executive. He left the Nuffield Organization in 1947 and later took over the chairmanship of B.O.A.C. His place at Cowley was taken by Reginald Hanks, who was one of the few executives to appreciate the ingenuity of Issigonis's design, and he gave the go ahead for the model's production, the Minor making its début at the 1948 Motor Show.

This lack of enthusiasm by Morris's management set the pattern for the relatively few changes made to the Minor during its 23-year production life. The first model, the Series MM, was initially produced in two-door saloon and touring forms, with a four-door saloon following in 1951. It was during that year the car's headlamps were moved from their original position in the radiator grille to the front wings in deference to the American lighting regulations, overseas sales being all important in those export conscious days. A painted radiator grille replaced the original plated one during the same year.

Following on from the creation of BMC in 1952, the Austin A30's 803 cc overhead valve engine took the place of the Series E side-valver that had served the model since its inception. This Series II Minor was joined in 1954 by the Traveller with composite wood and steel bodywork (following the same theme as the American station wagon). In 1957 the model was re-designated the Minor 1000 with the fitment of a more powerful 948 cc engine and at the same time a one-piece curved windscreen was introduced replacing the split screen that had been fitted since the model's inception. It had been initially employed because in the early post-war years glass manufacturers did not possess the facilities to mass produce curved glass windscreens, so split screens, made up of a pair of flat glasses, sufficed for some years. The Minor was also fitted with a new enlarged rear window at the same time.

The millionth Morris Minor was produced at the end of 1960: the first British car to achieve this noteworthy milestone. With its manufacture, a batch of replica cars bearing the *Morris 1000000* legend rather than the *Morris 1000* badge was manufactured in a memorable lilac livery. The

TOP **1948 Morris Oxford, Series MO.** *Announced simultaneously with the Minor, this 1476 cc side valve model was built until 1954.*

ABOVE **Sir William Morris** *(left) pictured with his new managing director, Leonard Lord, at Cowley in 1933.*

Minor kept its semaphore indicators for far longer than most and they were finally dispensed with in 1962 and replaced by fashionable flashers.

For 1963 came a larger capacity 1098 cc engine. The open version of the Minor was discontinued in 1969 and the last saloons were built in 1970, while the final Traveller left its assembly plant in April 1971. A total of over one and a half million Minors of all varieties had been produced during the 23-year production run.

BMC is formed

These developments were all somewhat removed from the year 1952 which saw the Austin and Morris companies join forces to create the British Motor Corporation. Although Morris had been Britain's largest manufacturer of the inter-war years, by the late 1940s Austin, directed by the aggressive Leonard Lord, was well ahead in production terms. With the creation of BMC Lord Nuffield at last took a back seat, was made the Corporation's honorary President, and the Morris design initiative was transferred to the Austin headquarters at Longbridge, with Leonard Lord effectively in charge of the whole combine.

The Series II Oxford that arrived in 1954 was a Cowley design, however, with an Austin 1489 cc engine under its bonnet. There was also a 1200 cc Cowley echoing pre-war Morris practice. The Isis name was revived for a 2.6-litre six-cylinder similarly styled saloon of 1956. A Series II version arrived in 1957, with right-hand gearchange, but the model was dropped the following year. The Oxford soldiered on, appearing in Series III form in 1957, while the Series IV, which lasted until 1959, was a Traveller with opening tailgate. The

Series V Oxford, introduced that year, was the corporate four-door Farina saloon, while the larger 1622 cc Series VI remained in production from 1962 to 1971.

The evolution of the revolutionary front-wheel-drive Mini has already been chronicled in the Austin section of this book. The Morris version was titled the Mini Minor and cost £536 which was £40 more than the basic Austin Seven. The transverse engine/front-wheel-drive layout was perpetuated for the 1100 model, introduced in 1962, and initially only available in Morris form. Unlike the Mini it had a Farina-styled body, derived from the Italian styling house's Austin A40, while the suspension also differed and was an interconnected Hydrolastic system. The model – there was an Austin version in 1964 – was destined to be Britain's top-selling car for close on a decade; a 1300 engine option arrived in 1968, a year in which the Morris name was discontinued from the saloons, though it continued on the Traveller versions until 1971. In 1966 came the Morris variant of the front-wheel-drive Austin 1800, introduced two years pre-viously. For 1969 there was also a high compression version with twin carburettors and larger front discs. The 1800 remained in production until 1975. Similar in appearance, the 2200, with 2227 cc six-cylinder overhead camshaft engine in the Austin Maxi manner, and also produced in Wolseley form, appeared in 1972. Output, however, was short-lived and only lasted until 1974.

Last Morris model

The Leyland take-over of BMC in 1968 had been a recognition that the high production/low profit front-wheel-drive 1100/1300 theme also required a rear-drive back up. Ford had displayed this with devastating effect with its Cortina range, introduced in 1962 and soon to take over as the country's top selling model. British Leyland's answer was the Morris Marina introduced in 1971, a year in which the 1100/1300 range became Austin-only models. The Marina followed the Morris Minor's proven formula of torsion bar independent front suspension and rack and pinion steering, while the 1275 cc

LEFT **Morris 1100.** *Introduced in 1962, this was Britain's top selling car for close on a decade. A 1300 option arrived for 1968. Output continued until 1974 but latterly in Austin form.*

TOP **1968 Morris Mini Minor.** *The Mini was produced in Austin and Morris forms until 1969 when it became a marque name in its own right.*

engine employed an all-synchromesh Truimph gearbox. It was available in saloon and coupé forms and there was also a 1.8-litre option along with the high performance twin carburettored TC. There was, briefly, an 18-22 Morris in 1975 and when the car was re-named simply Princess later in the year this left the Marina as the sole Morris car. In 1978 the 1.8-litre dispensed with its pushrod engine and it was replaced by a 1695 cc new O Series engine with belt-driven overhead camshaft. The Marina, however, was destined for only a further two years of life and it was replaced by the Ital in 1980.

This was essentially a face-lifted Marina with a new front by the Italian Ital Design styling house. In addition to the two previous engine options a 2-litre O Series engine was announced for 1981 and output continued, with manufacture latterly transferred from Cowley to Longbridge, until the end of 1983. After 70 years the Morris car was no more.

ABOVE **1979 Morris Marina.** This was British Leyland's answer to the Ford Cortina. Introduced in 1971 in 1300 and 1800 forms, its mechanical inspiration was the Morris Minor. The Marina, with a 1700 cc engine replacing the 1800 cc unit in 1978, was produced until 1980.

LEFT **1968 Monte Carlo Rally.** This was the last occasion the works Minis competed in the event. Paddy Hopkirk and Ron Crellin, pictured here, finished sixth.

RIGHT **Morris Ital.** The Marina was face-lifted for 1980 by Ital Design, and was accordingly renamed, with alterations to the front and rear body profile. It ceased production in 1983 as the last Morris car.

ROLLS-ROYCE

Britain's most famous marque name and born of Sir Henry Royce's genius, the spirit of his perfectionist ideals is still maintained in the current cars from Crewe.

LEFT **The famous Spirit of Ecstasy mascot** *created by artist Charles Sykes for Rolls-Royce in 1911 and still fitted to the current models.*

BELOW **Phantom I.** *Rolls-Royces were manufactured in America between 1921 and 1933. This Springfield-built car was once owned by actor Tom Mix, and featured in several films, including* Inside Daisy Clover *and* FBI Story. *Provided by Hal Blaine.*

Early in May 1904 three businessmen sat down to lunch at Manchester's newly opened Midland Hotel to discuss motor cars. The Midland has no doubt witnessed many such commercial meetings but this one triggered a chain of events that was to create the most illustrious of all names to be associated with the automobile. For, as a result, Rolls-Royce Ltd was established.

At first sight Rolls and Royce must have made unlikely dining companions. Frederick Henry Royce, who was 41 at the time, was a miller's son and largely self-taught, and had achieved commercial success in the face of overwhelming personal odds. By contrast, at 26 years of age, the Hon. Charles Stewart Rolls, a peer's son, had followed an assured aristocratic path to Eton and Trinity College, Cambridge, and was supported, to some extent, by a wealthy father. The final member of the luncheon party was Henry Edmunds,

who knew both men and had effected the meeting. His catalytic role must surely make him godfather of the Rolls/Royce alliance. To find out how this historic meeting came to take place, and what drew the two principal characters into the same unlikely orbit, we must examine the respective careers of Royce and Rolls and the times in which they lived.

Henry Royce

Frederick Henry Royce was born on 27 March 1863. His father, James Royce, described himself as a 'farmer and miller' on his marriage to Mary King. That took place in 1852 at Woodham Ferrers, Essex, which was Mary's home. In all, five children were born to the couple, Henry being the youngest. By the time of his birth the family had moved to Alwalton, near Peterborough, where James managed mills for the Ecclesiastical Commissioners, the body concerned with Church of England properties and stipends. History has cast James Royce as a shadowy, luckless figure but it should be remembered that agriculture was in a state of decline at the time, so how much was due to circumstances or personality is difficult to establish.

What we do know is that James took Henry and his other son, also called James, with him when he left the quiet banks of the River Nene for the bustling, friendless streets of London in the hope of obtaining work. Meanwhile his wife and daughters remained in Alwalton. The year was 1867 and Henry was four, but James Royce seems to have had as little success in London as he did in rural Lincolnshire. Ill fortune seemed to haunt the man for he died in 1872 at the early age of 41. This left nine-year-old Henry faced with the task of getting work for himself. For a time he sold newspapers for W.H. Smith and, at the age of ten, he became a telegraph boy in London's opulent West End. By all accounts Mary Royce did her best for her youngest but she seemed to have been ill-equipped for early widowhood. In later life Henry spoke little of his early years, but he did tell a close friend that at this time his food for the day was 'often but two slices of bread soaked in milk'.

Fortunately help was at hand, for his aunt had a little money and Henry's mechanical aptitudes were clearly developing because she managed to secure a £20-a-year apprenticeship for him at the Great Northern Railway Works at Peterborough, only a few miles from his birthplace. He was 14 at the time and he later recalled that there 'I acquired some skill as a mechanic but lacked technical, commercial and clerical experience.' The three years spent with the Great Northern instilled some stability in his all too insecure and unhappy life. Apart from benefiting from mechanical skills, he embarked on a bout of self-education, teaching himself those subjects he had missed when his energies were geared to survival. Elementary education, it should be remembered, did not become compulsory in England until 1888. So he sharpened up his mathematics and learned algebra, and began teaching himself the rudiments of the new power source that had clearly captured his imagination: electricity. By good chance the owner of his lodging, a Mr Yarrow, had a lathe in his garden shed, along with a carpenter's bench, shaping machine and grinder; tools that Henry was able to use to develop his skills in the working of metals.

Then, tragically, fate again intervened and his aunt found herself unable to continue payments for his apprenticeship. So, in 1879, he was again looking for work. He travelled north to Leeds where he worked for a firm of machine-tool makers who paid him 11 shillings for a 54-hour week. Later he was to remember starting work at 6 am and finishing at 10 pm for months on end. Then, by chance, he saw an advertisement for a tester with the London-based Electric Light and Power Company, which had acquired the patents and services of that versatile American inventor, Hiram P. Maxim. Royce got the job and moved back to London, taking lodgings in Kentish Town. He continued his self-education by night, also attending Professor William Ayrton's evening classes and other lectures at the Polytechnic in Regent Street.

Royce's ability and dedication must have made a good impression on his employers for in 1882, at the age of 19, he was sent to Liverpool to manage the firm's affairs in that city. His responsibilities included the supervision of the then somewhat precarious business of theatrical electric lighting, but his employment with the Lancashire Maxim and Western Electric Company was destined to be shortlived for the enterprise foundered.

Henry, however, had struck up a friendship with another young electrical engineer, a London doctor's son named Ernest Claremont. In 1884, when Royce was 21 and on a modest capital of £70 (Claremont contributed £50 and Royce, incredibly, £20) they set up an electrical business, renting a small room in Cooke Street, off Stretford Road in Manchester. In the first instance F.H. Royce and Co. produced lampholders, progressing to bells and eventually dynamos. It was these dynamos that gave Royce an opportunity to express his perfectionist ideals. He quickly grasped the importance of producing a unit with a sparkless commutator, thus eliminating a potential fire hazard: a crucial factor for any establishment installing a generating set, but particularly on board ship, or in a paper or cotton mill. Although trade fluctuated, and competition from America and Germany was an ever-present challenge, Royce and Claremont worked long hours and gradually their efforts were rewarded with success.

These factors of improved circumstances and stability, the first he had ever enjoyed, were no doubt considerations when in 1893, at the age of 30, Henry Royce married. His bride was Minnie, the daughter of Alfred Punt, a London printer; rather conveniently, Claremont married the other sister. F.H. Royce and Co also benefited, for Punt put money into the firm.

By 1894, just ten years after its inception, the business had grown sufficiently to become a public company and there was a change of name to Royce Ltd. Then the invention of the electric crane lent itself perfectly to Royce improvement and refinement, and soon attained a worldwide reputation for the company. By 1899 orders stood at an impressive £20,000. A works and foundry were established at Trafford Park, Manchester, which was Britain's first industrial estate. Royce's growing prosperity was apparent when he and his wife, along with Minnie's adopted niece Violet, moved into a specially built house in fashionable Legh Road, Knutsford, de-

signed by none other than the architect of Manchester Town Hall, Alfred Waterhouse.

The birth of the motor car

We should, perhaps, pause here to consider the birth and appearance of the motor car, which by the turn of the century was beginning to make its presence felt on Britain's roads. It was in 1885 that Carl Benz and Gottlieb Daimler, working quite independently of each other in Germany, had created self-propelled carriages powered by internal combustion engines that were saleable to the general public. The French were soon to take up the idea while the British, who clearly represented the most prosperous European market of the day, had to import vehicles from the Continent before their own industry got on a sound footing.

ABOVE **The Hon Charles Stewart Rolls** *(1877–1910), third son of Lord Llangattock, who died in a flying accident at the age of 32.*

ABOVE RIGHT **Sir Henry Royce** *(1863–1933), a self-taught mechanical genius, was made a baronet in 1930.*

BELOW **Royce's 10 hp car** *completed in 1904, awaiting its body. Was this the photograph that inspired Rolls to arrange a meeting with Royce?*

ABOVE Royce Ltd's cramped premises in Cooke Street, Manchester. In the foreground is a two-cylinder car with two four-cylinder models positioned centrally. The stairs on the right lead to the offices of Royce, company secretary John de Looze and to the drawing office and instrument room. The famous radiator has already made its appearance.

So when Henry Royce acquired his first horseless carriage it is no surprise to find that it was a French De Dion Bouton Quadricycle. Claremont and their friend and doctor H. Campbell-Thompson acquired similar machines. It was hoped that Royce, with the leafy lanes of Cheshire and Derbyshire now within easy reach, would lessen his work load. Maybe he was driven by the fear that those terrible, poverty-stricken days would one day return but his health, which had inevitably suffered during the privations of his youth, was never robust. So Campbell-Thompson suggested a break and, in 1902, Henry at last agreed and went on a ten-week cruise to South Africa with his wife, who had relatives there. On his return his doctor again took a hand, suggesting that Henry, to avoid over-exerting himself, should buy a motor car. Therefore a second-hand 1901 French Decauville was acquired. The arrival of the Royce car was drawing ever and inevitably nearer.

Royce was in for a nasty shock when he went to collect the Decauville, which had been conveyed to Manchester by train. Unfortunately it failed to start and Henry had to undergo the indignity of being pushed back to Cooke Street by four labourers while he sat at the steering wheel giving directions. The car was left in a shed and the following day Royce set about getting it running. In actual fact the Decauville was a fairly reputable make and its apocryphal reputation for crudeness and unreliability probably says

outset of the project, Royce employed light, yet strong, nickel steel for many chassis and engine parts and enough components to build three cars were produced. Royce worked ceaselessly on the project and all too often the instrument room foreman would arrive to start work at 6.30 am only to find his employer slumped over his bench, having worked throughout the night on the car, and then collapsed from sheer exhaustion. Much of the Royce car was actually produced at Cooke Street: the patterns, aluminium and bronze castings were made there, but the iron castings came from the Trafford Park works. Forgings were bought out from the Manchester firm of Mountford Brothers and, naturally, the car's ignition system was designed by Royce himself. A local carriage maker produced a simple four-seater body for the car.

By all accounts the 10 hp two-cylinder 1800 cc Royce performed well enough on its first outing. Naturally Henry took the wheel and drove the car on a 24 km (15 mile) run to his Knutsford home. The second car went to Ernest Claremont, who at first had not been over-enthusiastic about Royce Ltd entering the motor trade. Henry Edmunds, a director of the company, had the third car and he was destined to play a crucial role in the creation of Rolls-Royce Ltd. He acquired his share in the company almost by chance. Edmunds was a director of W.T. Glover and Co, a firm that was also based at Trafford Park and supplied Royce with electrical cables. It so

LEFT **1904 10 hp Rolls-Royce.** *This is the earliest surviving example of the marque and heralded the appearance of the Classically inspired radiator that features on all Rolls-Royces to this day. The engine was an 1800 cc two-cylinder unit, though later this was enlarged to 2 litres. Note that the driven rear wheels have more spokes than the front ones; a common practice in those days. Sixteen examples were eventually built and output continued until 1906. Provided by T. and E. Love.*

RIGHT **The 10 hp model** *featured in a 1905 Rolls-Royce catalogue, announcing C.S. Rolls's arrangements with the illustrious Barker coachbuilding concern. Even at this early date the silent running of Henry Royce's cars has been underlined. 15, 20 and 30 hp models were also offered, priced at £460, £650 and £900 respectively. The 20 was the most popular.*

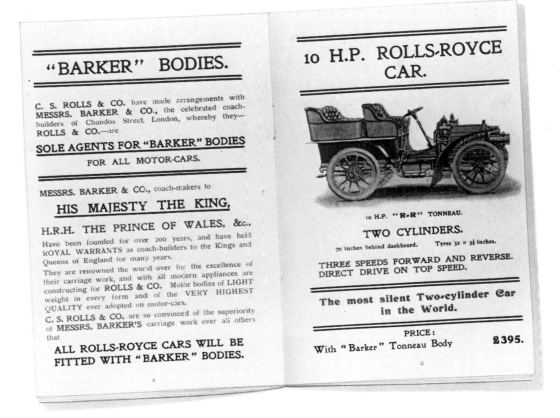

more about Royce's perfectionist standards than about shortcomings in the 10 hp two-cylinder car from Corbeil. As it happened, Royce's electrical business was not enjoying the buoyancy that had marked its formative years and, with that activity concentrated at Trafford Park, he decided to employ the spare capacity available at Cooke Street to enter the motor business. Doctor Campbell-Thompson's plan for Royce to take things easier by getting a car had gone seriously awry!

Early in 1903 work on the Royce car began. Henry was assisted by mechanic Ernie Mills, who was already acquainted with the works of the Decauville, and two electrical apprentices, Tom Haldenby and Eric Platford. From the very

transpired that Claremont decided to take a financial interest in Glover and he acquired shares from Edmunds in exchange for Royce stock. Henry Edmunds, also a pioneer electrical engineer, was a prominent member of the London-based Automobile Club of Great Britain and Ireland (later to become the RAC); a fellow member was the Hon. Charles Rolls, a pioneer motorist and third son of Lord Llangattock of Monmouth.

The Hon. Charles Rolls

Charles Stewart Rolls was born in London on 27 August 1877 though he grew up at The Hendre, the family's Monmouthshire country seat. His father was John Allan Rolls, the grandson of the seventh Earl of Northesk, who became Baron Llangattock in 1892 when Charles was 15. His education began at Mortimer Vicarage School, near Reading, Berkshire, and in 1891 he followed his two brothers to Eton.

He left Eton in 1894 and afterwards entered Trinity College, Cambridge, where he became an enthusiastic motorist, and soon after coming down he established the London-based C.S. Rolls and Co motor agency. There he sold foreign cars but was keen to market a good quality British one. It is here that Henry Edmunds, Royce director and friend of Rolls, enters the story. He sent photographs of the Manchester engineer's car to him and it seems likely that these were sufficient to encourage Rolls to travel to Manchester early in May 1904 to view the car and meet Royce. In the train's dining car, as they sped northwards, Rolls, with remarkable prescience, told Edmunds that his ambition was 'to have a motor

car connected with his name, so that in the future it might be a household word, just as much as Broadwood or Steinway in connection with pianos; or Chubb in connection with safes'.

On arrival in Manchester they met Royce at the Midland Hotel. Edmunds, who later recorded his impressions of the meeting, says that Rolls and Royce 'took to each other at first sight'. For, although they had such contrasting social backgrounds, both had practical engineering experience, shared an equal enthusiasm for electricity and both were of a parsimonious persuasion: Royce no doubt through circumstances, Rolls displaying a family trait. After lunch, Rolls inspected the Royce car and his response to it can be gauged by the fact that on his return to London he dragged his partner Claude Johnson from his bed to inform him, 'I have found the greatest motor engineer in the world.' Unfortunately that very day Johnson had committed C.S. Rolls and

Co. to finance a company to produce electric broughams, for which he harboured some personal enthusiasm. However, after some discussion, they decided to cut their losses in favour of Henry Royce's car.

The first Rolls-Royces

One outcome of the Manchester meeting was that an agreement was drawn up stipulating that C.S. Rolls and Co. would sell all the cars Royce Ltd could produce: the resultant vehicles would bear the name Rolls-Royce. This may sound a trifle unfair on Royce who had, after all, designed the car but the primary use of Rolls's name made marketing and alliterative sense. This agreement was finally signed on 23 December 1904.

A more immediate outcome of the meeting, however, was that work started at once on a batch of nineteen 10 hp cars and a new model, a three-cylinder 15 hp car, was initiated. Unlike the three 10 hp prototypes, these vehicles witnessed the introduction of the famous Classically inspired radiator fitted to all Rolls-Royces thereafter. Later in 1904 meetings were held between Johnson and the Royce company when it was decided to extend the range to include four-cylinder 20 hp and six-cylinder 30 hp cars. The earlier 10 hp and these later two models, in the interests of rationalization, shared the same cylinder blocks, pistons and connecting rods. In

1905 15 hp Rolls-Royce. *This three-cylinder car, now displayed at the Doune Motor Museum, Perthshire, Scotland, is the second oldest surviving Rolls-Royce and the only one remaining of the six examples produced. Owner is the Royal Scottish Automobile Club. The first owner was the Hon. Captain T. Dundas.*

December 1904 C.S. Rolls and Co.'s stand at the Paris salon displayed two-, three- and four-cylinder Rolls-Royces, along with the first 30 hp six-cylinder engine. Henry Royce's cars had made their international début.

The following year Rolls moved his London showrooms from Brook Street to nearby Conduit Street, premises the company occupies to this day. It was also in 1905 that two examples of a lightened 20 hp car ran in that year's TT race. Although Rolls in one of the cars dropped out, the other came second and the Light 20 entered the Rolls-Royce range. However, Rolls was luckier in 1906 and won the event.

The year 1905 also witnessed the appearance of a new Invisible Engine model, which seems to have been Claude Johnson's inspiration. The idea was that the car should resemble an electric brougham by its apparent absence of engine. So Royce adopted a more horizontally compact 3½-litre V8, which was tucked under the vehicle's floorboards. It seems that Sir Alfred Harmsworth (later Lord Northcliffe), founder of the *Daily Mail*, was also party to the model's conception because he came up with the idea of the 'Legalimit' variant. Although this looked more like a conventional car it would not exceed 32 km/h (20 mph), the legal speed limit of the day. Neither model was a success and, in all, only three V8-engined cars were built.

It soon became clear that the affairs of C.S. Rolls and Co. of London and the Manchester-based Royce Ltd required some tidying up. The obvious course of action was amalgamation and Rolls-Royce Ltd, echoing the name of the cars, was registered on 15 March 1906. Ernest Claremont became chairman of the new company with Rolls as technical managing director. Royce was chief engineer and works director and Claude Johnson commercial managing director. Royce and Johnson soon got down to the urgent business of planning a new factory as the cramped Cooke Street premises were obviously unsuitable for expansion. To finance this exercise it was subsequently decided to increase the company's £60,000 capital to £200,000 of which £100,000 would be open to public subscription.

The Silver Ghost

That year's London Motor Show was of enormous significance for Rolls-Royce. For not only did C.S. Rolls and Co.'s stand display the coveted Tourist Trophy, along with the winning car, but also a new 40/50 hp model was unveiled. A gleaming chassis was displayed and the lower half of the engine's crankcase was removed and a mirror revealed the six-cylinder power unit's internals. The model was Royce's masterpiece and was to mark a turning point in the company's affairs.

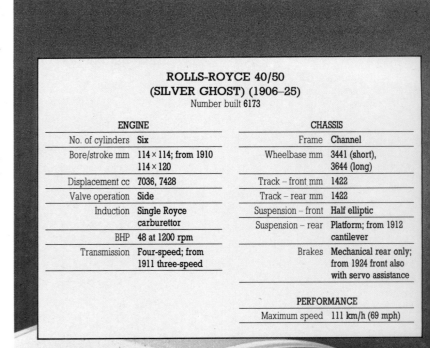

ROLLS-ROYCE 40/50 (SILVER GHOST) (1906–25)
Number built 6173

ENGINE			CHASSIS		
No. of cylinders	Six			Frame	Channel
Bore/stroke mm	114 × 114; from 1910 114 × 120			Wheelbase mm	3441 (short), 3644 (long)
Displacement cc	7036, 7428			Track – front mm	1422
Valve operation	Side			Track – rear mm	1422
Induction	Single Royce carburettor			Suspension – front	Half elliptic
BHP	48 at 1200 rpm			Suspension – rear	Platform; from 1912 cantilever
Transmission	Four-speed; from 1911 three-speed			Brakes	Mechanical rear only; from 1924 front also with servo assistance

PERFORMANCE	
Maximum speed	111 km/h (69 mph)

ABOVE AND RIGHT **1907 Silver Ghost.** *The most famous Rolls-Royce of all, named by Claude Johnson and retrospectively adopted for the 40/50 range. The engine is a 7-litre side valve six. This car has been in Rolls-Royce's ownership since 1948.*

It is what we now know as the Silver Ghost, Rolls-Royce's most illustrious car. Sharing the stand with that magnificent polished chassis was a majestic Pullman limousine, built by Barker and made possible by the new 40/50 chassis. This measured 4756 mm (15 ft 7¼ in) in length, making it more than 610 mm (2 ft) longer than the largest 30 hp car.

A larger chassis required a bigger capacity engine and it was here that Royce drew on the experience he had gained from his earlier designs, developing and refining the concept of the 30 hp six-cylinder model, which had suffered in its

early days from catastrophic crankshaft failure. For early in 1906, three 30s had broken their cranks while on test and Royce immediately set about remedying the problem. It is a peculiarity of the six-cylinder engine layout that it sets up excessive torsional vibrations that, if left unchecked, will produce exactly those symptoms that Royce experienced with the 30. He succeeded in preventing these breakages by removing the crankshaft balance weights and lessening the mass of the forward flywheel.

With the 40/50, however, Royce did not initially employ a

vibration damper, though an externally mounted one appeared in 1910 and this was contained within the crankcase the following year. Also, by increasing the bore by 13 mm ($\frac{1}{2}$ inch) and making a similar reduction in stroke, Royce assumed that he would be able to eliminate the crucial crankshaft vibration he had experienced with the 30. The crankshaft itself was considerably strengthened for the same reason. Like that on the 30, it had seven main bearings and was carried in the upper half of the aluminium crankcase, which was a great improvement on the earlier design. Another plus was the use of a fully pressurized lubrication system. The cast-iron, fixed-head cylinder blocks were arranged in two units of three, rather than three batches of two as with the earlier six. Also the overhead inlet valves were dispensed with, no doubt in the interests of quiet running: the 40/50's valves were all side mounted. The capacity was 7036 cc, increased to 7428 cc in 1910.

This description can do little justice to the impact the 40/50 made on its announcement. The car's extraordinary silence, its smooth running and undoubted refinement, to which should be coupled its sheer beauty, all contributed to a magnificent car that was head and shoulders above its contemporaries. Even more significant was the decision to discontinue all other Rolls-Royces, leaving the 40/50 in splendid isolation. For, if the new model was a masterpiece of design, then the one-model policy was a triumph of marketing. It should be remembered that at the time most manufacturers offered a bewildering variety of models intended to capture as many tastes and pockets as possible.

The credit should go to Claude Johnson for the one-model decision, which was taken in March 1908, 15 months after the 40/50's appearance. However, it should be seen against the background of a year that began with the local manager of the London City and Midland Bank having to grant Rolls-Royce a £20,000 overdraft. Johnson argued that the development of a new four-cylinder model (in succession to the 20) would cost thousands of pounds. There was no falling off in demand for the 40/50 and there were sound reasons for a one-model policy with a saving on tooling costs in the new factory by then well under construction.

LEFT **Claude Johnson** (1864–1926). Rolls-Royce's managing director, who died at the age of 61, having worked untiringly for the company since its inception.

BELOW **Silver Ghost.** E.W. (later Lord) Hives drove this car from London to Edinburgh in top gear in 1911. Provided by Kenneth Neve.

RIGHT **Silver Ghost**, one of the last examples to be built before World War 1. Provided by D.K. and R.A. Lankester.

The original intention seems to have been to establish the new factory in Manchester. Then a further four sites were contemplated, mostly in the Midlands, and Bradford was also considered. When Derby Town Council heard that Rolls-Royce was looking for a new factory site the company was offered the considerable inducement of cheap electricity on a long-term contract and the provision of all other essential services. A site was purchased from the Osmaston Estates Company and work began, Royce having the responsibility of planning the new factory and negotiating with contractors.

In the meantime Claude Johnson was engaged in obtaining valuable publicity for the 40/50. He took the 13th chassis (possibly the one that had graced the 1906 show stand), had it painted with aluminium paint to give a silver finish while the Barker Roi des Belges touring body was similarly resplen-

son's steadying hand and managerial ability.

After the attempt to ease Royce's work load came Charles Rolls's request to the board to relieve him of his 'irksome' duties. Then, in April, he resigned as a director of the company that bore his name. In truth, he had become totally absorbed in the world of aviation which initially had taken a tandem role with his motoring interests. A few months after he had left Rolls-Royce, on 12 July he was tragically killed in a flying accident at Bournemouth. He was 32 years old.

Royce, deeply affected by the death of Rolls, suffered a collapse in his own health. A complete rest was prescribed and Henry went to recuperate at the Norfolk seaside village of Overstrand, just south of Cromer. As it had become essential for him to receive professional nursing, Miss Ethel Aubin was provided by a local nursing home. She was destined to

dent. All the appropriate metal work was then silver-plated and, as was his way, Johnson decreed that the car should be named. It was called 'The Silver Ghost', 'Silver' because of its finish and 'Ghost' to reflect its remarkable silence.

Johnson then embarked on a positive orgy of runs and reliability trials which included two impressive runs from London to Edinburgh and Glasgow, in the latter instance also taking in the Scottish Reliability Trials. The car ran faultlessly throughout.

Work was progressing apace on the new Rolls-Royce factory at Nightingale Road, Derby, and it was duly opened on 8 July 1908 by Lord Montagu of Beaulieu, a friend of Rolls and Johnson, and champion of motorists' rights in the House of Lords. Derby was destined to be the home of Rolls-Royce cars until the outbreak of the Second World War in 1939.

Royce's ill health and its consequences
Claude Johnson's role in Rolls-Royce affairs was becoming increasingly important and, in March 1909, he was promoted from commercial managing director to chief executive. During the year, fears continued to grow about Royce's health, and in January 1910 it was announced that he had curtailed all his executive duties to concentrate fully on technical matters, taking the title of engineer-in-chief. It was the start of a difficult year for the young company and the fact that it emerged relatively unscathed says much for Claude John-

remain with Henry Royce until his death in 1933 and the fact that he survived until the age of 70, indeed outliving Claude Johnson, says much for Ethel Aubin's diligence and devotion.

It was decided that the South of France would provide the best possible climate for Royce's convalescence, so he and Nurse Aubin crossed the Channel and travelled to Tours by train. There they met up with Claude Johnson and a 40/50 fitted with a magnificent Barker double enclosed Pullman limousine body and named 'The Charmer'. They motored south to the village of Le Canadel on the French Riviera where Johnson already owned a house called Villa Jaune. Royce was captivated by the place, so Johnson immediately put arrangements in hand for the purchase of land adjoining his own grounds. Royce himself designed his house, which initially was called Les Cypres, changed in 1914 to Villa Mimosa. Soon after his first visit in 1911 Royce was taken seriously ill. A 40/50, converted to take an ambulance body, was swiftly dispatched to Le Canadel and he was driven back across France and on to London where major surgery was carried out by his doctor and old friend Campbell-Thompson. Fortunately Royce recovered from the operation and went to live for a time in Crowborough, Sussex; although he was visited by his wife Minnie, their marriage was at an end and thereafter he was solely dependent on Ethel Aubin.

Royce's illness, although it cost Johnson an enormous amount of time and effort, was to prove something of a blessing in disguise, both for the engineer-in-chief and the Rolls-Royce company. For in truth Royce was something of a liability at Derby: such is often the way with genius. His endless quest for mechanical perfection meant that there were constant interruptions with the process of production. He would not tolerate the slightest sloppiness among his workforce and was quite capable of dismissing an employee for the most trivial shortcoming. Clearly this could not go on and Royce's illness and resultant indisposition produced an elaborate compromise that, although somewhat unwieldy in concept, worked fairly well until his death in 1933. He was to spend the summer months, along with his design team, on the south coast of England, first at St Margaret's Bay, Kent, near Johnson's own house, and later, in 1917, at West Wittering, Sussex. Wintertime was spent on the French Riviera at his beloved Le Canadel, with his staff who worked in a special building known as Le Bureau. So it was that after leaving the Derby factory in 1910, Royce, except for one occasion, never returned.

Mention should be made of the famous Spirit of Ecstasy mascot, commissioned by Johnson, who felt that the motifs that some customers used to grace their Rolls-Royces were hardly worthy of the make. He therefore commissioned artist Charles Sykes to produce a company-approved mascot which was originally titled 'The Spirit of Speed'. Although Sykes conveyed the resulting statuette to Rolls-Royce in 1911 the mascot produced from it did not enjoy popular currency until after the First World War. Royce himself would never fit one. He considered that it spoiled the bonnet line.

Royce starts designing aero engines

The outbreak of the First World War in 1914 was to have an enormous and far-reaching effect on the Rolls-Royce company. This was because Britain was suffering from an almost total absence of home-produced aero engines. It is sobering to recall that, when war broke out, the Royal Flying Corps and the Royal Naval Air Service had not a single aircraft powered by a British aero engine. Those they did have were mostly of French manufacture, namely by Gnôme, Renault or Le Rhône. This was an unsatisfactory situation in time of peace, but potentially disastrous in war. As Rolls-Royce's Derby works was one of the country's most up-to-date car factories it was not surprising that in August 1914, the very month that war broke out, the Admiralty should ask the company to design an aero engine.

As ever, Claude Johnson's principal concern was the precarious state of Royce's health but, as he had refused to go to Le Canadel when war broke out, he settled down at St Margaret's Bay with A.G. Elliott and Maurice Olley and began work on the design of a water-cooled V12 engine: the prototype Eagle. However, before this power unit became a reality, Rolls-Royce manufactured some Renault and Royal Aircraft Factory 1A engines and, although this output continued into 1916, by that time the Eagle was well into production.

With this momentum established, Rolls-Royce moved decisively into the aero engine field. It was a market that was to be consolidated in the 1920s and expanded in the '30s to such an extent that by mid-decade Rolls-Royce was principally an aero engine manufacturer. In fact, the cars relied on profits generated in this lucrative market.

No reference to Rolls-Royce and the First World War would be complete without mention of the 40/50-based armoured car. Although rather basic conversions were available as early as September 1914, later these Rolls-Royces saw service in practically every theatre of war, from the Western Front to German West Africa. Although conditions hardly lent themselves to their extensive use in France and there were not sufficient machines to make a tremendous impact, nevertheless in the sands of North Africa and Arabia these armoured cars really proved their worth.

1924 Silver Ghost *with limousine body by Joseph Cockshoot of Manchester, pictured at Tiddington, Derbyshire. This is one of the last series of Ghosts, having been returned to the factory and fitted with front-wheel brakes. Provided by Rex Sevier.*

A HOST OF PHANTOMS

The two years that followed the end of the war witnessed an unprecedented boom in Britain. The pent-up frustrations of war resulted in a financial and emotional uplift that withered away at the end of 1920. The following year was dominated by a terrible depression, high unemployment and the collapse of many companies created in those heady post-war months. Claude Johnson was only too aware of these changes, and the 40/50 was a child of the Edwardian era: those sunny days when, for the Rolls-Royce clientele, it was always afternoon. The harsher realities of the 1920s convinced Johnson that Rolls-Royce must produce a smaller car more suited to the times. The outcome was the 20 hp car of 1922 and it marked the beginning of a two-model policy that continues to this very day. This smaller car, and its inter-war derivatives, are considered later (see page 214).

The New Phantom

Meanwhile, the Rolls-Royce board was contemplating the future of the 40/50. In truth, it was beginning to look its age and was becoming increasingly expensive to manufacture. After all, Royce had conceived the car back in 1906 and since then there had been enormous progress in automobile design, which had been stimulated by the technological advances of war. So, in September 1922, it was decided that work should begin on a 40/50 replacement, though the car that emerged in May 1925 was, in effect, simply a new engine fitted in the 40/50 chassis. It was announced that the new model would be called the New Phantom and the older car would henceforth be titled the Silver Ghost, a tribute to that famous and much-publicized 1907 example.

The new engine was only slightly larger than that fitted in the Silver Ghost, 7668 cc compared with 7428 cc. Inevitably it was a six-cylinder, though the Ghost's fixed cylinder head side-valve layout was replaced by a single detachable cylinder head containing pushrod-operated overhead valves.

1928 Phantom I. *This model succeeded the Silver Ghost in 1925 and it remained in production until 1929, when it was replaced by the Phantom II. This particular example was built for diamond magnate Otto Oppenheimer and is known as Black Diamond, with all the interior and exterior fittings being silver plated. There is even a secret compartment for diamonds. The coachwork is by Hooper.*

There was, however, one improvement the Phantom enjoyed that had also featured on the 1924 Silver Ghosts. This was the fitting of front wheel brakes, which were inspired by a system fitted to the 1919 H6 Hispano-Suiza. Royce had an H6 for scrutiny at Elmstead, his West Wittering home and design office, where he had moved in 1917. The year was 1921 and, taking the H6's braking system as his starting point, he proceeded to improve and refine the concept until it satisfied his own high standards. In November 1923 it was announced that front-wheel brakes would be fitted to the 1924 40/50s. The system was both ingenious and efficient. It relied on a power take-off from the gearbox which was transferred to the braking system via friction discs. When the brake pedal was applied this servo assistance operated the front brakes and also contributed to actuating the rear ones. From 1924 this arrangement became an integral part of the Rolls-Royce car right up until 1966 when the Silver Cloud III ceased production, and even until 1978 on the majestic Phantom VI.

It was therefore a natural progression for the New Phantom to benefit from these brakes. Although this car remained in production until 1929, it cannot be regarded as the company's most inspired model. A change in mechanical specifications came in 1928 with the adoption of an aluminium cylinder head but, in truth, that high Edwardian chassis looked a little awkward in the 1920s for, after all, only the engine had been designed in the post-war years.

Then tragedy overtook Rolls-Royce management. In April 1926 Claude Johnson caught a chill that quickly turned to pneumonia and he died at his London home at Adelphi Terrace on 11 April at the age of 61. Royce, on hearing the news, remarked: 'He was the captain. We were only the crew.' How right he was. Johnson's genius had honed and refined the Rolls-Royce image so that it became the most venerated marque name in the world. He had worked

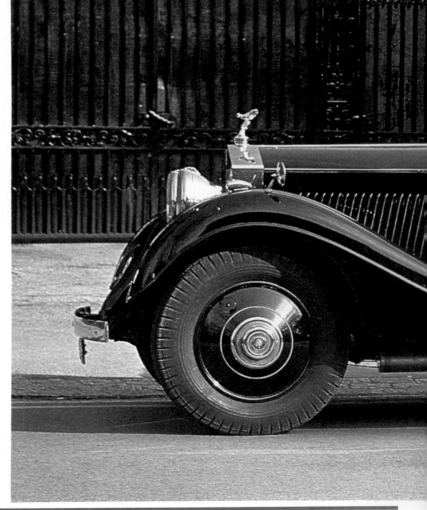

untiringly for the company, though much of his energy was absorbed in his later years in Rolls-Royce's unprofitable American venture at Springfield, Massachusetts, when between 1921 and 1933 the Silver Ghost and Phantom I were manufactured. He was succeeded as managing director by his brother Basil, but this proved a short-lived appointment and in 1929 he was replaced by Arthur Sidgreaves. Educated at the well-known Downside School, Sidgreaves had worked for Napier before joining Rolls-Royce in 1920, and at the time of his appointment he was the company's general sales manager.

LEFT **1932 Phantom II.** *The original owner was Prince Aly Khan; body is by Thrupp and Maberly. Provided by Richard Lowe.*

BELOW **1934 Continental Phantom II.** *A magnificent Gurney Nutting sedanca drophead coupé. Provided by Jim Bidwell-Topham.*

The Phantom II

In 1929, the year that Sidgreaves took up his appointment, Rolls-Royce announced the successor to the New Phantom, the Phantom II. Although the engine was substantially the same, the gearbox was now in unit with it but, above all, the new car had a simpler and lower chassis frame, similar in concept to the smaller 20 hp model. It was therefore fitted with half elliptic springs all round, whereas the Phantom I had retained cantilevers at the rear, which betrayed its Edwardian origins. The new car in closed form had its overall height reduced by 230 mm (9 in) compared with its lofty Phantom I equivalent. Most important of all, as far as the Rolls-Royce story is concerned, it was the last design that Royce saw through from beginning to end.

After the Phantom II had gone into production, Royce conceived the idea of producing a 'tuned-up' version, a project in which the company's sales staff showed little interest. The construction of the body was entrusted to Barker

and Royce dictated that the car should be finished in a light colour. So the body and wings were painted in a delicate shade of saxe blue. It was then coated with an artificial pearl lacquer, produced by finely grinding herring scales. The effect must have been sensational, with the light-blue bodywork gleaming through a shimmering 'oyster shell' finish. Similarly the interior was a model of delicacy. The soft calf hide had been specially imported from France and echoed the colour of the bodywork; the headlining was of a slightly lighter hue. The interior wood was sycamore and also faintly azure tinted. The car was completed in August 1930, just four months after it had been conceived. It was taken down to West Wittering and Ivan Evernden, chief body designer, later remembered that Royce first saw the car on a beautiful day with 'blue sky, blue sea and pearl blue car to match'. Thus the Continental Phantom II model was born.

It was in 1931 that Rolls-Royce acquired the bankrupted Bentley Motors, as detailed earlier in this book. Subsequent Bentleys were closely based on contemporary Rolls-Royces though the marque's sporting ambience was usually maintained.

The Phantom III

Of course, all these activities were taking place at a time when the world depression was at its nadir and it is a curious paradox that during these years luxury cars became increasingly more complex. In America, particularly, the V12 engine was enjoying some popularity. General Motors had the V12 Cadillac and Ford offered the Lincoln marque with a V12 engine from 1932. Packard, with a V12 tradition stretching back to 1916, was yet another American manufacturer to offer this configuration. Hispano-Suiza, Rolls-Royce's great Continental rival, had adopted the V12 in 1931. Bearing in mind that the layout was established Rolls-Royce aero engine practice, it was perhaps inevitable that the Phantom II's replacement should follow suit. The Phantom III, as the new

RIGHT AND BELOW **1936 Phantom III**. *This model, introduced in 1935, was the last Rolls-Royce to be designed regardless of cost; it had a 7-litre V12 engine and was the first Derby car to be fitted with independent front suspension. This example was built for heiress Barbara Hutton and the superbly elegant saloon body was by the French Saoutchik coachbuilding concern. Not all coachwork on this model managed to look so effective. Provided by the Briggs Cunningham Automotive Museum.*

ROLLS-ROYCE PHANTOM III (1936–9) Number built 717	
ENGINE	
No. of cylinders	V12
Bore/stroke mm	82 × 114
Displacement cc	7338
Valve operation	Overhead pushrod
Compression ratio	6:1
Induction	Single Stromberg carburettor
BHP	189 at 3650 rpm
Transmission	Four-speed
CHASSIS	
Frame	Box
Wheelbase mm	3606
Track – front mm	1536
Track – rear mm	1587
Suspension – front	Coil spring/wishbone
Suspension – rear	Half elliptic
Brakes	Mechanical with servo assistance
PERFORMANCE	
Maximum speed	140 km/h (87 mph)

model was called, represented the end of an era for Rolls-Royce, for it was the last model to be built regardless of cost; it required both a new engine *and* chassis; and Royce had a hand in its conception. Sophisticated as the new car was, somehow the magic of the Phantom II had been lost.

Although unable to leave his bed, Royce continued working. He designed a cottage for one of his farm workers and Evernden was dispatched to London to get the plans copied as there was no one available locally to do the job. While Evernden was in the capital, Nurse Aubin sent him a telegram to return to West Wittering immediately. As soon as he received this, Evernden caught the first available train but arrived too late. Frederick Henry Royce died at 7 am on 22 April 1933. He had lived to his 70th year. His ashes were eventually laid to rest at Alwalton, the village of his birth.

Inevitably Royce's place at the head of the design team was taken by Elliott, and work continued apace at Derby on the Phantom III. Code-named Spectre, the new car was announced in October 1935 at a chassis price of £1850 – and for the first time a Phantom was offered at a single chassis length. The 7338 cc V12 engine was a complex masterpiece, but it has to be said that Elliott paid more attention to mechanical refinement than the practicalities of a potential owner running one. The crankcase was cast in Hiduminium, an aluminium alloy developed by Rolls-Royce for its aero engine work, and produced by High Duty Alloys (hence its name). The cylinder heads were of the same material. Wet liners were employed and the overhead valves were actuated, via pushrods, from a central camshaft which, as on every Rolls-Royce engine from 1904 to the present day, was gear rather than chain driven. As if this innovation was not enough, the Phantom III was the first Rolls-Royce to be fitted with independent front suspension, and a General Motors-derived coil and wishbone layout was adopted.

The Phantom III remained in production until 1939 and when it ceased plans were already well advanced for a rationalized series of Rolls-Royce and Bentley cars that were to see fruition in the post-war years. With the end of the Phantom III went much of Royce's design philosophy: the era of producing cars with a seeming disregard for development costs was over.

BIRTH OF A SMALLER MODEL

Royce had been thinking in terms of a smaller car to augment the 40/50 during the First World War but it was not until 1919 that he got down to the serious business of conceiving a prototype. This was designated Goshawk the following year, in keeping with the company's policy of naming its aero engines and prototype cars after birds of prey. Royce, no doubt influenced by the racing Peugeot of pre-war days, opted for a twin overhead camshaft engine. It was rated at 21.6 hp, about half that of the 40/50, and followed Royce's established preference for six-cylinder engines. However, the project was short-lived, probably on the grounds of cost and noise from the upstairs camshafts.

Therefore in 1921, Goshawk II, unlike its predecessor, employed pushrod overhead valves and its prototype car was the subject of a first-rate journalistic scoop by the young Miles Thomas, then working for *The Motor*. This was in September 1921 and, although it was to be another year before the 20 hp was officially announced, Thomas was remarkably accurate in his account of the car, except that he referred to its having a four- rather than a six-cylinder en-

gine. It should be said that the production of a four was also considered, with an engine based on the 15.9 hp Humber unit and code-named Swallow, but it was not proceeded with.

The 20 itself was announced in October 1922 at a chassis price of £1100, which was £750 cheaper than the 40/50's. And unlike the larger car, it was possible to go along to Rolls-Royce's showrooms in London's Conduit Street and, for the first time, buy a Rolls-Royce complete with body, rather than just a chassis which was then completed to the customer's individual requirements. For Johnson had decided to offer the 20 with a standardized range of coachwork, designed in-house by Ivan Evernden and built by Barker. It ranged from a tourer at £1590 to an 'Enclosed Drive Cabriolet' for £1900, which was only £50 more than a completed 40/50 chassis. If, on the other hand, the customer required a coachbuilder and body style of his own choice, he could buy a 20 hp chassis in the usual way. It should be said that Royce looked upon the 20 hp purely as a stopgap. He insisted that the model should be dropped when the 40/50 market improved. Stopgap or no, the 20 and its derivatives became increasingly important to Rolls-Royce as the market for the larger and more expensive cars gradually contracted.

Rolls-Royce's decision to opt for a smaller model was undoubtedly a wise one for, when the 20 ceased production in 1929 and was succeeded by the 20/25, 2940 had been sold, making it the best-selling Rolls-Royce model of the decade. The new car was slightly larger in capacity than the old, 3699 instead of 3127 cc, but in general it followed a similar engine and chassis layout to its predecessor. It was also somewhat faster; whereas the 20 had been capable of 96 km/h (60 mph), *The Autocar* timed a 20/25 at just over 120 km/h (75 mph) in 1935. The model lasted until 1936 when it was replaced by the 25/30. Engine capacity was again increased, by enlarging the bore size to 4257 cc. Although the model looked like any other Rolls-Royce, below the surface some significant changes were taking place. Under the bonnet the most obvious difference was the fitting of a Stromberg carburettor. By contrast, the 20/25 had used a Rolls-Royce-designed unit but the Phantom III of the previous year had paved the way in that respect. Not only was the carburettor a proprietary unit but the 25/30 was fitted with SU fuel pumps, Lucas electrics, a Borg and Beck clutch and Marles steering.

These changes in specification were the result of the Rolls-Royce management beginning to get to grips with the crucial business of manufacturing costs. The whole problem sprang from Royce's fanatical pursuit of perfection. Amazingly, in the 1930s Rolls-Royce was about the only car company in the world to manufacture its own electrical equipment and to produce its own carburettors. This was a reflection of what Arthur Sidgreaves was later to describe as the 'Silver Ghost mentality' and the company tackled the problem soon after Royce's death in 1933.

FAR LEFT **1922 20 hp.** *The 20th 20 built, originally an Indian trials car and then sold to H.H. Maharana of Udaipur and returned to Britain in 1969. Provided by John Fasal.*

LEFT **1929 20 hp.** *This stately saloon by Arthur Mulliner is now resident in California, USA. Provided by Hy Lesnick.*

BELOW **1930 20/25.** *Originally a saloon by Barker, it was later re-bodied as a boat-tailed tourer, a popular style of the time. Provided by Mike Wilkinson.*

ROLLS-ROYCE 20/25 (1929–36)
Number built 3827

ENGINE		CHASSIS	
No. of cylinders	**Six**	Frame	**Channel**
Bore/stroke mm	**82 × 114**	Wheelbase mm	**3276**
Displacement cc	**3699**	Track – front mm	**1422**
Valve operation	**Overhead pushrod**	Track – rear mm	**1422**
Compression ratio	**4.6:1**	Suspension – front	**Half elliptic**
Induction	**Single Rolls-Royce carburettor**	Suspension – rear	**Half elliptic**
Transmission	**Four-speed**	Brakes	**Mechanical with servo assistance**

PERFORMANCE	
Maximum speed	**118 km/h (73 mph)**

1933 20/25. *The small car line, established by the 20, was continued with the 20/25, introduced in 1929 and produced until 1936 by which time 3827 had been built, making the model the best-selling Rolls-Royce of the inter-war years. This example has coachwork by H.J. Mulliner, a firm taken over by Rolls-Royce in 1959. Provided by Richard Barton.*

The following year William Robotham, head of Rolls-Royce's experimental department, made a fact-finding tour of the American automobile industry. He was aware that in some respects Rolls-Royce car manufacture had more in common with the early days of the motor industry than the 1930s, when many luxury car manufacturers were struggling for survival. As a result of his visit Robotham recommended that Rolls-Royce should cease producing its own components and should start buying them from the specialist manufacturers.

The 25/30 lasted a mere two years, with 1201 cars produced, and was replaced in 1938 by the Wraith. This used a welded, rather than a riveted chassis, which was a sign of the cost-conscious times, and independent front suspension. It was fitted for the first time on a small Rolls-Royce and was a variation on the system pioneered on the mighty Phantom III. The engine was considerably reworked and lightened. It was a 4157 cc six with an alloy cylinder block and wet liners that again echoed Phantom III practice. However, the Wraith was destined for a short production life and it was only manufactured up to 1939 when output was curtailed by the outbreak of the Second World War. In fact, only 491 Wraiths were built.

The production of this and the Bentley models was carried on against the background of disappointing sales and there is little doubt that, had Rolls-Royce been solely relying on

chassis production, by 1938 its financial position would have been very serious indeed. That year the company's car division accounted for only 4½ per cent of profits, the remaining 95½ being contributed by aero engine output.

POST-WAR RANGE EVOLVES

The rationalization programme for the production of Rolls-Royce cars laid down in the 1930s reached fruition in the post-war years. Before 1945 production amounted to around 1500 chassis per annum. After the Second World War, Rolls-Royce and Bentley car output could be numbered in thousands. Undoubtedly the most significant post-war model was the 1966 Silver Shadow, for not only was it the best-selling Rolls-Royce ever, but it was the first one to make significant

profits for the company since the 1920s. And with Rolls-Royce Motors cut adrift from its bankrupted aero engine offspring after 1973, the profitable Shadow played a pivotal role in the firm's survival.

In order to chronicle these post-war years we must first return to those days of the immediate pre-war era when the outbreak of hostilities was looming ever nearer. The Rolls-Royce Merlin aero engine went into production in 1935 and from then on the company's resources were concentrated on progressively increasing its output. This task largely fell on the broad shoulders of Ernest Hives and it was as a result of his untiring efforts that the Merlin engine made such a crucial contribution to the British war effort.

Hives, a native of Reading, Berkshire, was educated at Redlands School in that town and joined Rolls-Royce in 1908; later he became head of the company's experimental depart-

ABOVE **1936 25/30** The 20/25's successor was produced between 1936 and 1938. This close-coupled sedanca de ville by Gurney Nutting was originally built for motor agent Raymond Way. Provided by D. Buller-Sinfield.

LEFT **1937 25/30.** The North London-based Vanden Plas company was best known for its tourers but the firm also built some drophead coupés. This example features a hood that disappears when lowered. Provided by Philip Francis.

ment. After Royce's death in 1933, car and aero engine production diverged and Hives devoted his considerable energies to the latter cause. In 1936 he replaced Arthur Wormald as general works manager at Derby and with the outbreak of war against Germany in 1939 car production ceased there for good.

The Royal Air Force's inexhaustible demand for Merlins (they powered the Hurricane and Spitfire fighters) led to the establishment of two further factories for their manufacture. In 1939 the Air Ministry built a new works at Crewe and later the same year another factory was opened at Hillington, Glasgow. Both were administered by Rolls-Royce. Later, in 1941, another factory was established at Urmston, Manchester – but, unlike the Hillington and Crewe plants, Rolls-Royce exercised no control over it, this coming within the orbit of the Ford Motor Company. Also in the same year Packard began Merlin production in America.

With aero engine production occupying centre stage, the patterns and tooling for the Rolls-Royce cars were dispersed in and around the Derby area. With an eye to the future, William Robotham and his experimental department collected two complete sets of drawings for Rolls-Royce's postwar programme. One set was sent to Canada for safe keeping, to be followed by two experimental cars, while Robotham deposited the other with a bank in Ashby de la Zouche, about 12 miles from Derby. As it was believed that the Nightingale Road works would become a prime target for the German Luftwaffe, Hives decreed that all the company's technical staff should be moved to villages around Derby, though he remained to occupy the empty executive building throughout the war. So Robotham and his team eventually established themselves in the unlikely surroundings of a disused iron foundry on the outskirts of Belper.

The Clan Foundry, as it was called, witnessed the development of the Meteor tank engine, which was derived from the Merlin, and Robotham's excursions into tank design and technology. Not that the development of the next generation of Rolls-Royce cars was overlooked. In 1937 Robotham had been given the task of producing a rationalized range of cars and by 1939 four-, six- and eight-cylinder engines had been manufactured experimentally and tested. The eight-cylinder variant, in particular, saw sterling service during these war years: it was used by the company's transport department for its scattered technical staff. Named Big Bertha, its Evernden-designed seven-seater Park Ward limousine coachwork was removed and replaced by a 14-seater bus body. Bertha covered close on 160,000 km (100,000 miles) before the rear axle pinion gave out.

The six-cylinder engine also had plenty of use. There were a number of experimental Mark V Bentleys fitted with them but wartime constraints prevented Rolls-Royce carrying out long-term testing. So the company cannily lent them to various high-ranking officers and cabinet ministers who then proceeded to do their testing for them! Perhaps the most illustrious of these experimental Mark Vs was a 160 km/h (100 mph) vehicle, suitably dubbed 'Scalded Cat.' It considerably impressed Major-General Charles Dunphie, a member of the General Staff, and later chairman of Vickers, who

was on the look-out for a suitable power unit for an armoured personnel carrier. Although this particular project was still-born the dialogue between Rolls-Royce and the armed services bore fruit and the company's engines were extensively used for military vehicles after the war.

Although the war years were largely taken up with tank design, towards the end of hostilities Robotham again began to devote himself to getting the post-war range of Rolls-Royces up to scratch. The chassis and engines had been successfully tested and proved, but the problem lay with the production of bodywork. It was an area in which Rolls-Royce had no expertise for, as we have seen, until 1939 the company had only produced its cars in chassis form.

Robotham was convinced that the car division's survival depended on a substantial increase in production and this meant the adoption of machine-made pressed-steel bodywork instead of the handcrafted low-quantity coachwork they had used in the past. This view was confirmed by conversations with Rover's Spencer Wilks (Robotham had even mooted a far closer association between the two companies). The high cost of tooling demanded that the company had to produce at least 5000 uniform cars, which in many respects represented the antithesis of the Rolls-Royce formula of exclusiveness, quality and refinement. Robotham, however, commented 'I felt that we had no alternative but to buy these tools or go out of the automobile business' (*Silver Ghosts and Silver Dawn*, Constable, 1970). The tooling was expensive, around £250,000 and, although Hives gave the project his blessing, managing director Arthur Sidgreaves was not so easily won over. He demanded that the Rolls-Royce board should inspect a mock-up of the proposed design. So one was duly created and, although there was some disquiet among board members in response to the rather daring integral headlamps, approval was gained when Robotham pointed out that the tooling was already in an advanced state and, if work on it stopped, Rolls-Royce would lose its place in the Pressed Steel Company's queue. The decision was more than vindicated, for this body, designed by the talented hand of Ivan Evernden, remained in production for nine years as the Mk VI Bentley and the Silver Dawn.

Car production restarted

The Second World War came to an end in 1945 and, once again, Rolls-Royce had made an immeasurable contribution to victory. Not only had more than 166,000 Merlin engines been manufactured by the company and licensees, but others including the larger Griffon had been produced at Derby and, later, Crewe. It was the latter factory that was to be the home of the newly formed motor car division. In May 1945, the month the war in Europe ended, Sir Arthur

1956 Silver Wraith. *This touring limousine body is by James Young and just 639 long chassis Wraiths were produced between 1951 and 1958, compared with 1144 short chassis examples. Originally powered by a 4½-litre, six-cylinder engine, capacity was increased to 4.9 litres for 1956. Only coachbuilt bodies featured on these cars. Provided by Bob Barrymore.*

Sidgreaves (knighted in 1945), Rolls-Royce's managing director, announced the resumption of car production, although he was privately sceptical of the post-war market for Rolls-Royce cars. Although he made reference to the perpetuation of the pre-war theme, he underlined the benefits of wartime production methods along with a reference to 'standardized *coach*work'. Not *body*work you notice – that had nasty, mass-produced connotations.

BELOW RIGHT **1954 Silver Dawn.** *Although most were fitted with Bentley Mark VI type saloon bodies, there were some Dawns with special coachwork. This is a drophead coupé by Park Ward. Provided by Bob Barrymore.*

BELOW **1953 Silver Dawn** *'production' version. Provided by Darrell E. and Maybelle Barr.*

The following year Ernest Hives took over as managing director. In 1945 Dr Frederick Llewellyn Smith was made a Rolls-Royce director and the car division's general manager. He became its managing director in 1954. Educated at Rochdale High School, Lancashire, and Oxford and Manchester Universities, Llewellyn Smith had joined Rolls-Royce as a technical assistant in 1933. He had achieved international recognition in 1939 when, with Ernest Hives, he had presented a paper entitled 'High Output Aero Engines' to the World Automotive Congress of the Society of Automotive Engineers in New York, for which he was awarded the Manley Memorial Medal for an outstanding contribution to aeronautical science that year. Not unnaturally, the appointment disappointed Robotham, who had nursed the car division along during the war years, and he was given the title of Chief Engineer of Cars. However, in 1949, he was elevated to the Rolls-Royce board, becoming general manager of the

company's oil engine division the following year. His place at the car division was taken by Harry Grylls.

The Silver Wraith

This is to anticipate our story because after the end of the war in Europe the Crewe works had to be transformed from an aero engine to a car factory. Output began in 1946; the Mark VI Bentley was produced ahead of the Rolls-Royce mechanical equivalent, the Silver Wraith, the first example leaving the production line on 23 October that year. Although the Bentley was mainly produced with pressed-steel bodywork, the Silver Wraith was offered with a variety of coachbuilt bodies by in-house Park Ward together with Mulliner and James Young.

Under the bonnet of both cars was a 4.2-litre version of the B60 overhead-inlet/side-exhaust engine developed before the war. Departures from previous practice included a com-

bined block and crankcase casting and *belt-* instead of gear-driven dynamo and water pump. Henry Royce would not have approved! The new chassis was a channel section structure with a strong central cruciform. Coil and wishbone independent front suspension was employed and this demanded hydraulic brakes, the first to be fitted on a Rolls-Royce; the rear ones, however, were mechanically actuated, assistance throughout being maintained by the faithful gearbox-driven servo.

These difficult early post-war years brought a government initiative to encourage the British motor industry to sell its products abroad, thus generating valuable foreign currency. As has already been noted, Rolls-Royce had been selling cars in America since before the First World War and, although Mark VI Bentley sales there were small, there was clearly a need for a Rolls-Royce version of the Standard Steel Bentley. The result was the export-only Silver Dawn, identi-

cal to the Mark VI, apart from that noble radiator. The model is significant because it signalled the arrival of a common body shell for the Bentley and Rolls-Royce marques. The Silver Dawn became available on the home market late in 1953 and production ceased in 1955.

In 1950 the big car line was re-awakened with the appearance of the 5.6-litre Phantom IV, which was available only to royalty and heads of state. Consequently only 16 were manufactured during the six-year production life. This Phantom

had evolved from the wartime Big Bertha prototype. After the war it had had its bus body removed and this was replaced by an open-back, low-loading truck body. In this guise Big Bertha was used for transporting car, Merlin and Meteor engines, and at one stage it was charged with speeding. The police maintained that Bertha had attained 145 km/h (90 mph) at the time of apprehension, which the court found difficult to believe of a lorry. Later Bertha had the original limousine body replaced, a much more appropriate attire for a lady of such eminence.

In the latter half of 1951 the Mark VI Bentley and Silver Wraith and Dawn received enlarged 4½-litre engines, the pressed-steel bodied cars benefiting from a larger boot the next year. All these models (by then the Bentley was named the R type) ceased production in 1955 and were replaced by the Rolls-Royce Silver Cloud and Bentley S Series. (It is interesting to note that 'Silver Cloud' along with 'Silver Dawn' had been coined by William Robotham in the 1930s as possible names for what became the Phantom III!)

LEFT **1956 Phantom IV.** *One of two once owned by the Sheikh of Kuwait. At the time his country had only 32 km (20 miles) of road! Provided by Merle Norman Classic Beauty Collection.*

BELOW **1977 Phantom VI.** *This car was ordered by Bill Harrah of Reno, Nevada, who created the world's largest car collection. Coachwork is by Mulliner Park Ward. Provided by Mike Wilkinson.*

With the appearance of these new models in 1955 the Bentley and Rolls-Royce marques became ever more closely allied, with only the radiator and badging indicating the different makes. It was still possible, however, for the customer to specify a coachbuilt body on either marque if he so desired. The standard four-door saloon was again manufactured by Pressed Steel and the styling was the work of a new designer. John Blatchley had been chief draughtsman and designer of the famous Chelsea-based Gurney Nutting

BELOW **1966 Phantom V.** *Its predecessor, the Phantom IV, was only available to royalty and heads of state, but the V was offered for general purchase. The power unit is a 6230 cc V8, similar to that fitted to the contemporary Silver Shadow, and coachwork is by James Young. V production continued until 1968. A total of 832 was produced, compared with the mere 16 of its predecessor, and all had coachbuilt limousine bodies. Provided by Merle Norman Classic Beauty Collection.*

coachbuilding establishment before the war and had joined Rolls-Royce in 1939 at its power plant design office at Hucknall, Nottinghamshire. He transferred to the car division in 1946 and four years later became chief styling engineer. In that capacity he was responsible for the design of all Rolls-Royce bodywork from the Silver Cloud to the Silver Shadow.

The Silver Cloud still retained a chassis. It was a new box section one and was fitted with unequal length coil and wishbone independent front suspension. The engine represented the ultimate development of the overhead-inlet/side-exhaust six-cylinder theme. Its capacity was increased to 4887 cc and the new six-port cylinder head was fitted. This larger capacity engine had been foreshadowed in the Bentley Continental of 1954. The more powerful unit was also fitted to the Silver Wraith, which remained available as a coachbuilt option until 1959.

Automatic transmission arrives

A further landmark for Rolls-Royce came with the fitting from the outset of a four-speed General Motors-derived automatic gearbox on the Cloud. This unit had been available on the 4½-litre export version of the Silver Dawn from 1951 to aid the model's competitiveness on the American market, and was also optional on examples produced for home consumption from the 1954 season. Similar options were available on the Silver Wraith and the 'box was standardized on that model at the same time as it was fitted to the new Silver Cloud. This car remained in production until 1959, when it was replaced by the Silver Cloud II and Bentley S2 cars. Although externally

ROLLS-ROYCE SILVER CLOUD I			
(1955–9)			
Number built 2359			

ENGINE			
No. of cylinders	**Six**	Track – front mm	**1460**
Bore/stroke mm	**95 × 114**	Track – rear mm	**1460**
Displacement cc	**4887**	Suspension – front	**Coil spring/wishbone**
Valve operation	**Overhead pushrod**	Suspension – rear	**Half elliptic**
Compression ratio	**6.6:1**	Brakes	**Front hydraulic, rear mechanical with servo assistance**
Induction	**Twin SU carburettors**		
Transmission	**Four-speed**		

CHASSIS		PERFORMANCE	
Frame	**Box**	Maximum speed	**171 km/h (106 mph)**
Wheelbase mm	**3124 (short), 3225 (long)**		

identical, under the bonnet was a new aluminium wet liner 6.2-litre V8 engine, the finalized designs of which were completed by Charles Jenner shortly before his death. It was Rolls-Royce's first V8 since the short-lived Invisible Engine and Legalimit models of 1905 and its arrival no doubt contributed to the Silver Cloud II being the best-selling of the pre-Silver Shadow range, with a total of 2716 examples sold during its three-year production life. These cars were made until 1962 when they were replaced by the Silver Cloud III and S3 range, easily identifiable by their horizontally mounted twin headlights. In 1959 the Phantom line was re-activated for general sale by the advent of the V8 engine and a respectable 832 examples were produced before production ceased in 1968. Thus this Phantom V was the best-selling big Rolls-Royce since the days of the Phantom II.

Production of the small quantity limousine Phantom bodies was the responsibility of Rolls-Royce's Park Ward coachbuilding division, purchased in 1938, and in 1959 these facilities were expanded by the acquisition of H.J. Mulliner. In 1961 these coachbuilding interests were merged into a single company, H.J. Mulliner, Park Ward Ltd.

The Silver Shadow

If these developments related to a more traditional aspect of car manufacture, the Silver Shadow (and T Series Bentley) announced for 1966 was a far more progressive offering. Created under Harry Grylls's engineering direction, the Shadow represented three significant firsts for Crewe. Gone was the separate chassis, to be replaced by a monocoque body which was shorter and lower than the Silver Cloud. (This reduced frontal prospect meant that the Rolls-Royce radiator could be reduced in height to return to its finer pre-

LEFT **1959 Silver Cloud.** *This was the last Rolls-Royce to be six-cylinder powered and this car is one of the 121 long-wheelbase examples. The coachwork is a Park Ward touring limousine. Provided by Bob Barrymore.*

RIGHT **1961 Silver Cloud II.** *This Mulliner drophead coupé has a Radford Countryman conversion, the rear platform being for picnics and spectator sports. The back seat also converts into a bed. Provided by Bob Barrymore.*

BELOW **1963 Silver Cloud III,** *identifiable by its twin head lamps, pictured at Burbank Airport, California. Provided by Merle Norman Classic Beauty Collection.*

ROLLS-ROYCE SILVER SHADOW (1965–77)
Number built 19,412

ENGINE		CHASSIS	
No. of cylinders	**V8**	Construction	**Monocoque**
Bore/stroke mm	**104 × 91; from 1970 104 × 99**	Wheelbase mm	**3035**
		Track – front mm	**1460**
Displacement cc	**6230; 6750**	Track – rear mm	**1460**
Valve operation	**Overhead pushrod**	Suspension – front	**Independent wishbone and coil**
Compression ratio	**9:1**		
Induction	**Twin SU carburettors**	Suspension – rear	**Independent single trailing arm, coil**
Transmission	**Four-speed automatic; from 1968 three-speed**	Brakes	**Hydraulic disc**

PERFORMANCE	
Maximum speed	**187 km/h (116 mph)**

LEFT **1979 Corniche.** *The two-door Silver Shadow saloon and convertible took on the Corniche name in 1971. Mulliner Park Ward handled the interior. Provided by Kenneth Smith.*

ABOVE **1967 Silver Shadow.** *A two-door version of the Shadow appeared in March 1966. Paintwork and interior were by Mulliner Park Ward. From Merle Norman Classic Beauty Collection.*

First World War proportions.) Also new was the independent rear suspension along with a sophisticated self-levelling system. The drum brakes also departed, together with the gearbox-driven mechanical servo, to be replaced by hydraulic disc brakes all round. The engine was virtually a carryover from the Silver Cloud III, but with redesigned cylinder heads so that the sparking plugs were more conveniently positioned above the exhaust manifolds rather than underneath them. Power-assisted steering had been standard equipment on Rolls-Royces since the Silver Cloud II and the Silver Shadow employed a Saginaw system.

Fortunately the Shadow, and its Bentley equivalent, were to prove the most numerically successful models ever produced by the company and, by the time production ceased in 1980, no fewer than 32,300 examples had been built. About the only other significant change to the Shadow I's specifications came in 1970 when the engine's capacity was increased to 6.7 litres. The model had been refined in 1977 with the appearance of the Silver Shadow II, produced under Engineering Director John Hollings's direction. This boasted the standard fitting of air conditioning and the introduction of rack and pinion power-assisted steering.

Meanwhile, variations on the standard four-door saloon soon made their appearances. In the spring of 1966 came a two-door version by Mulliner Park Ward and late in the following year a convertible variant of this model appeared. Both were replaced in March 1971 by the Corniche which, although it shares the Shadow's dimensions, is distinguished by a lower roof line (on the saloon) and a deeper radiator shell. The Silver Wraith name was revived in 1977 for a long-chassis version of the Shadow, which offered a much roomier rear compartment and was perhaps rather more manageable than the contemporary Phantom VI. This Silver Wraith II was lengthened by Mulliner Park Ward.

The years that embraced the development and launching of the Silver Shadow should be seen against a background of some uncertainty about the future of Rolls-Royce as a car maker. Since the end of the Second World War the company had emerged as one of the world's leading manufacturers of jet engines and, although the car division retained strong emotional links with the aero engine child that had outgrown its parent, a split between the two activities seemed inevitable. This eventually happened but in a way that neither division would have ever dreamed possible.

It was in the 1960s that Rolls-Royce became deeply involved in the development of a new generation of 'Big Thrust' jet engines. In March 1968 the firm signed a contract with the American Lockheed Corporation which was to fit Rolls-Royce's new RB 211 engine to its forthcoming TriStar. Costs unfortunately spiralled and the British government stepped in with support. The situation was also complicated by Lockheed's own financial problems. Matters came to a head on 4 February 1971 when the impossible happened. Rolls-Royce Ltd, after a 65-year life, declared itself bankrupt. Edward Heath's Conservative government had no alternative but to nationalize the company in view of its defence commitments, technological prestige and skilled workforce. E. Rupert Nicholson was appointed receiver by the trustees for the debenture holders and on 23 February a new company, Rolls-Royce (1971) Ltd, was registered. (In 1977 it reverted to Rolls-Royce Ltd.) There is an ironic postscript to

this story for in 1981 Lockheed announced that the RB 211-powered TriStar, which first took to the air in 1972, would cease production in 1984. Tragically, the aircraft that led to Rolls-Royce overreaching itself had never made a profit.

Into a new era

The motor car, diesel and Continental light aircraft engine departments were not, however, nationalized. They continued trading under the receivership and in 1973 Rolls-Royce Motors was offered on the London Stock Exchange for public subscription. Since 1971, the car division, as it was then, has had a new managing director in David Plastow, the division's former marketing director.

A new model, the two-door Camargue, arrived in 1975. This time the company had gone to the Italian styling house of Pininfarina, who created a striking two-door saloon based on

LEFT AND BELOW **1982 Camargue.** *The most expensive Rolls-Royce in the current range at £83,122, this two-door model has fully automatic split-level air conditioning as an outstanding feature. Styling inside and out is by the Italian Pininfarina company, who daringly tilted the famous radiator four degrees from the vertical. Provided by Rolls-Royce Motors Ltd.*

LEFT **1980 Silver Wraith II (in background) and 1979 Silver Shadow II.** *The Silver Shadow proved to be the best-selling Rolls-Royce since the Silver Ghost and was produced between 1965 and 1981. The Silver Wraith is a long wheelbase derivative, so named in 1977. These are both Series II versions. Provided by Kenneth Smith.*

ABOVE **1982 Silver Spirit.** *This current model was introduced in 1981 while the long-wheelbase version is titled the Silver Spur. It is powered by a 6.7-litre V8 engine and, like its Silver Shadow predecessor, all independent suspension is employed, though in a refined form. Air conditioning is standard fitment. Provided by Rolls-Royce Motors Ltd.*

the Silver Shadow's floorpan. Above all, the Camargue was offered with air conditioning as standard. The system was the result of eight years' development by Rolls-Royce and not surprisingly, it made the Camargue the company's most expensive saloon, selling for £32,198 on its announcement.

Not that the big car line should be overlooked. The Phantom VI entered production in 1968. Originally powered by a 6.2-litre V8 engine, its capacity was increased to 6.7 litres (as on the Shadow II) in 1978 for an example produced by the company as a Silver Jubilee gift to Her Majesty the Queen. Also the introduction of a three-speed automatic gearbox meant abandoning the gearbox-driven mechanical brake

servo fitted to Rolls-Royces since 1924, which had survived on the Phantom range. All subsequent Phantom VIs have employed this new gearbox and the Shadow II-derived dual-circuit hydraulic brakes, although drums rather than discs are used.

It was in 1972 that work began on the Silver Shadow's replacement. Not surprisingly, the Shadow's mechanics and floorpan were largely retained and the Silver Spirit, as the new model was called, was announced in October 1980. The four-door saloon was styled in-house.

Rolls-Royce's output grew healthier in the 1970s and in 1975 it exceeded 3000 cars a year for the first time. The best year ever was 1978, with 3347 cars manufactured. Then two years later, in 1980, Rolls-Royce Motors' corporate status changed yet again with a merger with the Vickers engineering group. Ironically there had been some discussion between the two companies, along with some other car firms, back in 1917, but on that occasion Claude Johnson had decided that such an amalgamation would not have been in Rolls-Royce's interests. By 1980 it undoubtedly was.

For the company has successfully made the transition from hand assembling every car to quantity production, if 3000 or so cars a year can be so judged. But above all, every car still represents a tribute to Henry Royce's perfectionist ideals, though tempered by the practicalities of today's economics. Long may they continue to do so.

TRIUMPH

Born of a successful motorcycle manufacturer, Triumph cars showed promise but the firm was bankrupt by 1939. The name was revived after the war, only to disappear in 1984.

LEFT **1939 Triumph Dolomite** *with distinctive 'Fencer's mask' radiator grille.*

BELOW **Triumph range** *(foreground) – Herald Estate, Spitfire, GT6, TR6 and Herald saloon – pictured with contemporary Rover models following Leyland Motors's takeover of the latter in 1967. The creation of British Leyland was still a year away.*

Triumph's history has been one of switchback fortunes. The make was born in the 1920s but the following decade it went into decline and all but ceased to exist in 1939. In the post-war years Triumph, by then owned by Standard, again moved centre stage, expanded in the Leyland years and was finally extinguished in 1984.

Although Triumph sounds a very British name its founder was Siegfried Bettmann, a German immigrant. Born in Nuremberg in 1863 Bettmann came to London in 1884 intent on seeking his fortune. After a number of excursions into the business world he began exporting ready-made bicycles from the capital but then decided to manufacture them himself. Bettmann met up with fellow countryman Mauritz Johann Schulte in 1887 and a move was made to Coventry which was

then the centre of the world's bicycle industry. During his days in London Bettmann had sold his two-wheelers as Triumphs and in 1897 his firm was registered as the New Triumph Cycle Company. It was a natural progression for motorcycles to augment bicycle production with a Minerva-engined machine appearing in 1902.

However, car production was still some years away when in 1911–12 Bettmann became chairman of the Standard Motor Company of Coventry, a curious paradox as future events will reveal. By this time Bettmann had become a respected local figure and was Mayor of Coventry in 1913 and 1914, the first of the city's 559 mayors to be 'imported from abroad', as he later put it. The Triumph company's original premises

were in Much Park Street, Coventry, but in 1907 a move was made to a new, larger factory in Priory Street.

During the First World War the firm flourished with lucrative army contracts for Triumph motorcycles. After the cessation of hostilities the company decided to enter the car business though the first model did not appear until 1923. It was produced from a new works in Clay Lane in the Coventry suburb of Stoke in a building that had previously housed the Dawson car of 1919–21. The new Triumph was titled the 10/20 and was powered by a conventional 1.4-litre side-valve engine. The model along with a sporting derivative remained in production until 1926, a year after the 1.9-litre 13/30 had appeared. This was another orthodox side-valver but it had the distinction of being the first British car to be fitted with Lockheed hydraulic brakes though they were of the external contracting rather than the later internal expanding type. The 13/30 evolved into the 2.2-litre Triumph 15 which remained in production until 1930.

These cars sold tolerably well but the model that made a real impact was the 832 cc Super Seven introduced in 1927 and intended to follow in the wheel tracks of Austin's popular and pioneering Seven. Triumph's model was one up on Longbridge's baby as it offered its customers hydraulic rather than mechanical brakes which helped the car sell well both at home and abroad. The 1933 Super Eight followed and by the time output ceased in 1934 the combined sales of both models totalled a respectable 17,000 or so units. The six-cylinder Scorpion, effectively a Seven with two extra cylinders, made a brief appearance in 1932–33.

However, by the early 1930s Bettmann was approaching retirement and in 1933, his 70th year, he handed the running of the firm's affairs to Lieut.-Col. Claude Holbrook, who had

ABOVE LEFT **1923 Triumph 10/20**, *with 1393 cc four-cylinder side valve engine, the first car to carry the Triumph name. Output, along with its 13/35 successor, continued until 1926 with a total of around 2000 examples built*

LEFT **Super Seven.** *Introduced in 1927 the Seven and its Super Eight successor were to prove the best-selling Triumphs of the inter-war years, with about 17,000 examples produced. Production continued until 1934. Had the firm perpetuated this theme it might well have survived into the post-war years.*

ABOVE RIGHT **Donald Healey** *(standing by car) and Jack Ridley at the wheel of what was the prototype Monte Carlo model. They are pictured outside Triumph's showrooms in Priory Street, Coventry, following the 1934 Monte Carlo Rally after Healey had finished in third place in a Triumph.*

RIGHT **Triumph Southern Cross.** *Effectively a short-wheelbase Monte Carlo model with two seats. This version was sold between 1934 and 1937.*

been Triumph's general manager since 1919. Instead of pursuing the successful Seven theme – the model was to be the best-selling Triumph car of the inter-war years – Holbrook decided to move the firm's products up market and rather than compete with the likes of Austin, Ford and Morris decided to take on Alvis, Riley and the new SS marques. It was, with hindsight, a disastrous decision.

The Gloria range, 'The Smartest Cars in the Land', appeared for 1934 powered by overhead inlet/side exhaust Coventry Climax engines, built under licence by Triumph and introduced in a Super Nine model of 1932. These sporty cars were available in 1100 cc four and 1½-litre six-cylinder forms. In 1933 Donald Healey, with already a wealth of long distance rallying experience behind him, joined Triumph from Riley where he had been employed since 1931. Although initially experimental manager he later became the firm's technical director. He was soon publicizing the Triumph name in the Monte Carlo Rally, that he had won in 1931, and in 1934 he took a Triumph to third place in the event. A Monte Carlo model followed almost immediately.

A project that cannot have much helped Triumph's increasingly perilous finances, yet was none the less a fabulous extravagance, was born after Triumphs had put up a good showing in the 1934 Alpine trial. After the event, Healey, along with his friend Tommy Wisdom, motoring correspondent of the *Daily Herald*, and Claude Holbrook were bewailing the lack of a competitive British sports car to take on the Continental opposition.

The fabulous Dolomite

An outcome of this conversation was that Healey was given the go ahead by Holbrook to produce a vehicle which was

hardly in the Triumph tradition. As time was of the essence, Healey borrowed a 2.3-litre 8C Alfa Romeo that had been actively campaigned in Britain by the Hon. Brian Lewis, later Lord Essendon, for he had decided that Triumph would produce a British version of the design. Donald Healey also visited the Alfa Romeo factory in Milan where he met Vittorio Jano, the Italian firm's illustrious chief engineer and creator of the legendary P3 Monoposto.

The outcome of these activities was revealed at the 1934 Motor Show and was very un-Triumph like! The eight-cyl-

inder unit closely followed Alfa layout, the twin overhead camshafts driven by timing wheels in the centre of the engine with the two four-cylinder blocks either side of them. It was also supercharged in the best Alfa Romeo traditions, though the engine's capacity was 1990 cc, whereas the Italian car had a 2.3-litre motor. Suspension was by half elliptic springs front and rear while the hydraulic brakes had massive drums. A preselector gearbox was employed. Triumph's Frank Warner, who had styled the original Gloria range, designed a rakish two-seater body and the Dolomite's price was set at £1225. The cars certainly lived up to their good looks and had a top speed of around 177 km/h (110 mph). But despite these impressive specifications there were no buyers and in April 1935, in view of Triumph's deteriorating financial position, the project was scrapped after only three cars and six engines had been built. However, Donald Healey competed in the 1934 Monte Carlo Rally in a straight-eight Dolomite but a crash in Denmark prevented further progress. In 1935 he tried again in a Dolomite and finished in eighth place.

However, Triumph's over-riding problem was one of finance with losses amounting to £250,000 in 1935. The previous year the firm ceased producing the long-running Eight, and a Ten that had been introduced in 1933 was also discontinued. Therefore only Glorias were built in 1935 but they constituted the largest range of cars the company had ever offered which was hardly a recipe for survival. It consisted of the 9.5 hp Four, a 10.8 hp Four, a Vitesse Four, a 15.7 hp Six and a Vitesse Six of the same horsepower. Most exotic car in the range was the six-cylinder Flow-free model with fashionable fastback styling though it did not catch the public imagination and was withdrawn in 1936.

Nineteen thirty-five had seen Triumph car production transferred from Clay Lane to much larger premises in Holbrooks Lane, Coventry, a road that also played host to the thriving SS Cars. In a bid to raise some much-needed cash, in 1936 Triumph's motorcycle business was sold off to Jack

1938 Triumph Dolomite. *The Dolomite name was originally applied to the straight eight car of 1934 and revived for 1937 for this variation on the Vitesse model.*

Sangster, who in 1932 had rescued the Ariel motorcycle company. Sangster had inherited designer Edward Turner from Ariel and in 1937 Triumph's new Turner-engineered Speed Twin made its début and with it the firm's profits soared but this was little comfort to the now divorced car business.

A receiver appointed

Yet a further rationalization followed in 1936 when Triumph's car losses stood at £200,000 plus. In 1937 Triumph-built engines with overhead valves were introduced which gradually replaced the Coventry Climax units. There were 1½-litre

Gloria saloons while the Dolomite name was introduced for conventional 1.8-litre four- and 2-litre six-cylinder models. By 1938 only Dolomites were available and a curiously designated 1½-litre version of 1767 cc appeared. But the writing was on the wall. A cheap Triumph 12, based on the 1½-litre Gloria, was announced in 1939 but it failed to save the day. In June Lloyds Bank, the firm's principal creditor, appointed a receiver and Triumph cars were no more.

The Holbrooks Lane factory, which Triumph had only occupied for four years, along with the earlier Clay Lane works, were sold to the Sheffield-based Thomas Ward steel and engineering group who also bought the Triumph name. H.M. Hobson, the carburettor manufacturers, purchased the larger Holbrooks Lane works while Clay Lane was let to Armstrong Whitworth, who built sections of aircraft there though it was later damaged in the Coventry Blitz. It was not until 1944 that the Triumph name and the remains of the Clay Lane works were sold to the Standard Motor Company for

£75,000. Its managing director, Sir John Black, had been intent on establishing a second product line for a firm that had enjoyed considerable growth throughout the 1930s.

It had been back in 1903 that William Maudslay had begun producing cars in Coventry from 'standard' or interchangeable parts, a notable advantage over its contemporaries. During the 1920s Standard fared reasonably well but towards the end of the decade profits began to fall off and in 1929 John Paul Black became the firm's general manager. Prior to this appointment he had been running Hillman where, incidentally, he had married Miss Hillman, the proprietor's daughter, while Spencer Wilks, who was later to work wonders with the ailing Rover company, made another Miss Hillman his wife.

Black was responsible for revitalizing the Standard range of which the 1935 Flying models made a notable contribution, so that by the end of the decade it had joined the ranks of the country's top six motor manufacturers. Standard's growing presence was evident when it was requested to manage one of the government's shadow factories built in case of war which was constructed alongside the firm's works at Canley, Coventry. These were built with government money, managed by the car makers and were initially set up for the production of Bristol aero engines. Two further 'shadows' came within Black's orbit and in 1943 he was knighted for his services to the war effort.

Sir John could therefore look back on a successful business career but a thorn in his side was the young SS Cars for whom Standard provided engines. He was determined to challenge William Lyons's stylish and increasingly potent sports models, yet Standard's products were identifiably downmarket family saloons. But with Triumph Black could develop a new more expensive product line with a sporting image. So from 1944 Triumph would have a new home at the Standard works at Canley.

Post-war production

The first post-war Triumphs outwardly had little in common with their cheaper Standard stablemates. The 1800 Town and Country saloon featured distinctive razor-edged styling which had appeared on Rolls-Royce cars of the 1930s. As relatively small production was envisaged the work was entrusted to Mulliners of Birmingham, who were also

ABOVE AND RIGHT **1948 Roadster.** *This model, probably the last series production car in the world to be fitted with a dickey seat, was produced between 1946 and 1949; from 1948 it was Standard Vanguard engined.*

BELOW **1949 Renown.** *This Triumph started life in 1946 as the Town and Country saloon, having an 1800 cc four-cylinder Standard engine. It was radically re-engineered for 1949; a Vanguard type chassis was adopted along with that model's engine, gearbox and rear axle, and it was re-named Renown. This echoed Sir John Black's preoccupation with nautical titles; he had served with the RNVR during World War 1. Vanguard and Mayflower were named at the same time. Renown output continued until 1954.*

ABOVE Detail of the Triumph Roadster's dickey seat for the somewhat isolated rear passengers! The occupants were protected from the worst of the wind by the folding windscreen. Note the step on the left-hand side of the bumper to aid access. Demand was limited, and only 4501 were sold.

responsible for the saloon's styling. The engine came from nearer home, however, and was a 1.8-litre Standard four converted from side to overhead valve operation.

In 1946 the first of the sporting Triumphs appeared, though to modern eyes it was a somewhat dated design. The Triumph Roadster shared the saloon's 1800 cc engine but the bodywork was unusual because this convertible was fitted with a dickey seat (an occasional rear seat), at Sir John's insistence, which had enjoyed popularity in the 1920s! Not surprisingly the Triumph Roadster was the last series-production car to feature this archaic facility.

Standard, in the meantime, was developing a new saloon, the Vanguard, aimed at the home as well as the overseas market, an all important feature in those export conscious days. Its engine was a four-cylinder 2-litre wet liner unit which was also used to power the Ferguson tractors that Standard had manufactured since 1946. In 1948 the Vanguard's engine replaced the old Standard engine in the Roadster, though its fitment did little to help sales and the model was discontinued in 1949 after 4500 had been built. The following year the same engine was also fitted in the razor-edged saloon which was re-named 2000. In 1950 the saloon was re-worked receiving the Vanguard's chassis, suspension and steering and in this form it was named Renown and continued in production until 1954.

The Mayflower, a small saloon perpetuating the 2000's

styling, arrived in 1949 intended for sale in the American market though its engine was a 1.2-litre side-valver. But the coil and wishbone independent front suspension was new, previous Triumphs having relied on a transverse leaf and wishbone system. Not surprisingly, this latter-day Mayflower did not take America by storm; production only lasted until 1953 and amounted to close on 35,000 units.

Black was still trying to find his Jaguar challenger and in 1950 the TRX Roadster graced Standard's stand at that year's Motor Show. It had been styled three years previously by Walter Belgrove, who had been responsible for most Triumph styling since 1933 and had rejoined the marque under its new ownership. While the TRX was not positively disliked, its appearance certainly left something to be desired even though the company intimated that it would become a production model by giving it a selling price of £1206. This two/three-seater Roadster was Vanguard-engined and boasted such novelties as hydraulically operated headlamps, hood and windows! But it did not go into production and in 1951 Sir John made an attempt to take over the Morgan company, which had just started using the Vanguard engine in its Plus Four sports car. But these overtures were rejected so Black gave the go ahead for a cheap, no frills sports car which, like the Austin Healey, was aimed at the growing US market in the gap between the M.G. TD and Jaguar XK120.

TR2 triumphant

The car appeared at the 1952 Motor Show and has been retrospectively titled the TR1. Walter Belgrove was again responsible for the styling and a 1991 cc version of the Van-

TOP **1951 Mayflower.** *Similar in concept to the Renown was the Mayflower, introduced in 1950 and intended for the American market.*

ABOVE **1950 Triumph TRX.** *Intended as a replacement for the Roadster, it never went into production. Styled by Walter Belgrove, three examples were built on modified Standard Vanguard chassis.*

RIGHT **1959 Triumph TR3A.** *Externally similar to its TR3 predecessor but with re-styled full width radiator grille, it was first produced from mid 1957 for the American market until the beginning of 1958 when it became generally available elsewhere. With output of the 1991 cc Vanguard type engine boosted to 100 bhp, the TR3A remained in production until 1961.*

TRIUMPH TR2 (1953–5) Number built 8628	
ENGINE	
No. of cylinders	Four
Bore/stroke mm	83 × 92
Displacement cc	1991
Valve operation	Overhead pushrod
Compression ratio	7:1
Induction	Twin SU carburettors
BHP	75 at 4500 rpm
Transmission	Four-speed
CHASSIS	
Frame	Box
Wheelbase mm	2235
Track – front mm	1143
Track – rear mm	1155
Suspension – front	Independent wishbone and coil
Suspension – rear	Half elliptic
Brakes	Hydraulic drum
PERFORMANCE	
Maximum speed	167 km/h (104 mph)

guard engine was employed. The TR1's chassis had pre-war Standard Nine origins while the independent front suspension and rear axle had Mayflower ancestry. It clearly needed some development before it could enter production and this was undertaken at considerable speed by ex-BRM man Ken Richardson and chief chassis engineer Harry Webster.

By the time the re-named TR2 had entered production in 1953 the chassis, engine and body had been refined, all of which combined to improve considerably the car's handling and to raise its top speed from 144 km/h (90 mph) to around the 168 km/h (105 mph) mark. One of the more obvious changes was the previously exposed spare wheel being relegated to its own compartment, and a boot was introduced which considerably tidied up the rear end. There were few changes made to the car during its two-year production life. The most significant came in the autumn of 1954 when the depth of the doors was increased and sills introduced below them as owners were complaining about hitting kerb stones when they got out of their cars. Larger rear brakes were introduced at the same time.

ABOVE **1954 TR2.** *Triumph's sports car line really got into its stride with the TR2, produced between 1953 and 1955 when a total of 8628 was built, around twice the figure of its Roadster predecessor.*

In 1955 came the visually similar TR3 but with distinctive 'egg crate' radiator grille. There were modifications to the engine which pushed the brake horsepower up from 90 to 95, but the car had around the same top speed as its predecessor. In 1956 the TR3 was fitted with front disc brakes, a notable first for a British production sports car. In 1957 came the improved TR3A with new, full-width radiator grille, 100 bhp engine and better seats and trim. It remained in production until 1961 and was the most popular TR to date with over 58,000 sold, almost all of which found trans-Atlantic customers.

Michelotti takes a hand

The Triumph sports car range was thus well established with the TR range though, by contrast, the saloons were in the doldrums once the Renown had ceased production in 1954. But in 1959 came the Herald, arguably the most significant Triumph of the post-war years which effectively changed the marque's image with the general public as the first of a new generation of mass-produced saloons. How this transformation was effected is one of the most interesting stories to emerge from the British motor industry's recent history.

The early 1950s were a difficult time for Standard as the smallest member of Britain's major car makers. Like most British car manufacturers of the day Standard was beholden to an outside supplier for its mass-produced bodywork which came from Fisher and Ludlow's plant at Tile Hill, Coventry, where Vanguard, Mayflower and hulls for a new Standard Eight were produced. However, in August 1953 BMC announced that it was buying Fisher and Ludlow, following on from Ford taking over Briggs, its body supplier, earlier in the year.

Standard was thus in the unenviable position of having its body supply controlled by a competitor and the firm was also having its internal problems related to Sir John Black's increasingly dictatorial running of the firm's affairs. In early 1954 he was ousted in a boardroom coup and replaced by Alick Dick, who had joined the company as an apprentice and had been Black's personal assistant since 1945. Dick was all too aware of Standard's predicament and believed that the company's only real chance of survival was by merging with another motor manufacturer. Talks were subsequently held with both Rover and Rootes but did not prove fruitful. But his immediate concern was one of Standard's body supply and in 1954 Alick Dick reached an agreement with Mulliners of Birmingham, with whom the firm had close ties, for exclusive rights to their entire output of bodies. Mulliners agreed to this proposal but the decision caused difficulties for Alvis, Daimler, Lanchester and Aston Martin who had to look elsewhere for their bodies.

It was in early 1956 that corporate thoughts began to consider a replacement for the Standard Eight and its Ten

TRIUMPH HERALD (1959–61)	
Number built 100,275	
ENGINE	
No. of cylinders	Four
Bore/stroke mm	63 × 76
Displacement cc	948
Valve operation	Overhead pushrod
Compression ratio	8.5:1
Induction	Single SU carburettor
BHP	45 at 5800 rpm
Transmission	Four-speed
CHASSIS	
Frame	Backbone box section
Wheelbase mm	2324
Track – front mm	1219
Track – rear mm	1219
Suspension – front	Independent wishbone and coil
Suspension – rear	Independent swing axle and radius rod
Brakes	Hydraulic
PERFORMANCE	
Maximum speed	122 km/h (76 mph)

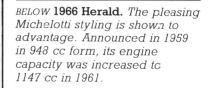

BELOW **1966 Herald.** *The pleasing Michelotti styling is shown to advantage. Announced in 1959 in 948 cc form, its engine capacity was increased to 1147 cc in 1961.*

BELOW RIGHT. The Herald's unconventional construction is revealed here. This was made possible by the use of a backbone chassis. The forward-opening bonnet section gives excellent access to the engine and front suspension. It was a type of construction that permitted the body sections to be produced from a number of different manufacturing sources. Mulliners produced the principal ones.

successor, which had sold well but were beginning to show their years. The intention was to have a new car that, significantly, was to be a Triumph rather than a Standard, on display at the 1958 Motor Show. Harry Webster, appointed the company's chief engineer in 1955, coded the new model Zobo, 'a Tibetan pack animal of indeterminate sex, crossed between a bull and a cow'! But the body problem seemed insuperable when BMC's Sir Leonard Lord confirmed to Alick Dick that Fisher and Ludlow would not undertake any further body contracts for Standard once existing agreements had been fulfilled. The only other body builder capable of taking on the job was Pressed Steel of Cowley and it had a full order book. The problem seemed insuperable.

Webster recognized that there was one way out of Standard's predicament and that was to give Zobo a chassis rather than a monocoque hull. This meant that the bodywork could be made in sections, deriving from a variety of small body builders, which could then come together like pieces of a jigsaw. As the new model was to be crucial to the company's survival it would have to be provided with some notable selling features and Webster decided on an all-independent suspension system, an almost unheard of specification for a cheap British car. Standard already possessed a good front coil and wishbone system which was serving the Standard Eight/Ten well, and this was adopted for the new model while a new swing axle arrangement was applied to the rear end. The engine would be the 948 cc unit from the Standard Ten, with improvements to cope with the additional weight of the chassis frame.

Zobo's mechanical specificiations were thus speedily resolved. It was then a matter of styling the new car. Unfortunately this was not anything like as straightforward because Walter Belgrove, who had styled most Triumphs over a 30-year period, had left the company in 1955 in the wake of a long-standing feud with engineering chief Ted Grinham.

For about a year Standard's styling department grappled with the problem of producing an impressive two-door saloon to mirror the Zobo's clever mechanical specifications. An ingenious feature, conceived at this early stage and again made possible by the use of a chassis, was that the entire front end of the car would hinge at its forward end permitting ready access to both the engine and front suspension. But all that emerged were dull and predictable shapes.

Time was running short when Harry Webster, who had been appointed engineering director in 1957, received a visit from Raymond Flower, who was designing the Meadows Frisky micro car and wanted to purchase some Standard Eight running gear. In the course of the conversation he mentioned that he was getting a prototype body completed within three months, an amazingly short time by British motor industry standards. Flower offered Standard the use of this facility and Webster readily responded.

As a result a TR3 chassis was sensationally rebodied within the allotted time and it was only after the work was completed that Webster discovered that it had been undertaken by the Vignale company in Italy to the designs of a young stylist named Giovanni Michelotti. It was to be the start of a long association with first Standard and, in later years, British Leyland, which was to prove mutually beneficial.

However, there was still the matter of Zobo's styling to be resolved and in September 1957 Harry Webster was on holiday in Italy and called in at Michelotti's Turin studio. He explained what was required and after discarding the original Standard styling, Michelotti came up with what was to be the Triumph Herald coupé. There followed two-door saloon, estate car and convertible bodywork and the car, by then named the Herald, after Alick Dick's boat, made its début a year late at the 1959 Motor Show. It was well priced at £702 and provided just the fillip Standard required. The Michelotti magic had completely changed the company's image.

It was not long before the TR sports car benefited from the Italian maestro's styling, the 1961 TR4 having new full-width bodywork with wind-up windows. Mechanically it was similar to the previous models though the front and rear track were slightly wider, and rack and pinion steering replaced the cam and lever layout previously used. The engine was of 2138 cc which had been introduced as an optional extra on the TR3A while an all-synchromesh gearbox was a further refinement.

Unfortunately for Standard Triumph, as the firm became in 1959, the British economy took a nosedive in the early 1960s and blew the recovery plan badly off course. In 1959 Dick had succeeded in extracting the firm from its manufacturing agreement with Massey Harris Ferguson so Standard got out of the tractor business. With the money received Dick purchased Mulliners of Birmingham and the former Fisher and Ludlow factory at Tile Hill. A new Herald assembly hall was built at Canley and in 1960 Standard bought Hall Engineering of Liverpool, who built the Herald's bonnet/front wing assembly. A further site was acquired at Liverpool for yet more expansion.

Leyland takes over

Nevertheless by the end of 1960 Triumph was in the red and the following year it was taken over by commercial vehicle manufacturers Leyland Motors. Alick Dick departed and Leyland brought in its own management team and there was a return to profitability in 1962.

The Herald was much improved by a capacity increase, to 1147 cc, in 1961 and the following year the Spitfire sports car, based on its chassis, made its manufacturing début. Although the model had been projected in 1960 and a prototype built, Standard Triumph had been unable to afford the necessary investment to put it into production but the Leyland take-over gave the project the green light. Initially it had an 1147 cc engine while a 1965 Mark Two version saw power upped from 63 to 67 bhp.

In the meantime the TR sports car range was further evolving and 1965 saw the arrival of the TR4A with trailing arm rear suspension and outwardly similar to the TR4. It was followed in 1967 by the TR5, the first of the TRs to dispense with the faithful and reliable ex-Vanguard wet liner four-cylinder engine. It was replaced by a 2½-litre six with fuel injection though the TR5 differed little visually from its predecessor. Performance was well up on the earlier model which had been capable of around 175 km/h (109 mph), the six-cylinder TR5 nudging 193 km/h (120 mph).

Also a six and the most refined Triumph of its day was the 2000 saloon, introduced in 1963. It boasted all-independent suspension, MacPherson struts at the front and semi-trailing arms at the rear, while the 1998 cc engine was inherited from the 1961 Standard Vanguard Six. Capacity was upped to 2½

litres in 1968, along with fuel injection, for an additional model, titled the 2.5 PI. Both options were perpetuated when the saloon was face-lifted for 1969, the fuel-injected version continuing until 1975.

A smaller six of 1596 cc had been fitted in the Herald chassis in 1962, the resulting Vitesse having its capacity increased to 2 litres in 1966. The same year saw the arrival of a six-cylinder version of the Spitfire theme, the GT6 coupé being powered by the 2000 saloon's 2-litre engine. However, the original swing axle rear, inherited from the Herald, was a questionable feature of the original model and a Mark Two version with revised wishbone rear appeared in 1968. The GT6 lasted for another five years before it was discontinued in 1973 as the American safety regulations became increasingly demanding.

LEFT **Spitfire 1500s** *in closed and open form in the compound of Triumph's factory at Canley, Coventry. Note that practically all of them are left-hand-drive examples, intended for export. The Spitfire made plenty of American friends.*

TOP **1967 Spitfire,** *Triumph's popular sporting model based on Herald components.*

ABOVE **1969 GT6.** *This six-cylinder car was produced between 1966 and 1973.*

Triumphs in competition

Triumph's sporting image had been continually nurtured by the factory and privateers during the 1950s and '60s. It had begun with the TR2 and the model's impressive first and second places in the 1954 RAC Rally, the same year that TRs were awarded the team prize and a Coupe des Alpes in the Alpine Rally. Also in 1954, TRs won the team prize in the TT and finished in 15th and 19th places at the Le Mans 24-hour race which highlighted the model's reliability but underlined the fact that the Triumph competitions department made no attempt to lighten the cars or power tune them. It was much the same story at Le Mans in 1955 with TRs finishing in 14th, 15th and 19th places. In 1956 Triumph TR3s participated in that year's French Alpine Rally, and won the team prize along with no less than five Coupe des Alpes awards. Nineteen fifty-seven saw a TR3 take a third place in the tough Liège-Rome-Liège rally and the same year a trio of TR3s won their class in America's Sebring 12-hour event. The newly introduced TR3A, by then 2.2-litre engined, won its class in the 1958 Alpine event and later in the year came fifth in the Liège/Rome rally.

There were exciting developments for the 1959 Le Mans when a twin overhead camshaft version of the TR3A appeared designated the TR3S. The model was rather special being 15.24 cm (6 in) longer than the production cars and lightened by the use of glass-fibre bodywork. The engines were special five-bearing crankshaft units developing 150 bhp instead of the standard model's 95. The rather prominent twin timing wheel covers on the front of the engine resulted in it being christened 'Sabrina' in tribute to a shapely actress of the day!

Unfortunately all three cars retired at their 1959 Le Mans début with engine trouble. TR3Ss appeared at Sarthe again in 1960 with minor refinements of wider track and rack and pinion steering. They ran without engine fans as two of the previous year's failures had been caused by blades disintegrating. But, although all the cars finished the event, stretched valves caused a loss of engine power and the TR3Ss did not complete the qualifying distance. However, it was a different story in 1961 when the trio finished in 9th, 11th and 15th places and also took the team prize. This was the last occasion that these special TRs were seen at the Sarthe circuit as they were sold off to American enthusiasts soon after the 1961 event.

The Herald had arrived in 1959 and it was not long before it appeared in competition, one winning a Coupe des Alpes in that year's Alpine Rally. Other TR3A victories that year were class wins in rallies across Europe: in Holland, France, Greece and Belgium while there were team prizes in the German and RAC events. There was also a class win for a privately entered TR3A in the 1960 Alpine and a Triumph win in that year's Tulip Rally.

A Herald won the 1961 Tulip while a TR4 achieved a class win and Coupe des Alpes award in the Alpine. There were more successes in the 1962 RAC Rally and in the 1963 Tulip, while in 1964 the factory entered two Spitfires for Le Mans, one of which finished in 21st place. In 1965 they did even better, taking 13th and 14th positions, and a Spitfire won its class in that year's Alpine. By then the 2000 saloon was finding its competitive feet and in 1965 the model was second and third in the Welsh Rally and achieved a fifth position in the RAC, which may have helped sales.

The 2000 and Spitfire continued to uphold Triumph honours in 1966 with the marque being placed fourth in the Circuit of Ireland event and seventh in the Geneva Rally. Although the cars were becoming less competitive, in 1968 a 2000 was third in the tough East African Safari. The model's 2.5 PI derivative was placed second and fourth in the 1970 World Cup Rally.

The 1960s had been pivotal years for Triumph. In 1964 the Standard marque was discontinued, for what had once suggested a car built of precision-made 'standardized' parts had latterly only projected a utilitarian image. So Triumph, which

had all but ceased to exist in 1939, now fortified by Leyland resources, became one of Britain's foremost marques. It was a position that was consolidated in 1968 when Leyland effectively gained control of an ailing BMC, and Triumph – which had been the first jewel in its corporate crown – moved progressively centre stage.

The Herald continued to soldier on. It received a 1296 cc engine for 1968 along with the Vitesse's angular bonnet and was retitled the 13/60. With its six-cylinder derivative it remained in production until 1971 after an impressive 12-year production run. It had been replaced the previous year by the Toledo 1300 and to discover that particular model's origins we must briefly retrace our steps to 1966. It was in that year that Triumph's 1300 saloon, which was the marque's first foray into front-wheel drive, made its début. The Michelotti-styled four-door saloon resembled a scaled-down 2000 and it boasted all independent suspension; coils and wishbones at the front and semi trailing arms at the rear. But the 1300 only lasted for four years to be replaced by the aforementioned Toledo with live axle and rear-wheel drive, though the front-wheel-drive theme was perpetuated by the 1500 which

ABOVE **1969 Toledo.** *Produced between 1970 and 1976, this was a rear-wheel-drive, 1296 cc powered model, based on the front-wheel-drive 1300 bodyshell of 1965–70 vintage.*

LEFT **1968 Triumph 2000.** *Introduced in 1963, the Michelotti-styled 2000 was powered by a 2-litre six-cylinder engine from the Vanguard Six. Suspension was all-independent, and the model was to remain a strong seller during its 14-year production life, output ceasing in 1977. There had been a facelift in 1969 and there were also 2½-litre versions with either carburettors or fuel injection.*

also featured an updated version of the 1300 body. The 1500 remained in production until 1973, thus ending Canley's seven-year flirtation with front-wheel drive. It was succeeded by the twin carburettored 1500TC, with rear-wheel drive, in the same body shell.

Also sharing similar styling to the Toledo/1500 was the Dolomite introduced in 1972 and destined to be the best-selling Triumph of the 1970s. Under its bonnet was a lively new 1850 cc four-cylinder overhead camshaft engine, the origins of which add yet a further dimension to the Triumph story. It had been at the end of 1963 that Saab had approached Standard Triumph, as the Swedish company had heard, via development engineers Ricardo, that the Coventry concern was intent on producing a new generation of engines similar in concept to one it wanted for its new front-wheel-drive 99 model intended for production in 1968. Saab would require between 30,000 and 40,000 units a year and the outcome was a 1709 cc overhead camshaft slant four which appeared in the 99 from the beginning of 1969. However, the Swedish firm was responsible for the development of the integral gearbox and final front-wheel-drive arrangements. Capacity was upped to 1850 cc from early 1971 and was increased again to 2 litres in 1972, the year in which Saab took over production from Triumph and also decided to undertake some redesign of the unit.

Sprint gets ahead

This then was the origin of the engine fitted in the Dolomite though the Saab used a single carburettor while the Triumph boasted twin Strombergs. The Dolomite was well received on its announcement and in its basic form was capable of over 160 km/h (100 mph). But there was a more exciting project in the pipeline and this emerged as the 2-litre Dolomite Sprint in 1973. (Incidentally this car was not the same capacity as the Saab 99 which was 1985 cc, as opposed to the Triumph's 1998 cc!) Not only did the Sprint benefit from this larger engine capacity but it was fitted with a potent alloy 16-valve cylinder head which boosted power to 127 bhp and the model's top speed to 185 km/h (115 mph).

It was a particularly ingenious arrangement which produced extra power at low cost. All this extra power demanded a more robust transmission than was available on the standard Dolomite, so the Sprint was fitted with the Triumph 2.5/TR6 gearbox along with a new rear axle and TR6 crown wheel and pinion. Here was an obvious challenger to the BMW market though total sales of 20,000 plus might have been better. In 1976 the entire Triumph saloon range was tidied up somewhat, the Toledo ceasing production and being replaced by a 1300 version of the Dolomite, while the 1493 cc engine became an option with the demise of the Triumph 1500.

Meanwhile the Spitfire sports car continued to sell well and by 1973 over 200,000 had been manufactured. The Mark Two of 1965 had given way to the Mark Three produced between 1967 and 1970 which was powered by a 1296 cc engine rather than a 1147 cc unit which had served the model since its 1962 inception. In 1970 came the Mark Four with a new close ratio gearbox and restyled front and rear ends. Early in 1973 the rear track was widened and the swing axle rear suspension modified. At the end of 1974 the model was redesignated the Spitfire 1500 when the engine from the 1500 saloon was introduced. The model benefited from new body contoured seats in 1977 and output ceased in 1980 after a record-breaking 18-year production run for a Triumph.

Rather less successful was the Triumph Stag two-plus-two convertible introduced in 1970. This had started life back in 1964 as a Michelotti-styled open version of the 2000 saloon intended for a 1968 launch powered by the now enlarged 2½-litre six-cylinder engine. It was coded Stag but as it met with directorial approval the name stuck and was seen through to the model's launch. Unfortunately for the Stag, the much-needed 2000 saloon facelift of 1968 got in the way (it remained in production until 1977), so the convertible's appearance was put back to 1970 by which time it had acquired a 3-litre V8 engine. It had been based on two overhead camshaft slant fours which Triumph had designed for Saab. But the Stag, which should have been the flagship of the Leyland fleet, developed a reputation for unreliability. This was mostly associated with its engine though production of the car continued until 1977.

The TR sports car line was revised in 1969 with the arrival of the TR6. Although the mechanics and 2½-litre fuel-injected six-cylinder engine were largely carried over from the TR5, the body was new and, for once, not the work of Michelotti, who was fully committed to other Triumph projects at the time. The restyling was therefore undertaken by the West German Karmann company and very popular it proved to be, for by the time the TR6 ceased production in 1976 close on 95,000 had been manufactured.

ABOVE **1972 TR6.** *Introduced in 1969, the TR6 had front and rear ends styled by the German Karmann company. The engine was a 2½-litre, fuel-injected six.*

LEFT **1970 Stag.** *Intended as the flagship of the Triumph range, the Stag was a controversial model from its inception and was built until 1977. The engine was unique to the car, a 3-litre V8, which had much in common with contemporary slant fours employed by Saab and Triumph.*

RIGHT **Triumph TR7.** *Last of the TR range, the 7 was produced at Speke, Canley and Solihull during a turbulent seven-year production life.*

ABOVE RIGHT **Triumph Acclaim.** *Last car to bear the Triumph name, it was introduced in 1981, a Cowley-built version of the Honda Ballade. It remained in production until 1984.*

The controversial TR7

It had been replaced on the American market the previous year by the TR7, the first TR without a chassis, which was intended to be British Leyland's corporate sports car, as detailed in the M.G. section of this book. The TR7 was initially offered in coupé form only because at the time of its inception the all-important American safety regulations demanded closed cars. Leyland stylist Harris Mann came up with a controversial wedge-shaped body while the engine was a 2-litre development of the Dolomite Sprint block and 1850 overhead camshaft eight-valve cylinder head. Suspension was by coil springs all round with independent struts at the front. The car was built at Triumph's factory at Speke, Liverpool, built by Leyland in 1968 and the firm's second works there. A prolonged strike culminated in the plant's closure in the spring of 1978 and TR7 production was transferred to Triumph's Canley base. The change of manufacturing location gave the firm's design staff the opportunity to make around 200 detail modifications to the sports car's specifications as early examples had been plagued with reliability problems. When output restarted in October 1978 the car was re-badged with a garland incorporating the Triumph name; hitherto a plain *TR7* had featured. A five-speed

was prepared by the competitions department based at the M.G. factory at Abingdon. There were successes such as the Boucles de Spa rally in 1977 and TR7s were second in that year's Scottish and third in the Mintex International events. The cars were V8 engined from 1978 and successes included firsts in the 24 Hours of Ypres and the Manx International Trophy. Subsequent results were a victory in the 1979 BP TV Rallysprint event, a third in the 1000 Lakes of 1980 and a

TRIUMPH TR7 (1975–81)		
Number built 111,648		
ENGINE		**CHASSIS**
No. of cylinders	Four	Construction	Monocoque
Bore/stroke mm	90 × 78	Wheelbase mm	2159
Displacement cc	1998	Track – front mm	1435
Valve operation	Overhead camshaft	Track – rear mm	1430
Compression ratio	9.25:1	Suspension – front	Independent
Induction	Twin SU carburettors	Suspension – rear	Radius arms and coil
BHP	105 at 5500 rpm	Brakes	Hydraulic, front disc
Transmission	Four-speed		
		PERFORMANCE	
		Maximum speed	174 km/h (108 mph)

gearbox option had been available in 1976–7 and was standardized in the latter year and all Canley-built cars were so equipped.

However, a restructured British Leyland, now titled BL Cars, decided that Triumph's Canley plant was no longer required as a manufacturing facility so, while the ageing Spitfire and Dolomite models were discontinued in 1980, TR7 production was that year transferred to the Rover factory at Solihull. It had been in the spring of 1980 that an open version of the TR7 was introduced which proved to be a great visual improvement over the closed car. During the same year the TR8, with Rover V8 engine, made its appearance on the American market, mostly in open form. A mere 2815 were built but a few escaped to Britain.

It had been rallying experience that had prompted the V8's introduction. British Leyland had returned to the competitive fray with the TR7 in 1976 when a quartet of cars

seventh in that year's Lombard RAC Rally which was the last occasion that the factory sponsored a TR7 competitive entry.

The TR7 ceased production at Solihull on 5 October 1981 after a stormy six-year production in three different manufacturing locations. Numerically it had been the most successful model in the TR range with over 111,000 examples built, but in America it had been selling against the respected but outdated MGB. So the TR7 remained a controversial model to the end, maybe haunted by the memory of early examples that had clearly been in need of further development.

On 7 October 1981, two days after the TR7 had ceased production, a 'new' Triumph appeared, though the Acclaim saloon, readied for the 1982 season, was a Cowley-built version of the Japanese Honda Ballade, discontinued in 1984. It was a striking contrast to the 1970s when Triumph had been one of Britain's foremost makes. Now the name has gone.

GLOSSARY

Axle ratio: In order that torque can be increased at the road wheels, a permanent gear ratio is incorporated into the rear axle's final drive, usually of between 3.5 and 6 to 1.

Badge engineering: A manufacturer's use of a basic body shell, endowing it with permutations of styling, trim and mechanical specifications and selling it under different make and model names within the corporate umbrella. The British Motor Corporation's Farina-styled four-door saloon of 1959, which appeared under the Austin, M.G., Morris, Riley and Wolseley names, is a good example.

BHP (Brake horsepower): The horsepower available at an engine's flywheel which is described as such because it is usually measured by the application of a brake.

Cantilever suspension: A half-elliptic spring, anchored at its rear end and centre to a car's body or chassis, so that, in effect, it becomes a quarter-elliptic one. Unusual in the post-war era, though the 1955 2.4-litre Jaguar is a notable example.

Compression ratio: This is the ratio of cylinder volume with the piston at its lowest possible position, to that with the piston at its maximum travel. As the compression ratio increases, a petrol of higher octane rating is required.

Cotal electric gearbox: A French device similar to a pre-selector gearbox (see below) but employing electrical power, via magnets, to actuate the brake bands of an epicyclic gear train. This meant that the gears were selected by a small electrical switch which could be conveniently positioned anywhere in a car's driving compartment.

Crankshaft: The principal revolving shaft in the engine which converts the reciprocating action of the pistons and connecting rods to rotary motion.

Crown wheel and pinion: The rear axle mounted pinion, which is connected to the car's propeller shaft, meshes with the crown wheel which transmits power, via the differential, to the half-shafts and thus to the road wheels.

De Dion rear axle: A suspension system almost exculsively used at the car's rear. This employs an additional dead axle, usually placed behind the body-mounted differential casing, which reduces the unsprung weight and improves roadholding. Drive is transmitted by universally jointed half-shafts. First used on the French de Dion steam vehicles of the late 19th century, the system was subsequently employed on the firm's cars, discontinued after 1914, but revived by Daimler-Benz on its W125 Grand Prix single-seater of 1936 and destined to appear on racing cars for the next 20 or so years. Used on sports cars, it also featured on the Rover 2000 saloon and is still employed on the current Aston Martin V8.

Drophead: Usually used in relation to open two-seater coupé bodywork that features a folding hood and wind-up windows.

Dry sump lubrication: Often used on high-performance cars, this system ensures that cool, clean oil is supplied to the engine. The reservoir is usually mounted at the front of the car to maximize the cooling effect. Two oil pumps are sometimes used with the system, one pumping lubricant from the reservoir to the engine bearings, while the other scavenges any surplus oil from the engine's sump.

Elliptic springs: Inherited from horse-drawn carriages, they consist of a number of leaves of spring steel clamped together. Before the Second World War, practically all cars used half-elliptic springs front and rear but, in the post-war era, the advent of independent front suspension meant that only the rear suspension was so equipped.

Fixed head: A coupé with a fixed roof.

Fuel injection: A system that dispenses with carburettors, and usually the inlet manifold, and meters a fine spray of petrol into each combustion chamber from an engine-driven pump. It was first fitted on the 1954 Mercedes-Benz 300SL of 1954 and the first British car to offer the system was the Triumph TR5.

Gear ratio: The ratio between the input and output speeds of a train of gear wheels. Many cars have a top gear ratio of about $4\frac{1}{2}$ to 1 which indicates that the engine's crankshaft is rotating $4\frac{1}{2}$ turns to every revolution of the road wheels.

Hydragas: An interconnected, all-independent suspension system produced by Moulton Developments in conjunction with British Leyland and introduced on the Austin Allegro of 1973. It is similar to the earlier Hydrolastic system (see below), but with nitrogen gas rather than rubber as the suspension medium.

Hydrolastic suspension: An interconnected all-independent system devised by Moulton Developments in partnership with the British Motor Corporation and introduced on BMC's Morris 1100 in 1962. Each wheel has its own suspension unit with rubber, in compression and shear, acting as the elastic element and fluid interconnection between the car's front and rear.

Independent front suspension: A system where the rise and fall of one road wheel has no direct effect on the wheel on the opposite side of the car.

Limited slip differential: Used on high-performance cars to permit the half-shafts not only to rotate at varying speeds if the road conditions demand this, but will also transmit torque to only one wheel if the other's adhesion, as in the case of wheelspin, is unacceptably low.

Live axle: An axle, the function of which is to transmit power, as opposed to a dead axle which does not.

MacPherson strut: A cheap, popular and effective independent suspension system where the coil spring and damper tube are combined in one big, near vertical member fixed to the wheel hub at the bottom and to a flexible mounting to the body structure at the top. The system is completed by a lower wishbone at the strut's bottom end to resist horizontal braking and acceleration forces. Named after Earle S. MacPherson, vice president in charge of American Ford engineering in the late 1940s and '50s, its British début was on the Ford Consul/Zephyr models of 1951.

Marque: A make of car, i.e. Austin, Morris, etc.

Monocoque: See unitary construction.

Over-bored: When an engine's bore is enlarged to increase the capacity of the engine. The British Motor Corporation's Mini, for instance, had an 803 cc capacity on its 1959 announcement, with a 57 × 76 mm bore and stroke. The 998 cc Mini Cooper, by contrast, retained the 76 mm stroke but its bore was increased from 57 to 64 mm.

Overdrive: The fitment of an overdrive unit to a gearbox, which usually operates on top gear, but sometimes third gear on a four-speed 'box, provides an additional gear so that engine revolutions are reduced by 20 to 25 per cent. This permits a high cruising speed at lower engine revs which improves petrol consumption and prolongs engine life.

Overhead camshaft engine/twin cam: The overhead camshaft with its close proximity to overhead valves results in their more efficient operation and is often used in conjunction with a hemispherical cylinder head. Twin overhead camshafts, as pioneered on the 1912 Peugeot, were for many years confined to racing and costly sports cars until 1948 when William Lyons's XK120 Jaguar showed that it could be mass produced. The XK engine remains in production at the time of writing.

Panhard rod: Usually transversely employed to tether a rear axle with coil spring suspension to prevent excessive sideways movement from taking place.

Pre-selector gearbox: A gearbox, introduced in Britain in the 1920s and used by Armstrong Siddeley and Daimler into the post-war era, it embodied the epicyclic gear train as used by Lanchester in 1900. Basically, it reduced the gear-changing principle to two separate and, above all, silent operations in the days before gearbox synchromesh (see below). The driver selected the gear he required by operating a stubby lever but the 'box would not change gear until the 'clutch' pedal was operated.

Pushrod engine: A power unit where the overhead valves are operated, via rockers, by long steel tubes, in their turn actuated by the revolving lobes of a side-mounted camshaft.

Rack and pinion steering: Steering gear usually used in conjunction with independent front suspension. The rack, housed in a tubular casing, meshes with the pinion which in turn is connected to the vehicle's steering wheel.

Radial engine: Derived from aircraft practice, separate cylinders were arranged in a circular pattern around the axis of the engine's crankshaft.

Radius arms: Rods attached to the car's body, or chassis, and rear axle to cope with the driving and braking forces.

Semi-trailing arms: An independent rear suspension system with two arms pivoting at an oblique angle to the car's longitudinal axis with the wheel hub carriers at the other end. The layout permits a certain amount of wheel camber as well as vertical movement.

Side-valve engine: An engine where the valves are mounted alongside the cylinders in the block. The simplest form of engine layout, the side-valve unit was used extensively on cheap cars during the inter-war years but was superseded in the post-war era by more efficient cylinder head located overhead valves. Ford, however, continued to build side-valve engines right up until 1959 (100E and Popular models).

Spaceframe: A light and rigid chassis/body structure, introduced on racing cars in the 1950s, of welded-up, thin-diameter tubes so that all members were either in tension or compression.

Spoiler: An aerodynamic tab attached to the front of a car or rear fin to aid tyre adhesion and stability.

Straight eight: Engine where eight cylinders are positioned in line. The world's first production straight eight was the Type 8 Isotta Fraschini of 1919 and the last British car to feature the layout was the Rolls-Royce Phantom IV which ceased production in 1956.

Supercharger: A system whereby an additional amount of air and fuel vapour is forced into the combustion chamber by an engine-driven compressor. Consequently, more fuel is burnt and the engine produces more power. First offered as standardized fitment of the 6/25/40 PS and 10/40/65 Mercedes models of 1921, and later employed on many sports cars of the inter-war years, superchargers were predominantly used on racing cars until the mid-1950s. Blown: supercharged; unblown: unsupercharged.

Swing axle: A cheap form of independent rear suspension where only the inner ends of the drive shafts are articulated. This allows considerable changes in wheel camber but reduces the capacity of the tyres to grip the road at moments when maximum adhesion is vital. Popularized by the Volkswagen Beetle and used in Britain on the Triumph Herald.

Synchromesh: A device, first introduced on the 1929 Cadillac by the American General Motors corporation, which simplified gear changing by equalizing the speed of the gears before engagement. This resulted in a straightforward and, significantly, silent movement.

Targa top: Introduced on the Porsche 911 and 912 sports cars early in 1966 and named after the Targa Florio Sicilian road race that Porsche had won five times (1956, '59, '60, '63, and '64). It consisted of an unobtrusive roll-over hoop bordering a fixed or movable rear window with a soft detachable hardtop. This offered the pleasures of open-air motoring in the summer with a snug interior for the winter.

Torque: Literally a twisting motion; the turning tendency of a shaft. In a car engine the crankshaft receives torque from the downward motion of its pistons.

Torque converter: Normally used in conjuction with an automatic gearbox, it replaces the conventional clutch and is basically the same as a fluid flywheel but with one important difference. The

former consists of two bowl-shaped moving parts with their rims not quite touching and each lined with 20 or more vanes. The impeller is attached to the engine's crankshaft, and its opposite number, called a turbine, is attached to the automatic gearbox's input shaft. When the engine is ticking over, oil is pushed by the impeller into the turbine, though without sufficient force to make it rotate. However, when the driver accelerates, impeller speed increases as does the force exerted by the oil and the turbine begins to turn. With a torque converter there is an additional small vaned wheel called a reactor located between the two. At normal speeds this turns at the same speed as the turbine but when extra power is required, for instance when a car is started from rest, the reactor is locked motionless and its vanes direct oil back from the turbine into the impeller in a far more efficient way than is possible with a fluid coupling.

Torque tube: A tube containing a car's propeller shaft, rigidly attached to the rear axle and jointed to the back of the gearbox. The tube thus takes the driving thrust of the vehicle rather than the rear springs, so these are freely shackled.

Torsion bar: Patented by Ferdinand Porsche in 1931, the torsion bar is, in effect, a coil spring straightened into a rod. One end is firmly secured to the car's chassis while the other is attached to the road wheels, often via a wishbone layout, the twisting motion of the bar providing the suspension medium. Extensively used on post-war British cars such as the Morris Minor and Jaguar XK120.

Turbocharger: A supercharger; but, instead of being driven by the engine and thus absorbing power from it, the turbo runs independently of it. It is driven by the engine's exhaust gases, utilizing what would otherwise be waste heat energy. BMW briefly offered the world's first production turbocharged car with its 2002 model in 1973, though Saab subsequently took the concept up, offering it on their 99 model of 1978.

Unitary construction: Up until the mid-1930s practically all cars used a chassis frame to which the engine, suspension and body were attached. The arrival of unitary construction, also sometimes called monocoque bodywork, saw the chassis frame eliminated and replaced by a rigid body structure built up from a series of pressings, spot-welded together to create a strong, rigid box-like structure. The principle was pioneered by Lancia with its revolutionary Lambda model of 1922, while the *Traction Avant* (front-wheel-drive) Citroën of 1934 represented a further step along the technological road. Britain's first unitary construction car was the 1938 Vauxhall Ten and by the mid-1950s most mass-produced saloons had unitary hulls.

V8, V12: Engines where the cylinders are arranged in a V formation resulting in a shorter but wider engine. Current British cars employing the layout are the Aston Martin V8, Rover 3500 and Rolls-Royce Silver Spirit (V8) and Jaguar XJ12 and XJ-S (V12).

Watt's linkage: Named after James Watt, who is best remembered for improving the steam engine with the addition of a separate condenser in 1765. Subsequently, he produced a parallel motion linkage to keep the connecting rod of his 1783 double acting steam engine vertical. The principle is used on a car's rear suspension to permit movement in a vertical plane.

Wet liner: Engines where the cylinder bores are in direct contact with the cooling water and are detachable from the block. Popularized by the *Traction Avant* Citroën, it inspired the production of the 1948 Standard Vanguard engine, a unit that was also used in the pre-1967 range of Triumph TR sports cars.

Wet sump lubrication: The conventional type of engine lubrication where the underpart of the crankcase serves as an oil reservoir.

Wishbone and coil spring suspension: A popular variety of independent front suspension, introduced on the 380 Mercedes-Benz sports car of 1933. The system consists of sets of transverse links connecting the top and bottom extremities of the individual carriers to the body structure. An intermediate coil spring provides the suspension medium.

Acknowledgements

The publishers wish to thank the following organizations and individuals for their kind permission to reproduce the photographs in this book:

Special Photography by: Ian Dawson 2–3, 4–5, 8–9, 10, 12 left, 20 above and below, 20–1, 37, 90–1, 91 above right, 92 above and below, 93, 94–5, 96 above, 96–7, 98–104, 104 inset, 105 below, 106–13, 114–5, 115 centre and below, 116–7, 116 below, 117 below, 119 and inset, 120–1, 122–3, 124–5, 124 above, 148–9, 152 and inset, 155–6, 155 above left, 156 and inset, 157 inset, 158, 159 above, 160, 165, 170, 172 left, 172–3, 174–5, 176–9, 178–9, 179, 181, 195 right, 212–3, 215 above and below, 220–9, 229 right, 232; Chris Linton 11, 150–1, 155 below left, 157, 158–9, 162, 164, 166, 166–7, 168 inset, 171 above and below, 173 below, 176 below, 180 above and below, 194–5, 198, 200–1, 202–3, 204 below, 205–9, 210, 210–1, 214, 216–9, 230–1, 231 inset, 233; Nicky Wright 39 above, 73 below, 82–3, 84, 87 below, 186, 234–5, 240 below.

Aston Martin Lagonda Ltd/Roger Stowers 15 left, 22, 23, above left and right, 30–1, 33 top, 33 below, (Michael Sargent Studio) 37 above; Austin Rover Group Ltd 50 above and below, 51 below, 193 above and below, 251 above; *Autocar* 115 top; British Motor Industry Heritage Trust 38 above left, right, and below left, 40 above right, 44 above and below, 46 below right, 62, 68 above right, 149, 150, 153, 161, 168–9, 182–3, 185 below, 187 above, 188 left, 188 below right, 191 above and below, 192 below left, 241 below, 245 right; Neill Bruce 18 below, 21 above left, 28, (Nigel Dawes Collection) 29, 32–3, 34 below, 45, 56–7, 60–1, 85 above, 190 above, 250 above; Geoffrey Goddard 16 above and below, 17 below, 18 above, 21 above right, 24, 25, 26–7, 30 centre left, 42–3, 43 inset 51 above, 52–3, 54 above and below, 67 below, 72, 74 left, 77 below, 78–9, 81 above and below, 128 below, 130 above, 130–1, 135 above, 138–9, 140, 141 below right, 183 below right; LAT 14–15, 27 below, 33 centre above, 35 below, 123 inset, 125, 134 above, 177; Lotus Cars Ltd 13 above, 127 left, 132 below, (Monitor Group) 132–3, 136–7, (Team Lotus) 141 above right, (Monitor Group) 142–3, 144, 146–7, 147 centre; T.C. March 91 below left, 95 right; Andrew Morland 27 above, 55, 58, 129 below, 237 below; *Motor* Magazine 105 above; National Motor Museum, Beaulieu 12 right, 17 above, 19 above and below, 23 below, 47 above, 48–9, 53 right, 61 above left, 65 above, 66, 68, below left, 69, 70–1, 77 above, 83 above, 86 above, 126–7, 128 above, 129 above, 137 inset, 145, 147 top, 189 below, 190 below, 192 below right, 238–9, 240 above, 240–1, 242 above, 244–5, 247 below right, 248–9, 249 right, 250 below; Rik Paul, 128; The Photo Source 47 below; Popperfoto 135 below; Cyril Posthumus 39 below, 61 below right, 62–3, 71 right, 73 above, 74–5, 76 above and below, 79 below, 80, 85 below, 86 below, 134 below, 141 above left, 185 above, 188 above right, 236 above; Peter Roberts 26 inset, 36–7, 40 below right, 40–1, 46 below left, 49 above, 59, 65 below, 67 above, 82 below, 131 below, 184, 187 below, 189 above, 192 above, 237 above, 242 below, 243 above, 246–7, 247 above right, 251 below; Rolls-Royce Motors Ltd 87 above, 88 above and below, 89 above and below, 196–7, 197 above left, right, and centre, 199, 202 left, 204 above; Paul Skilleter 64–5, 243 below; Andrew Whyte (British Leyland) 13 below, 46 above left, 235 right; Nicky Wright 1.

The publishers would also like to thank the owners who kindly provided the cars for photography.